‖‖‖‖‖‖‖‖‖‖‖‖‖‖‖‖‖‖‖‖‖‖‖‖‖‖‖‖

◁ **W9-DHH-359**

737-8263

168

Not For Resale
THIS IS A FREE BOOK
www.bookthing.org
THIS BOOK THING OF BALTIMORE, INC.

PLATE I. *Portrait Bust of* QUEEN NOFRETETE, *Wife of Ikhnaton*

Found in the studio of a royal sculptor at Amarna, with original colors
preserved as shown. (After Borchardt)

ANCIENT TIMES

A · HISTORY · OF · THE · EARLY · WORLD

VOLUME I · THE ANCIENT NEAR EAST

An Introduction to the Study of Ancient History
and the Career of Early Man by
JAMES HENRY BREASTED
Late Director of the Oriental Institute
in The University of Chicago

SECOND EDITION
REVISED AND LARGELY REWRITTEN

GINN AND COMPANY

COPYRIGHT, 1963, 1944, BY CHARLES BREASTED
COPYRIGHT, 1935, 1916, BY JAMES HENRY BREASTED
ALL RIGHTS RESERVED

Library of Congress Catalog Card Number: 66-18986

PAPERBACK EDITION

GINN AND COMPANY

Home Office:
Boston, Massachusetts · 02117

PREFACE

It is now eighteen years since the publication of the first edition of this book, and nearly twenty years since it was written. The progress made in the study of the Ancient World during these last twenty years, in spite of the obstacles resulting from the World War since 1918, has probably never been equaled in the history of humanistic research. At The University of Chicago the organization of the Oriental Institute, in the summer of 1919, has contributed substantially to this progress.

One of the most important developments has been the recovery of the evidence disclosing the life of man in the earliest Stone Age in Northeastern Africa by the Oriental Institute's Prehistoric Survey. Similar work in Western Asia, although not covering an extensive territory, has made it possible to sketch Stone Age development in the Near East as a whole, and thus to gain at least an outline of the prehistoric human development entirely around the Mediterranean. It is therefore no longer necessary to begin the Stone Age career of man with a résumé of it exclusively in France and Europe, as was done in the first edition of *Ancient Times*, and then, passing to the Near East for the origins of civilization, to return to Europe again, thus involving a confusing alternation of first Europe, then the Near East, and then Europe again. In the present edition of *Ancient Times* it has been possible to begin the human career with the Early Stone Age entirely surrounding the Mediterranean, including the Near East, and then to continue it in chronological sequence down through the origins of civilization and the subsequent developments of civilized life in the Near East alone, to the point when these influences passed over into Europe.

The range and importance of field research and discovery since 1918 have produced a series of discoveries of epoch-making importance. The Anglo-American Expedition at Ur has revealed a totally new and fundamentally important chapter in the development of earlier civilization in Western Asia. At Ras Shamra, in Ancient Phœnicia, the discoveries of the French expedition under Schaeffer have been of far-reaching importance. The expeditions of the Oriental Institute have likewise disclosed a whole series of new vistas in Assyria, in Babylonia, in Palestine, and also in Persia, where the excavation of the magnificent sculptured stairways at Persepolis has been perhaps the most notable of such disclosures.

While the puzzling Etruscan writing has not yet been deciphered, it is now evident that the Etruscans were a Western Asiatic people who migrated from Anatolia into the Italian peninsula. The resumption of excavation at Troy by Professor Semple of the University of Cincinnati has not yet progressed far enough to reveal all the important results which we may confidently expect from that famous site.

In the investigation of the great problem of the Hittites, substantial progress has been made in the last twenty years. The decipherment of Hittite cuneiform was successfully accomplished by Bedřich Hrozny of Prague during the World War. A good deal of progress has also been made in the decipherment of Hittite hieroglyphic, and it is safe to say that we shall be able to read it in the not distant future. The investigation of these philological problems in the study of the Hittites has been accompanied by extended field researches in the Hittite country of Asia Minor. The excavations of the Oriental Institute at the mound of Alishar, about one hundred and twenty miles east-southeast of Ankara, have for the first time revealed the material evidences of advancing civilization in Anatolia, both before and after the advent of the Hittites, beginning with the Late Stone Age at the bottom of the mound (at a depth of about one hundred feet) and working upward, disclosing stage after stage of human advance, from stone implements, through the discovery of copper, the production of bronze, and the introduction of iron, to a church of the Fifth Century of the Christian Era.

In Egypt the operations of the Harvard-Boston Expedition, under the leadership of Reisner, have given us a totally new revelation of the highly developed culture of the Pyramid Age, especially in the discovery of the tomb of the royal mother of Khufu, or Cheops, the builder of the great Pyramid of Gizeh. The discovery of the tomb of Tutenkhamon by Howard Carter has proved to be an epoch-making disclosure of the beauty and refinement of civilization under the Egyptian Empire, and has perhaps done more to interest a large public in the story of the human past than any other single discovery in the history of archæological research.

In Europe the project for a comprehensive excavation of ancient Athens has made very gratifying progress and has brought forth a large body of inscriptions which will prove invaluable sources of new knowledge still to be fitted into our historical accounts of ancient Greece.

So far as these discoveries have been contributed by the Oriental Institute, even though still unpublished, they have been available for this new edition of *Ancient Times*, and, besides presenting new facts, have contributed especially to the new series of illustrations in this volume. The discoveries of other expeditions, so far as they have been published and rendered accessible, have also been employed both in the revision of the text for the new edition and in the list of illustrations. It is safe to say that there has never before been available such a comprehensive range of illustrative material as this new volume now includes. As a result of all these discoveries the account of the history of civilization preceding the Greeks and the Romans has been entirely re-written, making this edition practically a new book.

It is a pleasure to express here the author's appreciation of the kindness of his colleagues and friends who have been willing to contribute photographs even before these were available in published form elsewhere. I take this opportunity of thanking the Duke of Alba; Professor Edson S. Bastin; the British Museum; the British Ordnance Survey Office, and O. G. S. Crawford, Esq., the editor of *Antiquity*; the British Royal Air Force Command, Baghdad, Iraq; Professor Edward Capps; Howard Carter, Esq.; M. Franz

Cumont; Sir Arthur Evans; the editor of *Forschungen und Fortschritte*; Professor Ernst E. Herzfeld; Bruce S. Ingram, Esq., editor of the *Illustrated London News*; Professor Franklin P. Johnson; the Metropolitan Museum of Art; Professor Percy E. Newberry; Professor Arno Poebel; Professor George A. Reisner and the Boston Museum of Fine Arts; Mr. John D. Rockefeller, Jr.; Professor Eckhard Unger; the University Museum, University of Philadelphia; Professor Thomas Whittemore and the Byzantine Institute.

Acknowledgment has been made under each cut in cases where monuments or figures have been redrawn from new publications.

To Dr. Edith Williams Ware I am indebted for constant attention to text and proof, for the compilation of index, bibliography, and assigned readings, and especially for a great deal of detailed labor on the extensive illustrative scheme.

In the first edition of *Ancient Times* the comments and suggestions of my old friend James Harvey Robinson were very helpful, and this is equally true of the present revision.

It is a pleasure also to acknowledge here the interest in the new edition evinced by the publishers, especially their constant coöperation in the development of the illustrations.

JAMES HENRY BREASTED

THE ORIENTAL INSTITUTE, *January, 1935*
THE UNIVERSITY OF CHICAGO

Note to readers: For your convenience the following features of Doctor Breasted's great classic—the preface, table of contents, list of colored plates, list of maps, bibliography and index—are reproduced in their entirety in each of the paperback volumes. *Volume I* covers pages 3-282; *Volume II* covers pages 283-554 and *Volume III* covers pages 555-795 of the hardback edition.

CONTENTS

VOLUME I

PART I. MAN BEFORE CIVILIZATION

PART II. THE ORIGINS AND EARLY HISTORY OF CIVILIZATION IN THE ANCIENT NEAR EAST

CONTENTS

VOLUME III

THE ROMANS

LIST OF COLORED PLATES

LIST OF MAPS

ANCIENT TIMES

PART I · MAN BEFORE CIVILIZATION

The Earliest REPRESENTATION *of Domesticated* HORSES *(about* 3000 B.C.)

An example of early picture-writing showing a group of nineteen horses, each represented by the animal's head only. The other signs are numbers, and it is probable that the whole is an inventory of the horses owned by some king or nobleman. The varying positions of the manes as represented on the tablet are significant. The *upraised* manes doubtless indicate stallions, while those that hang down probably indicate mares. The animals without any manes are presumably foals, too young to show any mane. The signs are incised on a clay tablet, discovered by the French at Susa, the ancient capital of Elam. It dates from about 3000 B.C. or possibly a century or two earlier. This evidence would therefore indicate that already at this early date the domesticated horse was found at the east end of the Highland Zone (§ 318), whence he gradually filtered into the Fertile Crescent during the next thousand years, so that he was common in the Age of Hammurapi (§ 212). We now know that around 2000 B.C. the domesticated horse was in use from the Caucasus through Anatolia to the Fertile Crescent, whence he reached Egypt during or after the Eighteenth Century B.C. The discovery, in Scania, in southern Sweden, of a horse's skull dating from about 2400 B.C., having a stone dagger driven deep into the forehead, led some prehistorians to believe that the horse was domesticated in northern Europe. There is now little support for this conclusion, and the evidence from the Orient indicates that the horse was domesticated somewhere in the general region northeast of Persia. There is some uncertainty regarding the date of his arrival in the Fertile Crescent, owing to the discovery of a surprisingly large percentage of the bones of the ancient wild ass (*onager*) in the Babylonian excavations of the Oriental Institute. In Fig. 91 and in our Elamite tablet above, the short ears of the animals represented have been regarded as conclusive evidence that they were horses. But the numerous bones of the wild ass in Babylonia suggest the possibility that all the horse-like animals shown in these representations might be regarded as wild asses, which we know were early used as draft animals in ancient Babylonia. If so, the domesticated horse was introduced among the most civilized peoples as late as 2000 B.C.

CHAPTER I · How Mankind began as Food-gatherers

SECTION 1. MAN'S EARLIEST WAYS OF LIVING

1. All readers of the story of Robinson Crusoe remember how interested they were in the way in which he managed to supply himself with shelter, tools, furniture, food, clothing, and the other things which he needed for living on the uninhabited island *How Robinson Crusoe began as a food-gatherer* where the terrible storm had cast him ashore. We recall that he had lost nearly everything he had except the clothing he wore. He had no food, but was later able to find young pigeons in nests, as well as turtles along the shore. He also gathered grapes, limes, and lemons. We should notice that he did not *produce* this food; he only *gathered* it as he found it. He was at first, therefore, merely a *food-gatherer*. He had no tools with which to work and at first no weapons with which to defend himself if he met a dangerous wild beast.

2. Later, however, when the storm had passed, the waves quieted and Crusoe could see the wreck of the ship not far from shore. Then he swam out to the ship, where he managed to lash together a raft out *How Robinson Crusoe became a food-producer* of pieces of wood and rope. Exploring the ship, he found tools, weapons, seed grain, guns, and many other useful things, which he carried back to the island on the raft. By the use of the tools he was able to build himself a house and make himself clothing, while the seed grain, when planted, brought him plenty of food. In this way he was freed from the need of food-gathering. He had become a *food-producer*. He was thus able to take possession of his island, which became his little world; and as he made it produce the food and other things he needed, he was able thereafter to lead a fairly comfortable life.

3

3. Now Crusoe was able to do this only because of the things which he found on the ship. If they had not been

Earliest man far worse off than Crusoe

there, he would have had to find some way of making them. And, indeed, there were certain necessities, like ink, of which the stock he found in the ship's supplies ran out, so that he had to make more. Crusoe, however, had known about these things and had used them in his own country; he could therefore make crude substitutes from memory, such as the spade which he cut out of wood. But the earliest men, who lived thousands on thousands of years ago, were in a much worse situation than Robinson Crusoe. We must think of the world in that long-ago time as if it were mankind's huge island, where the men who wandered about on it were not even as well off as Robinson Crusoe before he visited the ship and built his raft, because even if his wrecked ship had not been there to furnish him with tools, he would have *known* about the tools he had seen from childhood and often used in his own country. But the earliest men had never lived in a country which had tools and implements, for there were no such things anywhere in the world; and because they had never seen or heard of such things and did not even know that they could be made, the earliest men were at first entirely without them.

4. We all know that our grandfathers never saw an airplane or heard a radio when they were young, because these

Gradual invention of tools and implements; uncivilized life

things had not been invented. In like manner earliest men had never seen or heard of a tool of any kind, because no one in the whole world had even thought of such a thing or knew that such a thing was possible. The first men had nothing but their hands with which to supply their needs. They could not even speak or make a fire. They knew nothing about the many things which make our own lives so easy and convenient and interesting at the present day; all such things had to be invented one after another. Such inventions were made very slowly, and it was many thousands of years before the simplest of such inventions had gradually improved the lives of men. When only a few such improvements had been made, the life of early men was what we should call *uncivilized*.

5. After a very long time, however, men made such important discoveries and inventions that their manner of living lost its savagery and greatly improved. We call such men *civilized*. The list of all these Things necessary to civilized life discoveries and inventions is much too long to be learned here. Only the most important may be mentioned. First of all came *speech*; then followed a series of inventions. While they were still only *food-gatherers* men learned to make *fire* and produce wooden and stone *tools* and *weapons* needful in the *gathering* of food. Next they made two discoveries which changed them from *food-gatherers* to *food-producers*. The first of these was *cattle-breeding*, when men found out that they could tame wild cattle and sheep and keep them in pastures and stables; and the second was *agriculture*, when men first learned to plant and cultivate certain of the wild grasses so that these furnished their seed as food and became cultivated grains, or *cereals*, like wheat and barley. After this it needed only the discovery of *metal* and the invention of *writing* to equip men for civilized life and further advance.

6. There are still many uncivilized peoples on the earth, but people as completely uncivilized as the earliest men must have been no longer exist. Nevertheless, the Tasmanians, and what they had failed to learn lowest savage tribes found by explorers in modern times still led a life very much like that of our earliest ancestors. For example, the Tasmanians, the people whom the Dutch discovered on the island of Tasmania nearly three centuries ago, wore no clothing; they had not yet learned how to build a really roofed hut, but crouched behind a wind screen; they did not know how to make a bow and arrows, or even to fish, except by spearing. They had no goats, sheep, or cows, no horses, not even a dog. They had never heard of sowing seed or raising a crop of any kind. They did not know that clay would harden in the fire, and so they had no pottery jars, jugs, or dishes for food.

7. Naked and houseless, the Tasmanians had learned to satisfy only a very few of man's needs; they were still
Stone Age men. Yet that which they had
learned had carried them a long way beyond
the earliest men. They had a simple language,
with words for all the customary things they used and did every day. They could kindle a fire, which kept them warm in cold weather, and over it they cooked their meat. They had learned to make very good wooden spears, though without metal tips, for they had never even heard of metal. These spears, tipped with a sharp piece of stone, they could throw with great accuracy and thus bring down the game they neeided for food, or drive away their human enemies. They could take a flat piece of sandstone, and by chipping off the edges to thin them they could make a rude knife with which to skin and cut up the game they killed. They were also very deft in weaving cups, vessels, and baskets of bark fiber.

8. For several hundred thousand years earliest men lived a life far less civilized than that of the Tasmanians. This
savage life was scattered over wide areas of
the Old World. It entirely surrounded the
Mediterranean Sea. The savages lived on all
its shores and spread far inland: northward
to the North Sea and across the British Isles, southward far across Africa in what is now the Sahara Desert, and eastward beyond the Persian Gulf. It was in the region surrounding the *eastern end* of the Mediterranean Sea that civilization arose. We must therefore first turn our attention to the early Mediterranean world.

9. The lands of Europe and northern Africa were very different then from what they are today. Lofty forests not only
fringed the streams of Europe and clothed its
wide plains, but also covered some of the
Sahara Plateau, which at that time was a
green and well-watered region. Huge hippopotamuses wallowed along the shores of the rivers on both sides of the Mediterranean, and many a fierce rhinoceros, with a horn

Tasmanians, and what they had learned

Eastern Mediterranean region; home of earliest civilization

Early Mediterranean world; its climate and animals

three feet in length, charged through the forests. Enormous elephants, with gigantic tusks, herded with the last of the European mastodons. Myriads of bison grazed on the uplands, and the forests sheltered numerous herds of deer. Especially on the European side wandered vast herds of wild horses. Through Italy and Sicily, as well as at Gibraltar, land-bridges across the Mediterranean connected Europe and Africa. Thus most of these animals could wander *by land* from Africa to Europe or back again. The atmosphere was moist and warm, and echoed to the notes of many kinds of birds. This unbroken wilderness, filled with its myriads of creatures (fish, fowl, and animals great and small), extended entirely around the Mediterranean Sea.

FIG. 1. FIRE-MAKING WITHOUT MATCHES
by Modern Natives of Australia

The outfit is very simple, consisting merely of a round, dry stick placed upright, with the lower end in a hole in a dry tree trunk lying on the ground. The native turns the stick rapidly between both hands, and the friction finally generates sufficient heat to produce flame (§ 11)

10. With nothing to cover their nakedness, the early savages of this Mediterranean world roamed stealthily through the immense forests, seeking their daily food of roots, seeds, and wild fruits. They were also hunters, and they listened with keen and eager ear for the sound of small game which they might be able to lay low with their rough wooden clubs. Such weapons were so feeble that these savages often fled in terror as they felt the thunderous tread of the giant animals of the forest or caught dim glimpses of colossal elephants plunging through

Life and haunts of earliest men; their wooden weapons

the deep vistas of the jungle. At night, after cutting up the flesh of their prey with wooden knives and devouring it raw, the hunters slept wherever the hunt had led them. Not knowing how to make a fire to ward off the savage beasts, they lay trembling in the darkness at the roar of the mighty saber-toothed tiger.

11. At length, however, they learned about fire, per-

Man learns to kindle fire and use stone

haps when the lightning kindled a forest tree. They must have learned to fear it, too, as they viewed such terrible volcanoes as Etna and Vesuvius along the Mediterranean. It was a great step forward when at last they learned how to produce it themselves with the whirl-stick (Fig. 1). They could then cook their food, warm their bodies,

FIG. 2. *A Group of North American Indians making* FLINT WEAPONS

The farthest Indian is prying loose a large stone. This is the raw material, which is then taken by the middle Indian, who crashes it down upon a rock and shatters it into fragments. One of these fragments is then taken by the nearest Indian, who holds it in his left hand while he strikes it with a stone in his right hand. These blows flake off pieces of flint, and the Indian is so skillful that he can thus shape a flint hatchet. This process of shaping the flint by blows (that is, by *percussion*) was the earliest and crudest method and produced the roughest stone tools.
(After Holmes)

and harden the tips of their wooden spears with the fire. But their dull wooden knives they could not harden; and so they perhaps learned to make bone knives, or picked up a broken stone and used its ragged edge. When, not less than several hundred thousand years ago, they had learned to *shape* the stone to suit their needs (Fig. 3), and thus to produce a rude tool or weapon, they entered what we now call the Stone Age.

12. The stone weapons and tools which these savages then began to make did not rot and disappear like their bone and wooden ones. We can hold in our hands the very stone tools and implements with which early men maintained themselves in their long struggle to obtain food and to defend them- *Career of early man traceable in the surviving works of his hands* selves from their fierce animal foes, for these earliest men sometimes lost their stone tools and weapons. Later on, such implements were sometimes buried with their owners when they died. In the course of many thousands of years the number of such shaped stones became very large. We are able to find so many of them that they form for us something like a trail which these savage hunters left behind them. By this long trail of stone implements we can follow these early men and see how far they had advanced toward better methods of living. This advance is revealed to us by their increasing skill in shaping stone and by their improvement in some other industries which they gradually learned. In the specimens of their handiwork which still survive we can distinguish three successive ages, which we may call the Early Stone Age, the Middle Stone Age, and the Late Stone Age. Let us now observe man's progress through these three ages, one after another.

Section 2. The Early Stone Age

13. A stone tool or weapon made by human hands is called an "artifact," a word of Latin origin meaning "made by art" and related to the word "artificial." Stone *Archæology and study of earliest stone implements* artifacts, lying on the ground or turned up by the plow, were noticed by our ancestors centuries ago. Since then, for nearly a century, scientific men have been carefully searching for them, especially by systematic digging (called excavation). The study of man's early works is called archæology ; hence such digging is called archæological excavation, and we term a man who does such work an archæologist. The search for stone artifacts began in Europe, especially in France. There the rude stone tools and weapons of the Early Stone Age hunters of Europe and the bones of the huge animals they slew had sometimes been left lying side by side in the sand and gravel far up on the valley slopes where in these prehistoric ages the rivers of France once flowed, before their deep modern beds had been cut out by the water. They have been found in such large numbers in France that great museum collections of stone implements have been established there. Later, similar implements were found to be plentiful in other European countries also. Recent search in North Africa has likewise revealed stone artifacts, in an area stretching from Algiers to the lower Nile valley, and the same is true of Asia along the eastern shores of the Mediterranean. We are thus able to study thousands of stone weapons and implements from all the lands surrounding the Mediterranean. They reveal to us the fascinating story of man's earliest progress, after the Early Stone Age hunters had found that they could chip stones.

14. Although they perished probably in great numbers as their dangerous life went on, these savage hunters continued

Achievements and limitations of Early Stone Age man

for thousands of years the uncertain struggle for survival all around the Mediterranean Sea. They finally produced a most useful stone implement, which is commonly called a "fist-hatchet" (Fig. 3), and this they slowly improved. The fist-hatchet was the earliest widely used human device which has survived to our day. The Early Stone Age men learned, probably, to make additional implements of wood; but these have of course rotted and perished, so that we know nothing of them. Single-handed these brave hunters waged war upon all animals. There was not a beast which was not their foe. There was as yet no dog, no sheep, or fowl to which they might stretch out a kindly hand. The ancestor of the modern dog was then the fierce wolf of the forest, leaping upon the hunter unawares; and those beasts which were the ancestors of our modern domestic animals, like the horse, still wandered the forests in a wild state.

15. The earth, at this time so rich with life, both animal and vegetable, was, however, destined to pass through one of the most critical periods of its history.

Coming of the ice

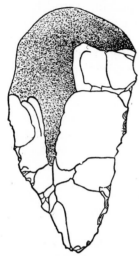

Fig. 3. A Flint Fist-Hatchet *of the Early Stone Age found in an Ancient Bed of the Nile*

Rough flint flakes older than the fist-hatchet still survive to show us man's earliest efforts at shaping stone. But the fist-hatchet is the earliest well-finished type of tool produced by man. They have been found all around the Mediterranean, as well as in other parts of the world. The original is about 7½ inches long. The drawing reduces it to about one third. It was usually grasped in the fist by the thicker part, and never had any handle. Handles of wood or horn do not appear until much later (cf. Fig. 19, 4 and 5). Traces of use and wear are sometimes found on such fist-hatchets. The above specimen was found by the Oriental Institute of The University of Chicago

Geologists have not yet found out exactly why, but for thousands of years the climate grew steadily colder and more moist. There was therefore an increasing snowfall, especially on the summits of the mountains. It is supposed that ice began to accumulate around these centers of snowfall. Finally there were formed great sheets of inland ice which covered much of the Northern Hemisphere. There is evidence that during the period of severest glaciation the ice extended southward in Europe until it covered England as far down as the Thames, and on the Continent it covered much of Germany. In Asia the ice came down far across Siberia, and it descended from the mountains of Armenia to the upper valley of the Tigris and Euphrates rivers. It was only here that the ice affected the region where civilization later arose. On the continent of North America the southern edge of the ice is marked by lines of bowlders carried and left there by the ice sheet. Such lines of bowlders (called moraines) are found, for example, as far south as Long Island, and westward along the valleys of the Ohio and the Missouri.

16. In Europe and the northern part of Western Asia the hunters saw the glittering blue masses of glacier ice, with Ice Age slows down their crown of snow, pushing through the human progress green of their forest abode and crushing down vast trees in many a sheltered glen or favorite hunting ground. Many of the animals so long hunted in Europe retreated to the warmer south, and the hunters were gradually forced to accustom themselves to a cold climate. The ice remained for thousands of years; then it slowly melted and retreated northward again. This forward and backward movement of the ice was repeated several times as the climate changed during a period of many thousands of years, which we call the Ice Age. When the ice came down for the last time, the Early Stone Age had ended. The improvement of stone tools and implements during this period had been very slow. It had advanced scarcely at all during all those thousands of years.

17. While the invasion of the ice thus made life very difficult for the Early Stone Age men on the north side of the Mediterranean, we see, by examining the map Stone Age men (p. 13), that the ice never reached the Medi- south of the Medi- terranean, and that the entire Southern Flat- terranean protected lands in North Africa, the region which we now from the ice call the Sahara Plateau, was never visited by the ice. The same atmospheric moisture which in frozen form built up the icy glaciers on the *north* side of the Mediterranean fell as plentiful rain on the *south* side. The Sahara Plateau was therefore well watered and covered with meadows, forests, and jungle growth. Across this fertile region the Early Stone Age hunters

---

* NOTE ON MAP, PAGE 13. After the Glacial Age, when the ice, which had pushed far south across large portions of Europe and Asia, had retreated for the last time, it was the men of the Great White Race who moved in and occupied these formerly ice-bound regions. So it came about that finally the people of this race inhabited the whole Northwest Quadrant, where eventually was produced the civilization which is ours today. The words "Great White Race" above represent the later spread of the race, but do not mean that they lived on the *ice*! In North Africa these people were dark-skinned, but nevertheless physically they belong to the Great White Race. This map is to be used with frequent consultation of the Racial Diagram of the Great Northwest Quadrant (Fig. 79).

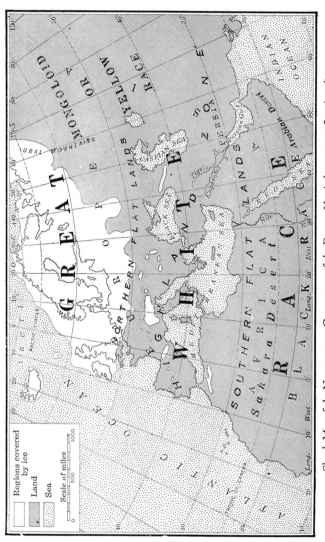

Sketch Map of the Northwest Quadrant of the Eastern Hemisphere in the Ice Age*

pursued the same big game which we saw them hunting on the north side of the Mediterranean. Sometimes they followed the game down into the wide and deep gorge which the Nile had already cut clear across the eastern end of the Sahara (see map, p. 13).

18. The Nile was at that time a much larger river than now. Like the Missouri River it sometimes shifted its bed and then never went back to the old one. One of the now dry beds of this larger early Nile, a stretch over fifty miles long parallel with the present river, has recently been discovered. On digging into its gravels, which are sixty feet deep, the archæologists found that it contained many of the stone weapons of the earliest hunters of the Southern Flatlands, who must have lost them there as they hunted on the banks of the river at least several hundred thousand years ago.

Weapons of the earliest Stone Age hunters found in the Nile gorge

19. At some time before the middle of the Ice Age, when the North African hunters were still in the Early Stone Age, the plentiful rains, which had long watered North Africa, began slowly to fail. The reason for this diminished rainfall is not yet clearly understood. The rainfall in Europe also decreased. As a result of the failing moisture the glacial ice in Europe began to shrink and to retreat toward the north, while the decreasing rainfall in North Africa caused the great Sahara Plateau slowly to dry up. Its parching vegetation gradually disappeared. During a period of many thousands of years the Sahara Plateau was slowly changed into the waterless desert which we know today. Thus, while the hunters on the north side of the Mediterranean were still suffering from the cold and the ice, those on the south side were being slowly driven from their plateau home by lack of water.

Drying Sahara Plateau slowly becomes uninhabitable

20. At this period the Nile valley was of the greatest value to these early hunters of the Southern Flatlands. The valley is a gorge, or canyon, more than thirty miles in width, with steep rock walls varying from a few hundred to a thousand feet in height. With its great river flowing down the gorge

FIG. 4. *The Heights of the* SAHARA PLATEAU *opposite Thebes*

Along the crest of the cliffs, shown in the background, the Early Stone Age hunters had a number of flint workshops. Worked flints are still scattered here so plentifully that one walks on them for hundreds of yards. The tops of these cliffs were the shores of a bay of the larger early Nile (§ 18). And on these shores the hunters sat chipping away at their flint weapons. Many thousands of years later the Nile River had shrunk to its present size, and the Egyptian emperors were having their tombs (§ 146) excavated in the walls of the cliffs which had been formerly cut out by the action of the river. In the center of the photograph may be seen the tomb entrances. The position of the tomb of Tutenkhamon, behind a low hill in the foreground, is indicated by an arrow. The embankment *A–B* is the rubbish from the modern excavation of this tomb

the valley offered the Early Stone Age hunters a new home with plenty of water. Therefore they shifted their dwellings down into the Nile gorge and made their homes along the banks of the river. Here the bottom of the great Nile trench, although it **Plateau man finds refuge in the Nile gorge** was as rainless as the desert, was watered by the river, which was plentifully fed from the rainy regions far south of the desert. Protected on both sides by practically rainless desert and unvisited by the ice or the cold of the north side of the Mediterranean, the great valley formed a *sheltered* home. Here the Early Stone Age hunters were soon to advance toward civilization much faster than the men of the same age in Europe, hindered as these prehistoric European hunters were by ice and arctic cold. The stone tools and weapons which reveal this advance to us have been found in great numbers, buried in the rock and gravel terraces formed by the river along its shores.

SECTION 3. THE MIDDLE STONE AGE

21. Thus while Europe was struggling with snow and ice the hunters of North Africa had found a warm and genial **Industries of the** refuge at the bottom of the great Nile trench. **Middle Stone Age** Nevertheless, when the ice came down for the **hunters** fourth and last time the European hunters of the Early Stone Age had finally improved their stone implements and their manner of living. Then began a new period which we may call the Middle Stone Age. Unable to build themselves shelters from the cold, the hunters of Europe took refuge in limestone caves, where they continued to live for thousands of years. We can imagine such a hunter at the door of his cave, carefully chipping off the edges of his flint tools. By this time he had finally left the rude old fist-hatchet far behind, and he had discovered that by *pressure* with a hard piece of bone he could chip off a line of fine flakes along the edge of his flint tool and thus produce a much finer cutting edge than by chipping with *blows* (or *percussion*), as his ancestors had done.[1] This discovery enabled him to produce a considerable variety of flint tools, — chisels, drills and hammers, polishers and scrapers. The new *pressure*-chipped edges were sharp enough to cut and shape even bone, ivory, and especially reindeer horn. The mammoth furnished the hunters with ivory, and when they needed horn they found great herds of reindeer, driven southward by the ice, grazing before the caverns in which these hunters were living.

22. With their new and keener tools the Middle Stone Age hunters worked out barbed ivory spear-points, which they attached to long wooden shafts, and each carried at his

---

[1] This new style of flint-chipping may have been brought in by an invasion of another people from the outside.

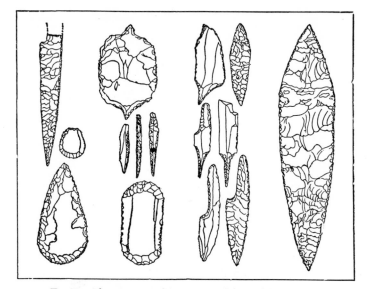

FIG. 5. *Flint* TOOLS *and* WEAPONS *of the Middle Stone Age*

From right to left they include knives, spear-points and arrow-points, scrapers, drills, and various edged tools. They show great skill and precision in flaking (see § 21)

girdle a sharp flint dagger. For straightening their wooden spear-shafts they invented an ingenious shaft-straightener of reindeer horn. Another clever device of horn or ivory was a spear-thrower, by which a hunter could hurl his long spear much farther and with greater force than he could before.

Middle Stone Age hunters' new weapons and skin clothing

Fine ivory needles found by excavation show that these people had learned to protect themselves from the cold and from the brambles of the forest wilderness with clothing made by sewing together the skins of animals.

23. Thus equipped, the hunters of the Middle Stone Age were much more dangerous foes of the wild creatures than were the men of the Early Stone Age. In a single cavern in Sicily archæologists have dug out the bones of no less than two thousand hippopotamuses which these Middle Stone Age hunters killed. In France one

Life of Middle Stone Age hunter

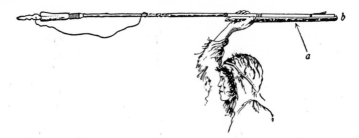

FIG. 6. *Modern Eskimo Hunter hurling a* SPEAR *with a* SPEAR-THROWER

The spear lies in a channel in the spear-thrower (*a*), which the hunter grasps at one end. At the outer end (*b*) of the spear-thrower is a hook (cf. Fig. 7, *B*), against which the butt of the spear lies. As the hunter throws forward his arm, retaining the spear-thrower in his hand and allowing the spear to go, the spear-thrower acts like an elongation of his arm, giving great sweep and propelling power as the spear is discharged. Modern schoolboys would not find it hard to make and use such a spear-thrower

group of such men slew so many wild horses for food that the bones which they tossed about their camp fires gathered in heaps, finally forming a layer in some places six feet thick and covering a space about equal to four modern city lots each fifty by two hundred feet. Among such deposits excavators have found even the bone whistle with which a returning hunter was able to announce his coming to his hungry family waiting in the cave. On his arrival there he found his home surrounded by piles of garbage. Amid foul odors of rotting flesh this savage European crept into his cave dwelling at night, little realizing that many feet beneath the cavern floor on which he slept lay the remains of his ancestors in layer upon layer, the accumulations of thousands of years (Fig. 11).

24. In spite of the darkness and savagery of their daily life these primitive hunters were standing just at the dawning of

Age of earliest art dawns

the first great light that entered the souls of men. Each of these savage hunters, when he lay down in his cavern at night, could close his eyes and see mind-pictures of the great beasts he had been pursuing all day. He could recall curious trees the shape of which might remind him of an animal, or he might turn as he lay and see a bulging mass of rock in his cavern, which looked like a horse. Thus there might arise in his mind the idea of *resemblance*: the animal and the tree that looked like it, the horse and the rounded rock that looked like the horse. As this thought continued, he began to be aware that resemblance might be produced by his own hands; that is, he could imitate the form of one object by shaping another like it. In this way the possibility of *imitation* awoke in his mind. In that moment art was born, and the soul of man entered a new world, the world of beauty, filled with a light that had never brightened his life before. For ages his *body* had been developing, but in this new realization that he might create beautiful forms out of the storehouse of his memory his *mind* grew and rose to a new and higher level. Sketches on small stones have been found, made by beginners just learning to draw. They are like modern studio exercises, and still show the corrections made by the more skilled hand of the master.

A   B

FIG. 7. *Two Views of a* SPEAR-THROWER *used by a Middle Stone Age Hunter*

(*A*) seen from the front; (*B*) seen from the side. It is carved of reindeer horn to represent the head and forelegs of an ibex. Observe the hook at the top of *B* for holding the butt of the spear-shaft. The spear-thrower and the bow were the earliest devices of man for hurling his weapons with speed

25. This new and *creative* age of man's prehistoric life has been revealed to us in an amazing series of works of art discovered in the Stone Age caverns of Europe. It is not a little surprising to find that these Middle Stone Age hunters of Europe could already carve, draw, and even paint with considerable skill. A Spanish nobleman who had crawled into a cavern on his estate in northern

Discovery of Middle Stone Age art

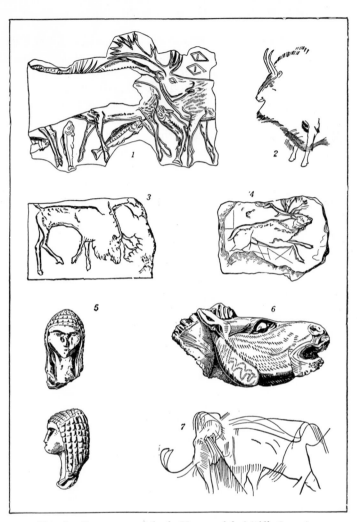

FIG. 8. CARVINGS *made by the Hunters of the Middle Stone Age*

The oldest works of art by man, carved in horn, schist, ivory, and the stone of cavern walls perhaps ten or fifteen thousand years ago. *1*, reindeer and salmon,—hunter's and fisherman's talisman; *2*, bison bull at bay; *3*, grazing reindeer; *4*, running reindeer; *5*, head of woman, front view and profile; *6*, head of wild horse whinnying; *7*, mammoth (an animal long since extinct), showing huge tusks and long hair

Spain was digging among the accumulations on the floor of the cave, where he had found flint and bone implements. His little daughter, who was playing about in the gloom of the cavern, suddenly shouted, *"Toros! toros!"* ("Bulls! bulls!"). At the same time she pointed to the ceiling. The startled father, looking up, beheld a never-to-be-forgotten sight which at once interrupted his flint-digging. In a long line stretching far across the ceiling of the cavern was a procession of bison bulls painted in well-preserved colors on the rock. For at least ten thousand years no human eye had beheld these cave paintings of a vanished race of men, till the eye of a child rediscovered them.

26. Other relics of higher life among these early men are few indeed. Nevertheless, even these ancient men of the Middle Stone Age believed in divine beings; they already had a crude idea of the life of the human soul, or of the departed person, after death. When one of their number died, they dressed him in his customary ornaments and supplied him with a few flint implements at least. Then they buried the departed hunter, protected by a rough circle of stones, in the cave beneath the hearth where he had so often shared the results of the hunt with his family. Here the bodies of these early men are found at the present day, lying under the successive layers of refuse which continued to collect over them for ages.

Religion in the Middle Stone Age

27. As the European hunters of the Middle Stone Age gained greater skill in carving and painting, they filled the caverns of France and northern Spain with pictures of the wild animals they hunted. Similar pictures are numerous in eastern Spain, not in caverns but on the rocks under the open sky; and likewise in North Africa, where they are found from Algiers entirely across the Sahara and eastward to the upper Nile. These widespread cave paintings and rock pictures, with much other evidence, reveal to us the Middle Stone Age hunters on both sides of the Mediterranean. We are now to see how their more favored situation in the Nile valley and their

End of the Middle Stone Age

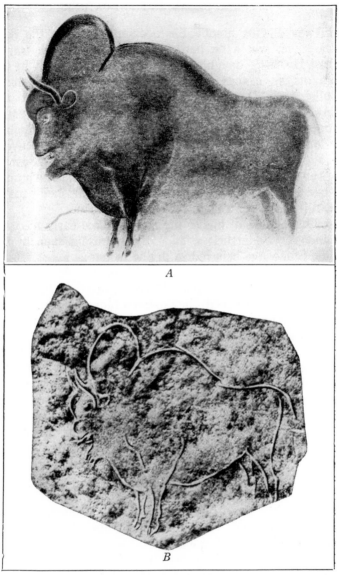

FIG. 9. CAVE PAINTING of a Bison (A) and the Artist's PREPARATORY SKETCH on a Small Stone (B)*

FIG. 10. NORTH AFRICAN ROCK DRAWING *of an* ELEPHANT *protecting her Young from the Attack of a Tiger*

The elephant mother throws her trunk around the young one to ward off the tiger, which is preparing to spring. This situation could not have lasted more than a few seconds; but the North African hunter's eye caught the scene, and he probably made a quick sketch then, which he afterward enlarged on a great rock in southern Algiers. The occurrence of such drawings, often in the most inaccessible regions of the desert, is further proof that the Sahara Plateau was, many thousands of years ago, a fertile region enjoying plentiful rains. (After Frobenius and Obermaier)

freedom from the rigors of the European Ice Age enabled the hunters of Egypt to become food-producers and thus to advance far beyond their rivals elsewhere, who long remained as before merely food-gatherers. The hunting life long continued, however; for it is now quite evident that the Nile gorge, with its lofty walls, had become a vast game preserve, where the animals of the Sahara Plateau, as we shall see, took refuge in enormous numbers. The presence of such great herds of wild game must have made the life of the Middle Stone Age hunter much easier.

* This remarkable sketch, scratched on a small stone of the same size as the photograph (*B*), was the ancient cave artist's preparatory study of the splendid bull bison, which he enlarged to nearly fifteen times the size of the sketch (*B*) when he laid out his great painting (*A*) on the cavern wall. He carefully copied on the cavern wall the lines he had scratched on the little stone, and then he finished his noble wall painting in a number of colors. Luckily for us, he threw away his little sketch (*B*), which was finally found by the archæologists some ten thousand years afterward in southern France. (*B* after Gaillard and *A* after Breuil)

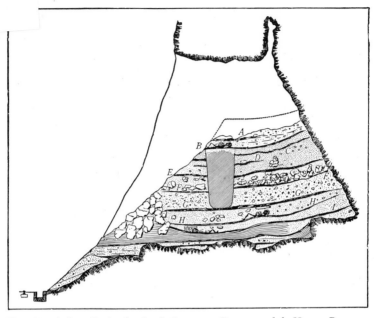

Fig. 11. A *Cross Section showing the* Layers of Rubbish *and the* Human Remains
in a Middle Stone Age Cavern

This cavern is at Grimaldi, on the Italian coast of the Mediterranean. The entrance is at the left, and the back wall at the right. We see the original rock floor at the bottom, and above it the layers of accumulations, 30 feet deep. The black lines *A* to *I* represent layers of ashes etc., the remains of nine successive hearth-fires, each of which must have been kept going by the natives for many years. The thicker (lightly shaded) layers consisted of bones of animals, rubbish, and rocks which had fallen from the roof of the cavern in the course of ages. The lowermost layers (below *I*) contained bones of the rhinoceros (representing a warm climate), while the uppermost layers contained bones of the reindeer (indicating a cold climate). Two periods, the Early and the Middle Stone Age, are thus represented,— the Early Stone Age below, the Middle Stone Age above. Five burials were found by the excavators in the layers *B*, *C*, *H*, and *I*; layer *C* contained the bodies of two children. The lowermost burial (in *I*) was 25 feet below the surface of the accumulations in the cave. These buried cave-dwellers crossed over from northern Africa and settled on the shores of Europe. Indeed, such prehistoric skulls and bones snow that several different races followed one another in Europe during the Stone Age. Since the above drawing was made, excavators digging in front of the cavern have penetrated to a depth of 60 feet below the original surface of the accumulations and have continued to find flint implements and other evidences of human occupation. (After Déchelette)

QUESTIONS

Section 1. Explain how Robinson Crusoe, after being at first merely a food-gatherer, became a food-producer. What things helped to make Crusoe a food-producer? What progress in invention have you noticed in your own lifetime? Describe the life of the Tasmanians in recent times. In what region of the world did civilization first arise? Describe this region and the life of the earliest men there. How can we trace the progress of early man?

Section 2. What is archæology? Describe the earliest stone weapon. Describe the life of the Early Stone Age hunter. What great change came over the life of the Early Stone Age man in Europe and Western Asia? Discuss the climate of North Africa during the Early Stone Age. What proof have we that the Sahara Plateau was habitable in early times? Why did the hunters on the Sahara Plateau retreat into the Nile valley?

Section 3. Where did the Middle Stone Age hunters take refuge after the coming of the ice? What improvements did they make in their stone tools? What new inventions were made? Discuss Middle Stone Age art. Draw a cross section of a cave with contents and describe (Fig. 11).

BIBLIOGRAPHY FOR TOPICAL STUDIES

Evidences of man's prehistory: BURKITT, *Our Forerunners*, pp. 7–35; BUXTON, *Primitive Labour*, chap. viii; COLE, *The Long Road*, chap. i; MARETT, *Anthropology*, pp. 30–59.

Art: BURKITT, *Our Forerunners*, chaps. ix–x; GARDNER, *Art through the Ages*, chap. i; OSBORN, *Man rises to Parnassus*, chap. iii; PEAKE-FLEURE, *Hunters and Artists*, pp. 77–95.

Chapter II · The Earliest Food-Producers

Section 4. The Late Stone Age

28. The floor of the Nile gorge was at first lacking in soil, but by the end of the Middle Stone Age the river had already

Coming of the black soil; Late Stone Age in Egypt

begun to carry down from the highlands of Abyssinia a great deal of black soil. Each season, as the summer rains of the Abyssinian mountains swelled the upper Nile, its waters rose above the banks. As they spread out over the bottom of the Egyptian Nile trench, these muddy waters left a thin layer of black mud. This sediment became at last a deep floor of black soil. It formed a strip wandering from right to left on each side of the winding river. At the present day this floor of black soil, including the strips of it on both sides of the river, is rarely more than ten miles wide. Living in the protected garden land thus formed, the Middle Stone Age men were able to advance to such improvements in manner of life that we must regard them as entering upon a new age which we call the Late Stone Age.

29. We have already learned that the animals which had so long inhabited the Sahara Plateau also found it necessary

Animals of the plateau seek refuge in the Nile valley; domestication

to take refuge in the Nile gorge in order to find food and water. The gorge was full of marshes, which offered a welcome home to vast flocks of wild fowl as well as to great herds of wild animals. On the north side of the Mediterranean the hunters had already learned to trap animals, even such large ones as the elephant. Down in the Nile gorge there was not as much room for these animals as they enjoyed in Europe or as they had once found on the plateau. As a result they were thrown into close contact with the human beings. Thus

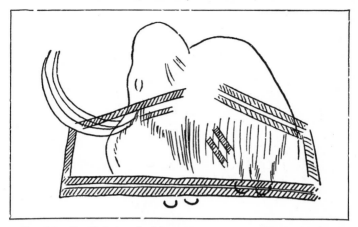

FIG. 12. *Cave Painting of a* MAMMOTH CAUGHT IN A TRAP *of Logs in Southern France*

This painting shows the early stage of man's ability to take wild animals captive At a later stage this practice led to domestication of animals. (Drawing after Capitan-Breuil-Peyrony)

the Middle Stone Age hunters found it easy to drive whole herds of them into the deep bays in the Nile-valley cliffs and to capture them there. At length it occurred to these hunters to close off such a bay with a stockade having only one entrance, or even to build a stockade of four sides with one gate, into which the game might be driven. Wild game thus fenced in formed a very valuable source of food "on the hoof" and was always ready for use. After a long time these captive animals lost their fear of men and gradually learned to live with them, thus becoming what we call domestic animals, the servants of men.

30. After a time the Nile-gorge people discovered another new and lasting source of food. Probably for thousands of years the women had been accustomed to gather the seeds of certain wild grasses and had ground them up for food. It was now discovered that such grasses could be planted and watered, so that they would grow better and produce a greater yield of eatable seed.

Discovery of agriculture

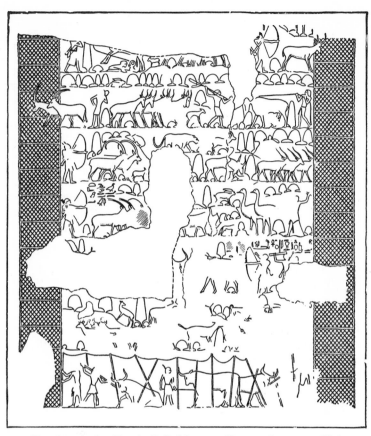

FIG. 13. *Ancient Egyptian Relief showing a* HUNTING INCLOSURE *filled with Animals*

This scene was placed on the wall of a tomb of the Feudal Age. The breaks and gaps are caused by damage to the wall. The wild animals have been driven into an inclosure made of netting. We see the hunters engaged in closing up one end (at bottom edge) by poles connected by lengths of rope, but the far end has been destroyed. Four men, who are armed with bows and arrows, are evidently bent on killing some of the game for immediate use. Other men, in the first and second rows, are using lassos for capturing the animals alive. The inclosure contains a fine catch, consisting of oryxes, gazelles, a leopard, hares, a jackal, ostriches, ibexes, addaxes, four stags, and even a porcupine. In the bottom row the men, who are setting up the final posts in order to close the trap, find it necessary to drive back the wild oxen, which are seeking to escape. (Drawing after Newberry)

Thus began the planting and harvesting of millet, barley, and wheat,[1] which were once only wild grasses.

31. After men began cultivating food in the field and raising it on the hoof, they became for the first time food-*producers*. Being therefore able to produce food *at home*, they found it less necessary to go out as hunters and kill wild animals for food. The wandering life of hunting, therefore, gradually changed. Groups of families settled down to live in one place, where it was possible to look after the tamed animals and to water the fields of grain. Most of the hunters finally became farmers and cattle-raisers, and thus began the age of agriculture and of animal husbandry which we may call the *Age of Food-production*.

Beginning of age of food-production and a settled life

32. We have seen that in this new Age of Food-production and settled life it was possible for men to make fixed homes. Their tools for this purpose were still made of stone, especially flint, but they had learned to use a gritty stone to sharpen the edges. By this method their stone tools were so much improved that we must regard the period as another Stone Age, which we call the Late Stone Age.[2] The homes which they made were at first only woven wattle huts daubed with mud. These were better equipped than formerly, for these

Ground stone tools; improvement of Late Stone Age life

---

[1] Oats and rye were still unknown and came in much later. The wild ancestors — that is, the wild grasses — from which our cultivated grains came have been discovered in Palestine and in Abyssinia, that is, both in Western Asia and in Eastern Africa.

[2] The Stone Age periods are as follows:

1. Early Stone Age (stone edge made by striking, or *percussion*) ⎱ Called Paleo-
2. Middle Stone Age (chipped stone edge made by *pressure*) ⎰ lithic Age by archæologists

3. Late Stone Age (stone edge made by *grinding*) ⎰ Called Neolithic Age by archæologists

In Europe, at least, it is probable that these successive improvements were the inventions of invaders of different races, who brought them in, rather than improvements introduced by the same race.

It is helpful to remember that we might also divide the prehistoric age into two periods, thus:

1. The Age of Food-gathering, including ⎰ *a.* The Early Stone Age ⎱ *b.* The Middle Stone Age

2. The Age of Food-production, beginning with the Late Stone Age

FIG. 14. *Stall-*FEEDING *of Semi-domesticated* ANTELOPES *and* HYENAS *along with Cattle*

The wild creatures, which were taken alive out of the inclosures (Fig. 13), were then stall-fed and partially if not wholly domesticated. Goats (*1*), gazelles (*4*, left end), addaxes (*4*, middle), oryxes (*4*, right end), ibexes (*4*, left), are all shown in the scene above, *eating at their mangers in stables* along with the large cattle (*2*). Many thousands of· years before the date of this wall relief these large cattle had been domesticated, and they became the ancestors of our own domesticated cattle. One important detail in the picture indicates that the Egyptians had practiced selective cattle-breeding from a very early date. The hornless breed of cattle (*2*, left end) is secured, or at least perpetuated, by selective breeding. At the bottom (*5*) captive hyenas are being stuffed with food. Among all these animals the Egyptians completed the domestication of the goats and large cattle shown here (*1*, *2*, and *3*); the others (*4*) were but partially domesticated and are now found only in a wild state, especially the hyenas (*5*)

early Nile-dwellers had noticed that clay will harden when heated in the fire. They were therefore able to make many pottery dishes, plates, pots, and jars for the household. At the same time the useful fibers of wild plants such as flax had been discovered, and the women had learned to cultivate these plants, to spin the fibers into thread, and to weave this thread into linen for their clothing.

33. All this happened so long ago that the traces of the little villages of wattle huts erected by the Late Stone Age Egyptians have been covered up under many Villages and cemeteries of Egyptian Late Stone Age feet of black soil, brought down since then by the Nile. Nevertheless scanty traces of several of their villages, on ground high enough to be above the reach of the Nile waters, have been discovered. They contained broken wooden sickles with flint edges, for use in harvesting grain, and also small circular pits used for granaries, in which were found small quantities of the grain itself. These are the oldest known evidences of agriculture. With these were bits of linen and pottery vessels, the earliest materials of this kind ever found. The villagers buried their dead along the margin of the black soil on the edge of the desert, at that time above the reach of the Nile waters. These cemeteries of the Late Stone Age men must have contained many graves much like the later one shown in Fig. 26; but unfortunately the cemeteries belonging to the Late Stone Age are now buried deep under the black soil, and nearly all of them are therefore still lost to us.

34. In one such cemetery, which has recently been found, the articles buried with the dead in one of the graves included a copper pin (Fig. 16, *11*). It is the Discovery of metal, about 5000 B.C. oldest implement of metal ever discovered in archæological excavation, for it can hardly be much later than 5000 B.C. It is interesting to follow in imagination the Egyptian who must have first discovered metal as he wandered into the Peninsula of Sinai, where the oldest copper mines are found. It may have been that in this vicinity (see map, p. 66) he happened to bank his camp fire with pieces of copper ore lying about on the ground. The glowing coals of his wood fire would finally roast the fragments of ore piled around to shield the fire, and thus the ore would be "reduced," as the miner says; that is, the copper in metallic form would be released from the lumps of ore. Next morning, as the Egyptian stirred the embers, he would discover in the ashes a few shining beads of metal. We can

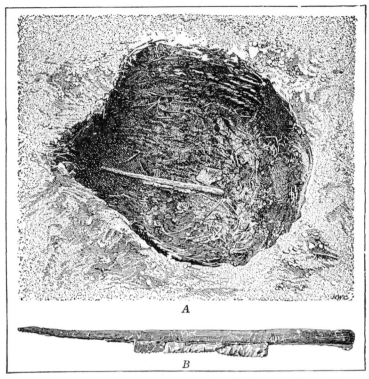

A

B

Fig. 15. *Late Stone Age* Wooden Sickle *(B) with Saw-Tooth Blade of* Flint, *found in Straw-Lined* Granary *(A)*

This prehistoric granary was a shallow pit dug in the earth. Wet mud was smeared on the floor and sides of the pit, and then it was lined with straw. A number of such granaries were found together. Most of them were empty but some contained quantities of wheat, barley, and other grain. The wooden sickle (*B*) found lying on the bottom of this granary (*A*) is nearly two feet long. A dark, gluelike mass holds the three saw-toothed pieces of flint in place to serve as the cutting edge of the sickle, and they remain fixed as firmly in their groove as they were on that day thousands of years ago when the Stone Age Egyptian dropped the sickle in the pit and perhaps forgot all about it. (After Miss G. Caton-Thompson)

imagine how he may have picked them up and turned them admiringly as they glittered in the sunshine. As the experience was repeated he discovered that these strange, shining beads had come out of the pieces of stone around his fire.

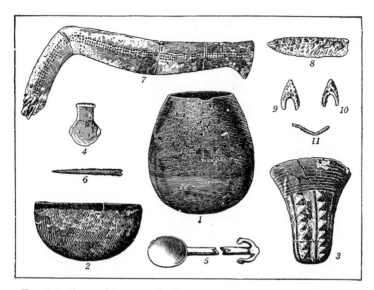

FIG. 16. *Group of* ARTICLES *found in a Late Stone Age Egyptian* CEMETERY

The Late Stone Age Egyptians had learned that clay hardens when baked; they therefore used baked clay for their purely hand-molded household vessels (*1–3*). The thinness and quality of this ware (jar, *1*), the beautifully rippled surfaces (bowl, *2*), were never improved upon by the later Egyptian potters, even after they had invented the wheel to aid them. The Late Stone Age Egyptians employed ivory or bone for cosmetic jars (*4*), spoons (*5*), and needles (*6*), wood and flint for implements (*7–10*). Toward the end of the Late Stone Age they learned to use copper for pins (*11*) or ornaments. Ivory spoons (*5*) were placed in the grave before the face of the dead man and at his hands, so that he might use them for eating his food in the next world. The bone needles (*6*) were used to sew garments of woven material as well as of skin, and were similar to the needles of Middle Stone Age man in Europe. Object *7* was an ancient Egyptian boomerang and probably the ancestor of the Australian boomerang. Saw-edged knives of flint (*8*) and many flint arrowheads (*9* and *10*) are found, but the bows have not been recovered; perhaps they were considered too valuable to be buried.
(Drawing after Brunton)

35. Without knowing it this man stood at the dawning of a new era, the Age of Metal; and if this Egyptian wanderer could have seen it, the little bead of shining copper which he drew from the ashes might **Dawning of the Age of Metal** have reflected to him a marvelous vision of the future, with metal buildings, great bridges, huge factories roaring with the noise of thousands of machines of metal, and vast stretches

of steel roads along which thunder hosts of rushing locomo-
tives. For these things of our modern world, and all they

signify, might never have
come to pass but for the
little bead of metal which
the wondering Egyptian
held in his hand for the
first time on that event-
ful day long, long ago.
Since the discovery of
fire many thousands of
years earlier, men had
made no conquest of the
things of the earth which
could compare in impor-
tance with this discovery
of metal. This took place
not later than about the
year 5000 B.C., that is, at
least about seven thou-

FIG. 17. *Rock Drawing of* HUNTER *with*
Earliest BOW AND ARROWS

This Middle Stone Age hunter is pictured
on the rocks in eastern Spain. He is about
to draw his bow, which he holds in his left
hand along with three arrows. These hunters
of eastern Spain came from North Africa.
(Drawing after Obermaier and Wernert)

sand years ago. But it was to be many centuries before copper tools and weapons came into common use. During this
long period, and for some time after, the Late Stone Age life
went on just as if metal had not been discovered.

36. Meantime the hunters on the north side of the Mediterranean had continued to lead their food-gathering life of
Final retreat of the   the Middle Stone Age, without cattle, grain,
ice in Europe   pottery, ground stone tools, or linen clothing.
The signs left by the ice, as it was drawing back northward
for the last time, have led geologists to think that it reached
its present latitude nearly nine thousand years ago. At this
point, therefore, the men of the Middle Stone Age on the
north side of the Mediterranean entered upon weather conditions which gradually became like those of today.

37. While the ice was retreating for the last time on the
European side of the Mediterranean, and while the North
African plateau continued to dry up, influences from North

Africa began to reach the European hunters toward the close of the Middle Stone Age. These influences entered Europe along three routes. There were the two land-bridges at Gibraltar and Sicily (§ 9), which at that time still connected Africa and Europe. The North African hunters seem first **North African influences reach Europe by land-bridges** to have passed across these land-bridges carrying the bow and arrow, which they had probably invented, and accompanied by the wolflike creatures which they had tamed and which later became stanch friends of man, — the familiar domesticated dogs. The bodies of these hunters, showing clearly their African origin, have been found buried in the cavern of Grimaldi in Italy. It is not impossible that later some of the men of the Nile gorge, with more roving tendencies than the others, wandered across North Africa and passed over these same land-bridges into Europe, and it is highly probable that they took with them their domesticated animals. In this manner, no doubt, there passed over to Europe from Africa also wheat and barley, linen and pottery, together with ground stone tools and implements, of which exactly the same styles and types are found both in Egypt and among the Swiss lake-dwellings (§ 42).

38. The *third* route by which North Africa was connected with Europe was a water route by way of the large island of Crete (see map, p. 146). Since this island is only about one hundred and eighty miles from the coast of Africa, it served as a mid-way station and shortened the voyage across **North African influences reach Europe by the Cretan route** the Mediterranean from Africa to Europe. Sir Arthur Evans, in his excavations in Crete, dug down through the remains of palaces of the ancient Cretan kings, and *under* them he found the walls of houses containing *ground* or polished stone axes used by the Late Stone Age men who lived in these houses. In one of the rooms lay a copper ax from Egypt, probably the earliest metal tool ever found in Europe. This copper ax shows very clearly what the Egyptian ships were bringing to Crete and how the earliest metal reached Europe.

39. In Europe it was especially beside rivers and water-courses, where there were fertile soil and extensive pastures,

Earliest European food-producers on the lower Danube

that the early communities of food-producers in the Late Stone Age located their settlements. The most important of the European river valleys in this age was that of the Danube. In its lower course the valley expands into what are now the far-spreading and productive plains of Hungary. This region of the lower Danube extends down toward western Asia Minor, through which the Late Stone Age life of Western Asia passed over into eastern Europe, bringing with it cattle-breeding and the cultivation of grain. It is probable that the wide grain fields and extensive pastures of Hungary supported the first large farming communities of Europe as increasing numbers of men abandoned the hunting life and settled down here in fixed dwellings. From the farmers of the Danube the pastoral and agricultural life passed up the great river into the heart of Europe. The remains of the Late Stone Age settlements which at this time spread westward from Hungary disclose great improvements in the manner of living.

40. While the earliest of these settlements began with wattle huts, we shall now see that improved, ground-edged

Tools of Late Stone Age man in Europe

tools afterward made possible the construction of wooden houses. If we examine the equipment of the Late Stone Age workmen we find that they had a list of tools almost as complete as that of the modern carpenter. Besides the ax they had chisels, knives, drills, saws, and whetstones, made mostly of flint but sometimes of other hard stones. They had learned also either to attach a wooden handle by lashings around the ax-head or to fit the ax-head into a deer-horn handle, or even to bore a hole in the ax-head and insert a handle. These tools, as found today, often display a polish due to the wear which they have undergone in the hands of the user.

41. It is a mistake to suppose that a man could not do good and rapid work with such stone tools. In a recent experiment in Denmark a modern mechanic had his steel ax taken away

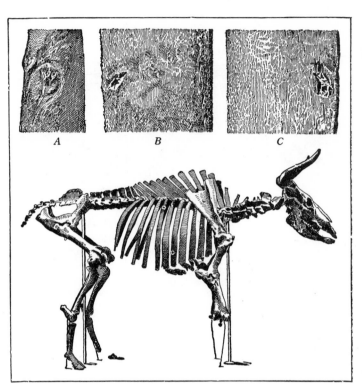

FIG. 18. *Skeleton of a* WILD BULL *bearing the Marks of the Late Stone Age Hunters'* ARROWS *which killed him in the Danish Forests, probably some Nine Thousand Years ago*

A Late Stone Age hunter shot him in the back near the spine (see *upper* white ring on skeleton). The wound healed, leaving a scar on the rib (*A*, above). Later another hunter shot him, and this time several arrows pierced his vitals. One of them, however, struck a rib (see *lower* white ring on skeleton) and broke off. Both sides of this wound, still unhealed, with the broken flint arrowhead still filling it, are shown above in *B* and *C*. While the wounded bull was trying to swim across a neighboring lake he died, and his body sank to the bottom ; and the pursuing hunter, on reaching the lake, found no trace of him. In the course of thousands of years the lake slowly filled up, and water 10 feet deep was followed by dry peat, of the same depth, which covered the skeleton of the bull. Here he was found in 1905, and lying with him were found the flint arrowheads that had killed him. His skeleton, still bearing the marks of the flint arrowheads (*A*, *B*, *C*), was removed, and set up in the museum at Copenhagen

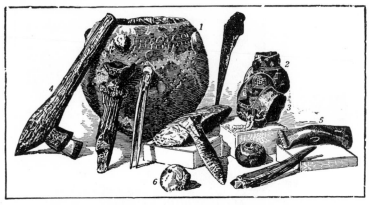

FIG. 19. *Part of the* EQUIPMENT *of a Late Stone Age* LAKE-DWELLER

This group contains the evidence for three important inventions made or received from the Near East by the men of the Late Stone Age: *first*, pottery jars, like *2* and *3*, with rude decorations, — the oldest baked clay in Europe, — and *1*, a large kettle in which the lake-dwellers' food was cooked; *second*, ground-edged tools like *4*, a stone chisel with ground edge, mounted in a deer-horn handle like a hatchet, or *5*, a stone ax with ground edge, and pierced with a hole for the ax-handle; and, *third*, weaving, as shown by *6*, a spinning "whorl" of baked clay, the earliest spinning wheel. When suspended by a rough thread of flax 18 to 20 inches long, it was given a whirl which made it spin in the air like a top, thus rapidly twisting the thread by which it was hanging. The thread, when sufficiently twisted, was wound up, and another length of 18 to 20 inches was drawn out from the unspun flax to be similarly twisted. One of these earliest spinning wheels has been found in the Swiss lakes with a spool of flaxen thread still attached. (From photograph lent by Professor Hoernes)

from him. In its place he was given a stone ax, and although he was not accustomed to the use of stone tools, he was able, **Effectiveness of stone tools** in ten working hours, to cut down twenty-six pine trees eight inches in thickness and hew them into logs. Then the *entire work of hewing out the planks and timbers and building a house was done by one mechanic with stone tools in eighty-one days*. It was therefore quite possible for the men of the Late Stone Age to build comfortable dwellings and to attain a degree of civilization far above that of savages.

42. The most plentiful traces of the earliest wooden houses in Europe are to be found in Switzerland. Here groups of families of the Late Stone Age built their villages of wooden

FIG. 20. *Surviving Remains of a Swiss* LAKE-VILLAGE

After an unusually dry season the Swiss lakes fell to a very low level in 1854, exposing the lake bottom with the remains of the piles which once supported the lake-villages along the shores. Thus was the existence of such villages discovered. It has now been shown that this low level of the water was the *original* level, when the above village was built. It stood, therefore, as we see it here, on the dry land *beside* the lake, and not over the water, as was formerly believed. In the course of thousands of years the water of the Swiss lakes has risen and covered the old shores, including the remains of the pile-villages, and has thus produced the incorrect impression that they were built over the water, and that the piles had been driven into the lake-bottom. Among the projecting piles were found great quantities of tools, household furnishings, and implements like those in Fig. 19; also dugouts and fish nets, wheat, barley, bones of domestic animals, woven flax, etc. There they had been lying some five thousand years. Sometimes the objects were found in two distinct layers, the lower (earlier) containing only *stone* tools, and the upper (later) containing *bronze* tools, which came into the lake-village at a later age and fell down on top of the layer of old stone tools already lying there

houses upon platforms stretching in long lines along the shores of the Swiss lakes. These platforms were supported by piles driven into the ground. Such villages, or groups of *pile-dwellings*, are com- Swiss lake-villages of Late Stone Age monly called *lake-villages*. In a few cases they finally grew to be quite large. At Wangen not less than fifty thousand piles were driven into the ground for the support of the village (see remains of such piles in Fig. 20).

43. The lake-villagers lived a life of peace and prosperity. Their houses were comfortable shelters, and they were supplied with wooden furnishings and pottery Life of Swiss lake-dwellers hand-formed, that is, without the potter's wheel. The hillsides looking down upon the lake-villages were green with fields of barley, wheat, and millet. This new source of food was a plentiful one; more than a hundred bushels of grain were found by the excavators on the lake bottom under the vanished lake-village of Wangen. Up the hillside now stretched also the lake-dweller's little fields of flax beside the growing grain. Their women sat spinning flax before the doorways, and the rough skin clothing of their ancestors had given way to garments of linen.

44. At first no one person owned these fields of wheat, barley, or flax; but after a time each household gradually gained **Social effects of** the right to cultivate a particular field, and **agriculture** finally they came to set up a claim to it. Thus arose ownership of land. It was to be a frequent cause of trouble in the future life of men, and out of it came the long struggle between the rich and the poor. This system of land ownership established more firmly the settled agricultural life in and around the villages, because it was necessary for the villagers to remain near the little fields where their women had hoed the ground for planting, that they might care for the crop and gather the grain when it ripened.

45. On the other hand, the possession of grass-eating animals feeding on the grasslands created a different class of **Flocks and herds;** men, who did not lead a settled life. The pas- **wandering, or** turage was not everywhere plentiful enough **nomadic, shep-** to permit keeping the cattle always in one **herd life** place. At times the cattle-keepers were obliged to seek pasturage somewhere else; and thus they came to follow a roving life, transporting their wives and children, and driving their flocks about in order to pasture them wherever the grasslands offered food. Such people, made up of herdsmen and shepherds, we call *nomads*, and they still exist today. While the farmers remained settled on their rich farm lands, the nomads took possession of the grasslands which stretched from the Danube eastward along the north side of the Black Sea and thence far over into Asia.

46. Thus grain and cattle created two methods of life side by side, — the settled, agricultural life of grain-raising and the wandering, nomad life of cattle-breeding. It is important to understand these two classes of people, because the grasslands became the home of a numerous *unsettled* population. Such grasslands often became too crowded with the nomad peoples, who then overflowed and overwhelmed the towns and the agricultural settlements. We shall see later Europe invaded over and over again by the hordes of nomads coming in from the eastern grasslands.

Age-long conflict between nomads and townsmen

47. The *settled* communities of the Late Stone Age at last began to leave behind them something more than fragile wooden houses and wattle huts. Toward the close of this age the more powerful chiefs in the large settlements learned to erect tombs, built of large blocks of stone. These tombs are still found fringing the western coast of Europe from the Mediterranean around Spain to the southern Scandinavian shores. There are at the present day no less than thirty-four hundred stone tombs of this age, some of considerable size, on the Danish island of Seeland alone. In France they exist in vast numbers and imposing size, and likewise in England. The enormous blocks in some of these structures were mostly left in the rough; but if cut at all, it was done with stone chisels. Such structures are not of masonry that is, of smoothly cut stone laid with mortar. They cannot be called works of architecture, — a thing which did not as yet exist in Europe.

Buildings in Late Stone Age Europe

48. When we look at these monuments of the Late Stone Age, still surviving, they prove to us the existence of the earliest towns in Europe ; for near every great group of stone tombs there was a town where the people lived who built the tombs. The remains of some of these towns have been discovered. They show us that men were learning to live together in larger numbers and to work together on a large scale. It required power over men and successful management of them to raise the earth walls of such a town, to drive fifty thousand piles supporting the lake-village at Wangen (Switzerland), or to move great blocks of stone for building the chieftain's tomb.

Earliest towns in Europe; the rise of government

FIG. 21. *Air View of the* GREAT STONE CIRCLE *at Stonehenge, England*

The circle is about one hundred feet across, and a long avenue connecting it with the neighboring Late Stone Age town is still traceable. Stonehenge dates from the beginning of the Copper or Bronze Age (about 2000 B.C.) and marks the end of the Late Stone Age in western Europe, which produced nothing more than this rude architecture in stone until the coming of the Romans. It is thought by some that Stonehenge marks the burial place of certain Stone Age chieftains.
(Courtesy of British Ordnance Survey Office and the editor of *Antiquity*)

In these works we see the beginnings of government under the rule of a leader. We may call such a government a state, and many little states, each made up of an earth-walled town with its surrounding fields, and each under a chieftain, grew up in Late Stone Age Europe. Out of such beginnings nations were later to grow.

49. Furthermore, the stone structures (§ 47) furnish us very interesting glimpses of the life of the Late Stone Age

Festivals and athletic contests of Late Stone Age Europe

towns. Some of them suggest to us whole communities coming out from the towns on feast days and marching to such places as the huge stone circles at Stonehenge in England (Fig. 21). It has been thought that here they held contests and athletic games in honor of the dead chief buried within the stone circles. Festival processions probably once marched down long avenues marked out by mighty stones. Today,

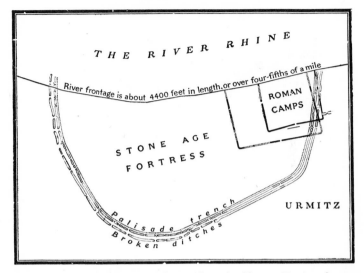

FIG. 22. PLAN *of the* DEFENSES *of a Late Stone Age Town at Urmitz, Germany*

This town was located on a level plain along the river Rhine, just north of the modern city of Coblenz. Excavations show that the defenses consisted of two lines of ditches (now very much broken), which describe a rough semicircle surrounding the city on three sides and extending at both ends of the town to the bank of the Rhine, which formed the defense on the fourth side. Just inside the inner ditch was a wooden palisade, the course of which is marked by the *innermost* line inside the ditches on the plan. Not all of the entrance causeways have been found, but the excavator thinks that there were about twenty-two entrances to the fort, each having a causeway leading across the palisade trench and both ditches. The entrances were probably closed with gates made of irregular wooden beams. It is believed that the entrance causeways enabled the defenders of a settlement to make sudden sallies against a besieging enemy from different points, and all at the same time. Long after the houses and defenses of this Late Stone Age town were in ruins, Roman soldiers built a small and then a larger fortress in one corner. (Drawing after Lehner)

silent and forsaken, they stretch for miles across the fields of the modern farmers, to remind us of forgotten human joys, of ancient customs, and of beliefs long revered by the vanished peoples of Stone Age Europe.

50. While such monuments are relics of the Late Stone Age people at play, other remains show them to us at their work. Men were beginning to adopt trades; for example, some men were probably wood-workers, others were potters,

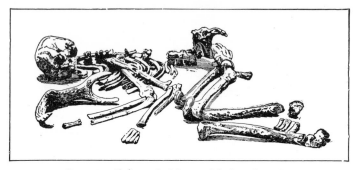

FIG. 23. *Skeleton of a* MINER *of the Late Stone Age*

The skeleton of this ancient miner was found lying on the floor of a flint mine in Belgium, under the rocks which had caved in and crushed him. Before him, just as it dropped from his hands at the instant of the cave-in, lies the double-pointed pick of deer-horn with which he was loosening the lumps of flint from their chalk bed when the rock ceiling fell upon him

and still others were already miners. These early miners burrowed far into the earth in order to reach the finest deposits of flint for their stone tools. In the underground tunnels of the ancient flint mines at Brandon, England, eighty worn picks of deer-horn were found in recent times. At one place the roof had caved in, cutting off a gallery of the mine. Here, behind the fallen rocks, archæologists found two more deer-horn picks bearing a coat of chalk dust in which were still visible the marks of the workmen's fingers, left there as they last laid down these tools thousands of years ago.

Rise of trades at the end of the Late Stone Age; mining

51. Business relations between the villages already existed. Such beginnings of commerce sometimes carried things far and wide. An outstanding example of this was an especially fine variety of French flint, found scattered today in many parts of Europe and recognizable by its color. The amber gathered on the shores of the Baltic was already passing from hand to hand southward to the Mediterranean. Stone implements found on the islands around Europe show that men of this age lived on these islands, and they must have had boats strong enough

Business in Late Stone Age

to carry them thither. Several of the dugouts of the lake-dwellers have been found lying on the lake bottom among the

FIG. 24. VERTEBRA *of a Late Stone Age* MAN *with a Flint Arrowhead sticking in it*

The arrowhead (*A*) struck the victim full in the pit of the stomach. It must have been driven by a powerful bow, for it passed clear through to the spinal column, producing peritonitis and death. (Photograph furnished by the great French archæologist Déchelette, who himself fell in battle not long after sending this photograph to the author)

piles, but vessels with *sails* had not yet been invented in Europe. The business of such an age was of course very simple. There were no metals and no money. Buying and selling were only exchange of one kind of wares for another kind. In all Europe there was no writing, nor did the inhabitants of the mainland of Europe *ever* invent a system of writing.

52. But the intercourse between these earliest villages was not always peace- **Wars of the Late** ful. The earthen **Stone Age** walls and the wooden stockades with which such towns were protected show us that the chieftain's war-horn must often have summoned these people to repel the enemy. Grim relics of these earliest wars of Europe still survive. A skull taken out of a tomb of this age in Sweden contains a flint arrowhead still sticking in one eyehole, while in France more than one human bone has been found with a flint arrowhead driven deep into it. A stone coffin found in a Scottish stone heap contained the body of a man of huge size, with one arm almost severed from the shoulder by the stroke of a stone ax. A fragment of stone broken out of the ax blade still remained in the gashed arm bone.

53. Such was the life of Late Stone Age men on the north side of the Mediterranean near the close of this period, about three thousand years before Christ. Long before this, portions of the Gibraltar and Sicilian land-bridges had sunk

beneath the water, and Europe was separated from Africa as it is today. The Late Stone Age villages on the north
Late Stone Age Europe at a standstill side of the Mediterranean were no longer connected by land directly with Africa and the Nile valley. Thus the older roads by which they had probably received cattle and grain were closed to them, and no more inventions from Egypt could reach them by those routes. But the sea route by way of Crete was always open, and the civilization of Western Asia, which we shall study later, was also entering Europe across the Ægean Sea, around the Black Sea, and especially, as we have seen, up the valley of the Danube. Nevertheless, after changing from the hunting life to the settled life beside their grain fields and on their pastures, the Stone Age men of Europe made little or no progress. They were still without *writing* for making the records of business and government; they were still without *metals* [1] with which to make tools and to develop industries and manufactures; and they had no *sailing ships* in which to carry on commerce. Without these things they could go no farther. Meanwhile these and many other possessions of civilization were being discovered or invented on the other side of the Mediterranean in Egypt and Western Asia, — in the lands which we now call the Near East. [2]

54. As we leave Europe to follow the story of the Ancient Near East let us remember that we have been following
Westward movement of civilization man's *prehistoric* progress as it went on all around the Mediterranean for several hundred thousand years after he began making stone implements.

[1] Metal was introduced in *southeastern* Europe about 3000 B.C. and passed like a slow wave, moving gradually westward and northward across Europe. It probably did not reach Britain until about 2000 B.C. Hence we have included the great stone monuments of western Europe (like Stonehenge) in our survey of Stone Age Europe. They were erected long after *southeastern* Europe had received metal but before metal came into common use in *western* Europe.

[2] The term "Far East" is used today to include Japan, China, and India. The term "Near East" became very common during the World War, especially in connection with the relief work called "Near East relief," and is now the most convenient name for the lands grouped about the eastern end of the Mediterranean, although the word "Orient" is still a correct designation of the same region.

In the Near East, beginning before 4000 B.C. and during the thousand years from 4000 to 3000 B.C. (see diagram, Fig. 41), men slowly built up a high civilization, forming the beginning of the *Historic Age*.[1] Civilization thus began in the Near East, where it is between five and six thousand years old. There it long flourished and produced great and powerful nations, while the men of the Late Stone Age in Europe continued to live without metals or writing. As they gradually received these things from the Near East the leadership of civilization both in peace and in war shifted slowly to Europe. As we turn to watch civilization gradually appearing in the Near East, with metals, government, writing, great ships, and many other creations of civilization, let us realize that its later movement will steadily carry us from east to west as we follow it from the Near East to Europe.

QUESTIONS

Section 4. Discuss the conditions in the Nile valley leading to the domestication of animals. Explain what is meant by "the Age of Food-production." Tell something of the life of the earliest Nile men and how we know about them. Describe the probable manner of the discovery of metal. Which metal was it? What great change in Europe ended the Middle Stone Age? How did North African cultural influences reach Europe? Where were the earliest large food-producing communities in Europe? Discuss carpentry with *ground* stone tools. Describe the lake-villages and the life in them. What were the social effects of agriculture? Discuss stone structures and the life they reveal, — industries, traffic, and war. What important things did the Late Stone Age in Europe still lack? Is civilization possible without these things? Where did these things first appear?

---

[1] We may best describe the Historic Age by saying that it is the age beginning when written documents were first produced by man,— documents which tell us in written words something of man's life and career. All that we know of man in the age previous to the appearance of writing has to be learned from weapons, tools, implements, buildings, and other things (bearing no writing) which he has left behind. These are the things from which we have been learning something of the story of prehistoric man all around the Mediterranean (see Chapter I). The transition from the Prehistoric to the Historic Age was everywhere a slow and gradual one. In the Near East this transition took place in the thousand years between 4000 and 3000 B.C.

BIBLIOGRAPHY FOR TOPICAL STUDIES

Industries of the food-producers: BURKITT, *Our Early Ancestors*, pp. 50–72; BUXTON, *Primitive Labour*, chaps. iii–iv, ix; CHILDE, *Most Ancient East*, chap. iii; CLELAND, *Our Prehistoric Ancestors*, pp. 83–104 and Fig. 53; COLE, *The Long Road*, chap. iii.

Stone implements: British Museum, *Flints*; BURKITT, *Our Early Ancestors*, pp. 102–122; *Our Forerunners*, pp. 65–93; CLELAND, pp. 136–147.

Civilization of the lake-dwellers: CLELAND, pp. 148–168.

NOTE. Below we see the photograph of a group of stone grinders, or mortars, in which early food-producers of North Africa ground the grain which they had learned to plant and harvest. These household flour-mills were found in the remotest regions of the desert on the west of Egypt, hundreds of miles from the Nile. The fact that such mortars were once used in this now dry and desolate portion of the Sahara is further evidence of the existence of a period when the great Sahara Plateau had not yet become desert and early men could still live there and produce their food. The explorer's sun helmet at the right end furnishes a scale for the size of these grinders.

PART II · THE ORIGINS AND EARLY HISTORY OF
CIVILIZATION IN THE ANCIENT NEAR EAST

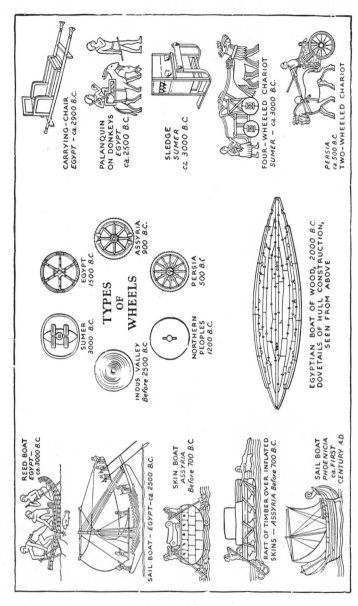

CARRYING-CHAIR
EGYPT - ca.2900 B.C.

PALANQUIN
ON DONKEYS
EGYPT
ca.2500 B.C.

SLEDGE
SUMER
ca.3000 B.C.

FOUR-WHEELED CHARIOT
SUMER - ca.3000 B.C.

PERSIA
ca.500 B.C.
TWO-WHEELED CHARIOT

TYPES
OF
WHEELS

SUMER
3000 B.C.

EGYPT
1500 B.C.

ASSYRIA
900 B.C.

PERSIA
500 B.C.

INDUS VALLEY
Before 2500 B.C.

NORTHERN
PEOPLES
1200 B.C.

EGYPTIAN BOAT OF WOOD, 2000 B.C.
DOVETAILS OF HULL CONSTRUCTION,
SEEN FROM ABOVE

REED BOAT
EGYPT-
ca.3000 B.C.

SAIL BOAT – EGYPT-ca.2500 B.C.

SKIN BOAT
ASSYRIA
Before 700 B.C.

RAFT OF TIMBER OVER INFLATED
SKINS – ASSYRIA Before 700 B.C.

SAIL BOAT
PHOENICIA
ca.FIRST
CENTURY A.D.

TRANSPORTATION in the Ancient Near East

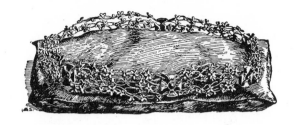

CHAPTER III · The Story of Egypt: The Rise of Civilization and the Pyramid Age

SECTION 5. THE FIRST UNION OF EGYPT AND THE RISE OF CIVILIZATION

55. As we take up again our study of the early Near East we return to Egypt. We remember how we followed the hunters of North Africa from the drying plateau down to the well-watered floor of the Nile valley, and we recall how these hunters learned to feed herds of once wild cattle in stockades and to plant fields of grain. Grain, of course, cannot grow without water, and these early Egyptians, living in a country without rain, had to make a simple machine for lifting water from the river or from canals filled by the river. In this way the irrigation trenches were kept full of water until the grain ripened. The Egyptians of today still continue to use the ancient water-lifting machine (Fig. 25), and our ancestors inherited it in the well sweep once common in New England.

Agriculture and irrigation

56. The soil of Egypt (§ 28) was enriched each year by the overflow of the river; for the muddy waters of the Nile continued to rise above its banks every summer, then to spread

NOTE. The TIARA, or DIADEM, at the top of this page was found resting on the head of an Egyptian princess of the Feudal Age as she lay in her coffin. The diadem had been placed there nearly four thousand years ago. It is in the form of a chaplet, or wreath, of star flowers wrought of gold and set with bright-colored, costly stones, and is one of the best examples of the work of the Egyptian goldsmiths and jewelers. It is shown here lying on a cushion.

far over the flats, and to stand there long enough to deposit a very thin layer of rich earthy sediment. In time this sedi-

Soil and area of Egypt, ancient and modern

ment filled a large bay at the mouth of the river and formed what we now call the Nile Delta. At the present day the Delta and the valley above, as far as the First Cataract (see map, p. 66), contain together over twelve thousand square miles of cultivable soil, about the area of Massachusetts and Connecticut. In the Late Stone Age, however, the area which could be cultivated must have been much smaller, for at that time the valley was still largely occupied by extensive marshes, and only here and there between the marshes was it possible to plant and harvest a crop. Furthermore, the fierce and rapid current of the river in the valley above the Delta made the shores there less easy to cultivate. But in the Delta, where the river branched out into smaller streams with slower currents, the marshes were easier to reclaim for cultivation.

Fig. 25. *An Egyptian* Shadoof, *the Oldest of* Well Sweeps, *Irrigating the Fields*

The man below stands in the water, holding his leather bucket (A). The pole (B) of the sweep is above him, with a large ball of dried Nile mud on its lower end (C) as a lifting weight, or counterpoise, seen just behind the supporting post (D). This man lifts the water into a mud basin (E). A second man (in the middle) lifts it from this first basin (E) to a second basin (F), into which he is just emptying his bucket. A third man (G) lifts the water from the middle basin (F) to the uppermost basin (H) on the top of the bank, where it runs off to the left into trenches spreading over the fields. The low water makes necessary three successive lifts (to E to F, to H), continued without ceasing, night and day, for one hundred days. The weird and plaintive songs of the shadoof-worker are heard day and night along the Nile

57. Gradually the people of the Delta outstripped the dwellers on the upper river and became more advanced in their manner of living. This advance led to the first regulations of community life, which finally became government. Government is Leadership of the Delta and rise of government an extensive organization for conducting the affairs of a community or nation. It grew up very slowly as a community felt the need of a leader. The people might first need him to help them defend themselves against their enemies in war, but the leadership of a warrior chieftain did not always result in very good government. Much more useful in the community was a leader to control and guide the men who were appointed to look after the trenches and canals which brought in the water to irrigate the fields. The need of good men to manage this irrigation system, as we call it, would gradually lead to better government.

The overflow of the river (called the inundation) often clogged the canals with mud, so that the men of a whole group of villages would go out together to dig out and clear the canals. They knew that if they did not do so there would be no water for the grain fields, no harvest, and finally no bread. The leader of one of these groups of Delta villages probably became in time a local chieftain who controlled the irrigation trenches and canals of the district. To him the people of the district were obliged to carry every season a share of the grain or flax which they gathered from their fields. These shares of grain or flax were the earliest taxes, and the chieftain's control of the canals and collection of such taxes formed the earliest government.

58. Eventually some one of these Delta chieftains, who was probably both a good irrigation engineer and a good fighter, conquered the rival chieftains in the other districts and united all the Delta into a kingdom which we call Lower Egypt, for it The Two Kingdoms: Lower Egypt and Upper Egypt was lower on the river. The King of Lower Egypt wore a red crown like this: ⨄, with a curious spiral in front. There must have been a long line of such Kings of Lower

Egypt, probably lasting for several centuries, but we know the names of only six. They are important, for they are the earliest known royal names in human history. In the same way there also arose another kingdom, extending up the Nile valley from the southern apex of the Delta to the region of the First Cataract. This stretch of over five hundred miles of the valley proper we call Upper Egypt, for it is on the *upper* course of the river, although lower on the map. The King of Upper Egypt wore a tall white crown like this: ⌂. Of these Kings of Upper Egypt there must likewise have been a long line, but their names are unknown to us.

59. These two kingdoms, Upper Egypt and Lower Egypt, were the earliest known nations. Their rule probably reached **The Two Kingdoms: Copper-Stone Age** back nearly seven thousand years, that is, nearly to the year 5000 B.C., and lasted for some centuries. There was a capital in each kingdom, where the king lived, while the people lived along the river in villages. The royal buildings and the huts of the peasants have all disappeared, but on the edge of the desert behind each village the people buried their dead in shallow pit-graves. The excavation of these graves shows that metal was very little used; for the art of mining was still hardly known, and little metal was to be had. As long as men continued to use metal only for making a few copper pins, or beads for the women, or an occasional tiny chisel, metal played an unimportant part in daily life. Stone tools and weapons still continued in common use.

60. There must have been much traffic between the Two Kingdoms, for they were of course connected by the Nile. **First union of all Egypt** Being thus in close contact, they often fell out with each other, and there were many wars between them. Finally, perhaps in the Forty-third Century B.C., although we are not sure about the date, a powerful King of Lower Egypt, whose name we do not know, marched southward out of the Delta and conquered his rival, the King of Upper Egypt. In this manner the Two Kingdoms were united under one king, who became King of

Upper and Lower Egypt. In order to show that he was ruler of both kingdoms he wore a new, double crown like this:

Fig. 26. *Looking down into the* Grave *of an Egyptian of the First Union*

An oval pit four or five feet deep. The body is surrounded by pottery jars which once contained food and drink

𝄞, made up of the two older crowns of the once separate kingdoms (pp. 53–54). He ruled the earliest known government controlling a population of several millions.

61. We shall call this first Kingdom of Upper and Lower Egypt the First Union as a matter of convenience, although this was not its ancient name. It lasted probably over eight hundred years, and had many kings, who lived at Heliopolis (or Sun-City), the first capital of Egypt (see map, p. 66). Situated midway between the Two Kingdoms, Heliopolis always remained the most sacred and influential of Egyptian cities. The history of the First Union is the most important chapter in the entire human story, because civilization arose in the age of the First Union. The people of the two united kingdoms made very important advances resulting in the production or invention of the remainder of those things which modern peoples regard as necessary to civilization (§ 5). Let us now see what those things were. *Place of the First Union in history*

62. We have seen that agriculture greatly improved human conditions and made it possible for men to give up the hunting life and to live in villages surrounded by little grain fields. But those grain fields had, up to this time, been cultivated by hand with the hoe, — a slow and laborious method of work. It greatly limited the amount of land which could be cultivated. Only very small fields of grain were possible. Finally it occurred to some clever Egyptian that he might lengthen the handle of his hoe so that it could be fastened to a yoke *Beginning of plow culture; introduction of agricultural machinery*

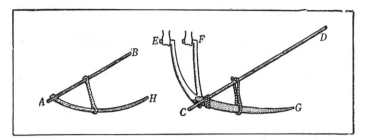

FIG. 27. *An Egyptian Wooden* HOE *(Left) and the Wooden* PLOW *(Right) which grew out of it*

The handle of the hoe (*A–B*) has been lengthened to become the beam of the plow (*C–D*). The upper end (*D*) of the beam was fastened to a yoke which was attached to the horns of the two oxen. To guide the new ox-drawn hoe, handles for the plowman's use (*E* and *F*) were necessary. These were attached at the point where the beam (*C–D*) and plowshare (*C–G*, once the hoe blade *A–H*) met. The first plows had only one handle, affixed to one side of the juncture of beam and share, but the Egyptians soon discovered the advantage of attaching two handles

resting on the horns of two oxen. By affixing handles to the new machine the farmer could then guide it across his fields as the oxen dragged it along before him (Fig. 28). Thus hoe culture was transformed into plow culture.

This invention of the first agricultural machinery marked a new epoch, for it enabled man to begin the use of animal power, that is, power other than the strength of man or woman. In this way much greater power was for the first time applied to the work of cultivating the fields. This meant as much for the increase of food among ancient men as the introduction of improved agricultural machinery has meant in the wealth and progress of the United States. Thus Egypt became the first great agricultural nation. The annual income in grain was not only a source of greatly increased wealth to the people and the government, but also the first *portable* wealth. With it loans could be made, taxes paid, and business debts settled. In an age before there was any money this new and portable form of wealth made an enormous difference and aided in carrying the Egyptians forward toward civilization.

FIG. 28. PLOW CULTURE *as compared with the Older and Much Slower Process of* HOE CULTURE

This drawing, based on ancient Egyptian reliefs, shows us the immense advantage in power and speed gained by the man who yoked his oxen to the plow and plowed an acre in a day, while the man who bent all day over the hoe could not possibly do more than scratch the surface of a quarter of an acre. The plow thus multiplied by at least four the amount of acreage that might be put under cultivation. The total harvest of the entire country, therefore, was likewise multiplied by four; the people had four times as much grain as before; the king received four times as much taxes

63. The large increase in the extent of the cultivated fields made the central government of the whole nation more important than ever, for the enlarged area of cultivation required an immensely increased amount of water for irrigating the fields. The little local systems of canals were united into one enormous national system, which was controlled from the capital. The irrigation administration thus centralized in the hands of the king was without doubt the first great administrative machine in the history of human government. The king must have been much interested in his Department of Irrigation, for without it he could not expect the farmers to raise large crops or pay taxes into his treasury.

First national irrigation system

64. The important place occupied by agriculture in the government of the Egyptians may be seen in the names which were adopted for the different seasons of the year. There were three seasons in their first calendar, and they bore the names "Inundation," "Coming Forth" (meaning the coming

Agricultural cal-
endar

forth of the fields from the inundation that had covered them), and "Harvest." The people who gave these names to the three seasons must have been irrigating *farmers*, since they named the seasons from the inundation and the condition of the cultivated fields.

65. Each of these three seasons was four months long, and the month was measured by the moon. In like manner the

Moon calendar

North American Indians used to measure time by moons (that is, the period from one new moon to the next), and they would speak of a journey of sixty days or so as a journey of two moons, meaning two months. Unfortunately the moon-month varies in length from twenty-nine to thirty days, and it does not evenly divide the three hundred and sixty-five days of the year. The Egyptians, however, showed themselves much more practical in removing this inconvenience than did their ancient neighbors in other lands (§ 179).

66. Probably long before the First Union the people of the Nile valley had discovered the number of days in a year, al-

Thirty-day month
and first practical
calendar

though they did not at first know that their reckoning of three hundred and sixty-five days overlooked a fraction of about a quarter of a day. Retaining the twelve-month year which was derived from the use of the moon-month, they decided to have a calendar year of twelve months as before, but each of these twelve months under the new calendar was to have thirty days. These twelve thirty-day months thus formed a short year of three hundred and sixty days, to which the new calendar added five feast days, a kind of holiday period five days long at the end of the year. This gave them a calendar year of three hundred and sixty-five days as before. Having the months all of the same length, it was the most practical and convenient calendar ever adopted.

67. By means of astronomy it is possible to compute the date when this calendar year was invented and introduced, and we now know that this great invention was made in 4236 B.C.[1] This is the earliest dated event in human history.

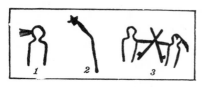

FIG. 29. *Part of a Dakota Chief's List of Seventy-one* NAMED YEARS

Lone Dog, a Dakota chief, had a buffalo robe with seventy-one named years recorded on it, beginning in 1800, when he was a child of four. A year when whooping cough was very bad was called the Whooping-Cough Year; its sign shows a human head coughing violently (*1*). Another year, very plentiful in meteors, was called the Meteor Year, and its sign was a rude drawing of a falling meteor (*2*). A third year saw the arrangement of peace between the Dakotas and the Crows; its sign was therefore two Indians, with differing style of hair, indicating the two different tribes, exchanging pipes of peace (*3*). Thus, instead of saying, as we do, that a thing happened in the year 1813, the Indian said it happened in the Whooping-Cough Year, and by examining his table of years he could tell how far back that year was

It is important to remember also that this early Egyptian calendar, invented in the Forty-third Century B.C., is the very one which has descended to us after more than six thousand years, — unfortunately with inconvenient alterations in the lengths of the months. For these alterations, however, the Egyptians were not responsible, and even the additional quarter of a day, necessitating a leap year of three hundred and sixty-six days every four years, was finally known to the Egyptians.

Earliest fixed date in history

68. The months in this calendar were numbered, and thus furnished a very practical means of identifying any particular *month*. It did not, however, furnish any way of identifying a particular *year*. If we are dealing only with the *current* year, we may date a business agreement or the time when a payment falls due by simply mentioning the month and the day of the month; but if we are dealing with events in some other year, or if we wish to refer to an occurrence of several years back, the *year* must in some way be identified. Our convenient system of *num-*

Years identified by names

[1] The date, 4241 B.C., formerly calculated for this event, contained a small error in the factors used. After this error is corrected, the calculation gives 4236 B.C. as the correct year.

bering years beginning with some great event, like the birth of Christ, was still unknown. In order to have some means of identifying a particular year when it was long past, the Egyptians gave each year a name after some important event which had happened in it. This method is still in use among the North American Indians and even among ourselves, as people in Chicago say "the year of the great fire," or as English people say "the year of the armistice." We find the earliest written monuments of Egypt dated by means of named years.

FIG. 30. PICTORIAL MESSAGE
Scratched on Wood by Alaskan Indians

A figure with empty hands hanging down helplessly, palms down, as an Indian gesture for uncertainty, ignorance, emptiness, or nothing, means "no." A figure with one hand on its mouth means "eating" or "food." It points toward the tent, and this means "in the tent." The whole is a message stating, "There is no food in the tent"

69. Lists of year-names then began to be kept. As each year-name usually mentioned some great event, these lists of year-names were thus lists of such events; and when we find one, it is a very instructive record of important happenings. The earliest year-list of this kind in human history now surviving, called the Palermo Stone (because it is preserved in the museum at Palermo, Sicily), began about 3400 B.C. and contained, when complete, the names of some seven hundred years, ending about 2700 B.C. Later the Egyptians found it more convenient to number the years of each king's reign, and then to date events in the first year of King So-and-so or the tenth year of King So-and-so. Finally they had lists of past kings covering many centuries.

Lists of years and kings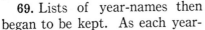

70. Such records were at first only pictures, like those of the Dakota chief's list of years (Fig. 29). As time went on, the *business* of the government and the people made it necessary to have records of transactions. A farmer, for example, might want to know how much he had paid as taxes. He might scratch a rude picture

Pictorial records

of his basket grain-measure and a number of strokes on the mud wall of his hut, to indicate the number of measures of grain he had paid. The use of these picture signs was the earliest step leading toward writing. Such picture writing survives in use among the still uncivilized North American Indians. The Alaskan natives send messages in picture form, scratched on a piece of wood. Fig. 30 might be read by one man, "No food in the tent," while another might read, "Lack of meat in the tepee" or "No game in the camp." Such pictures thus conveyed ideas only, without representing the *exact words*. Among the American Indians the desire of a chief to record his own brave deeds also led to picture records of them (Fig. 31). It should be noticed again that the *exact words* are not indicated by this record, but the chief's brave

FIG. 31. PICTORIAL RECORD *of the* VICTORY *of a Dakota Chief named Running Antelope*

This Dakota Indian prepared his autobiography in a series of eleven drawings, of which this is but one. It records how he slew five hostile braves in a single day. The hero, Running Antelope, with rifle in hand, is mounted upon a horse. His shield bears a falcon, the animal emblem of his family, while beneath the horse is a running antelope, which is of course intended to inform you of the hero's name. We see the trail of his horse as he swept around the copse at the left, in which were concealed the five hostile braves whom he slew. Of these, one figure bearing a rifle represents all five, while four other rifles in the act of being discharged indicate the number of braves in the copse

action is merely so suggested that it might be put into words in a number of different ways. Such purely picture records had already been made in Egypt under the Two Kingdoms long before the First Union, and they continued to be used occasionally even after the end of the First Union (Figs. 32 and 37).

71. But this picture stage, beyond which native American records never passed, was not real writing. Two steps had

to be taken before the picture records could become *phonetic writing*, and both of these steps were taken under the kings

First step leading from pictorial to phonetic stage of the First Union. These two steps were as follows: *First*, each object drawn had to gain a fixed form, always the same and always recognized as the sign for a *particular word* denoting that object. Thus, it would become a habit that the drawing of a loaf should always be read "loaf," not "bread" or "food"; the sign for a leaf would always be read "leaf," not "foliage." [1]

72. The *second* step then naturally followed; that is, the leaf 🍃, for example,

Second step leading from pictorial to phonetic stage might become the sign for the *syllable* "leaf" wherever it might occur. By the same process 🐝 might become the sign for the syllable "bee" wherever found. Thus, with a means of writing the syllables "bee" and "leaf," the next step was to put them together, 🐝 🍃, and they would then represent the word "belief." Notice, however, that in the word "belief" the sign 🐝 has ceased to suggest the idea of an insect. It now represents only the *syllable* "be." That is to say, 🐝 has become a *phonetic* sign.

73. If the writing of the Egyptians had remained merely a series of pictures, such

Advantage of phonetic signs words as "belief," "hate," "love," "beauty," and the like could never have been written. But when a large number of their pictures had become phonetic signs, each representing

Fig. 32. *Example of Egyptian* Writing *in the* Pictorial Stage

Interpretation: Above is the falcon, symbol of a king (cf. the falcon on the shield of Running Antelope in Fig. 31), leading a human head by a cord; behind the head is a thicket of papyrus plants growing out of the ground, to which the head is attached; below is a single-barbed harpoon head and a little rectangle (the sign of a lake). The whole tells the picture story that the falcon king led captive the men of the Harpoon Lake in the Papyrus Land (that is, the Delta)

---

[1] We are of course obliged to use *English* words and syllables here, and consequently the signs also are not Egyptian but are devised for this demonstration.

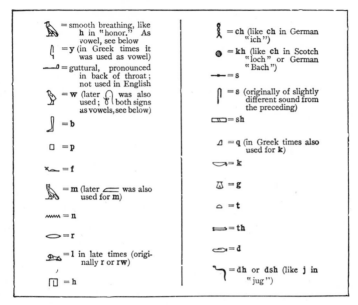

FIG. 33. The Egyptian ALPHABET

Each of these letters represents a consonant. The Egyptians of course *pronounced* their words with vowels as we do, but they did not *write* the vowels. This will be clear from a study of Fig. 34. Just as the consonants *w* and *y* are sometimes used as vowels in English, so three of the Egyptian consonants came to be employed as vowels in Greek times. The first letter (smooth breathing) was thus used as *a* or *e*; the second letter (*y*), as *i*; and the fourth (*w*), as *u* or *o*

a syllable, it was possible for the Egyptians to write any word, whether that word meant a thing of which they could draw a picture or not. This possession of *phonetic* signs was what made real writing for the first time. It arose among these Nile-dwellers earlier than anywhere else in the ancient world.

74. Egyptian writing contained at last over six hundred signs, many of them representing whole syllables, like ✎. The Egyptian scribes gradually learned many groups of such syllable signs. Each group, like ✎, represented a *word*. Writing thus became for them a large number of sign-groups, each group being a word, and a series of such groups formed a sentence.

Syllable signs and sign-groups

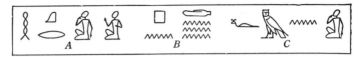

FIG. 34. An Egyptian Word (A) and Two English Words (B) and (C)
written in Hieroglyphic

The first three signs in word *A* are *ch-n-r* (see Fig. 33); we do not know the
vowels. The word means "pauper" (literally, "hungry"); as it denotes a person, the Egyptians added a little man at the end. Before him is another man with
hand on mouth, an indication of hunger, thirst, or speech. These two are old pictorial signs surviving from the pictorial stage. Such pictorial signs at the end of a
word have no phonetic value and are called *determinatives*. *B* is an English word
spelled for illustration in hieroglyphic. The first three signs indicate the letters
p-n-d, while the three wavy lines form the determinative for "water"; hence
p-n-d spells "pond." *C* is another English word in hieroglyphic. The first three
signs indicate the letters *f-m-n*, and the last sign is the determinative for "hunger";
hence *f-m-n* spells "famine." With the alphabet and the above determinatives
the student can put English words into hieroglyphic; for example, "man" (*m-n*
and determinative of man), "drink" (*d-r-n-k* and determinative of man with hand
on mouth), "speak" (*s-p-k* and same determinative), or "brook" (*b-r-k* and determinative for "water," as in "pond")

75. Nevertheless the Egyptians went still farther, for they
finally possessed a series of signs each representing only a
Alphabetic signs, *letter,* — that is, *alphabetic* signs, or, as we say,
or letters   real letters. There were twenty-four letters
in this alphabet, which was known in Egypt by the end of
the First Union, that is, by the Thirty-fifth Century B.C.
It was thus the earliest alphabet known. At that time the
Egyptians might have written their language with twenty-
four alphabetic letters if the *sign*-group habit had not been
too strong for the scribes, just as the *letter*-group habit is
strong enough with us today to prevent the introduction of
a simplified phonetic system of spelling English. If we smile
at the Egyptian's sign-groups, future generations may as
justly smile at our often absurd letter-groups.

76. It was probably under the kings of the First Union
that the Egyptians invented their *writing materials.* They
Invention of writ-   found out that they could make an excellent
ing materials   paint or ink by thickening water with a little
vegetable gum and then mixing in soot from the blackened
pots over the fire. Dipping a pointed reed into this mixture,

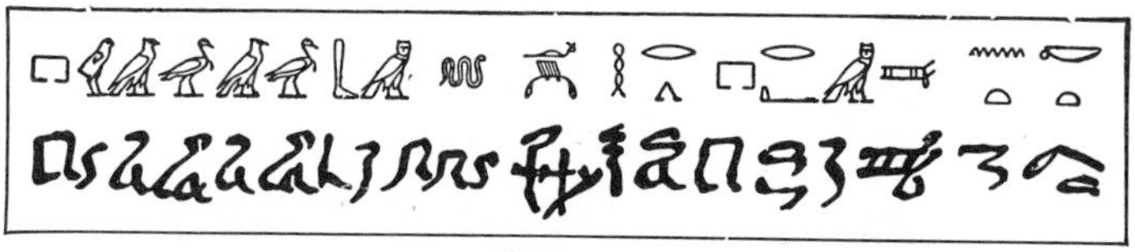

FIG. 35. *An Example of Egyptian* HIEROGLYPHIC *(Upper Line) and its Equivalent in the* RAPID RUNNING HAND *(Lower Line) written with Pen and Ink on Papyrus and called* HIERATIC, *the Writing of All Ordinary Business*

The daily business of an Egyptian community of course required much writing and thousands of records. Such writing, after it began to be done with pen and ink on papyrus, soon became very rapid. In course of time, therefore, there arose a rapid, or running, hand in which each hieroglyphic sign was much abbreviated. This running hand is called *hieratic*. It corresponds to our handwriting, while hieroglyphic corresponds to our print. In the above example the signs in the lower row show clearly that they are the result of an effort to make quickly the signs in the hieroglyphic row above (compare sign for sign). We must notice also that the Egyptians wrote from right to left, for this line begins at the right and reads to the left. Vertical lines, that is, downward reading, were also employed (Fig. 58). A third, still more rapid and abbreviated hand, corresponding in some ways to our shorthand, arose later (Eighth Century B.C.). It was called *demotic*, and one of the versions on the Rosetta Stone (Fig. 203) is written in demotic

they found they could write very well. They also learned that they could split a kind of river reed, called papyrus, into thin strips, and that they could write on them much better than on bits of pottery, bone, and wood, which were all they had at first. Desiring a larger sheet, they hit upon the idea of pasting their papyrus strips together with overlapping edges. This gave them a very thin sheet; but by pasting *two* such sheets together, with the grain crossing at right angles, they produced a smooth, tough, nearly white or pale-yellow paper. The Egyptians had thus made the discovery that a thin vegetable membrane offers a most practical surface on which to write, and the world has since discovered nothing better. In this way arose pen, ink, and paper. All three of these inventions descended to us from the Egyptians, and paper still bears its ancient name, *papyros* [1] (Latin, *papyrus*), but slightly changed.

---

[1] The change from *papyros* to "paper" is really a very slight one, for *os* is merely the Greek grammatical ending, which must be omitted in English. This leaves us *papyr* as the ancestor of our word "paper," from which it differs by only one letter.

77. The invention of writing and of a convenient system of records on paper has had a greater influence in uplifting

Importance of introduction of writing the human race than any other achievement in the life of man. It was then and is now more important than all the battles ever fought and all the constitutions ever written.

78. Writing must have aided greatly in

Commerce of the First Union the transaction of business. Under the First Union we find numerous paintings of many-oared Nile boats on the pottery jars found in the graves of the period. These are the earliest boats of which we have any knowledge. They show us that the river towns were car-

Fig. 36. Boat *carrying the Standard of a Trading Town, painted on a* Pottery Jar *of the First Union*

These many-oared boats were probably the first vessels to be constructed with wooden hulls. The standard is mounted on the top of a pole set up beside the smaller deck-house. The symbol on the standard is the figure of a bird. A mooring rope is hanging from the bow. The antelopes, ostriches, and plants scattered around in the background represent the scenery through which the boat passed. (Courtesy of the Metropolitan Museum of Art)

rying on brisk trade with each other; for each boat carries on a pole a standard, the symbol of the town from which it came. The cemeteries of the First Union have thus far yielded about three hundred of these standard-bearing boats, and two hundred and twenty-two of these came from the western Delta. This shows us how the old kingdom of Lower Egypt was leading in commerce. It indicates also that the seaport of Egypt on the Mediterranean was already at the western corner of the Delta, where Alexander the Great later founded Alexandria,

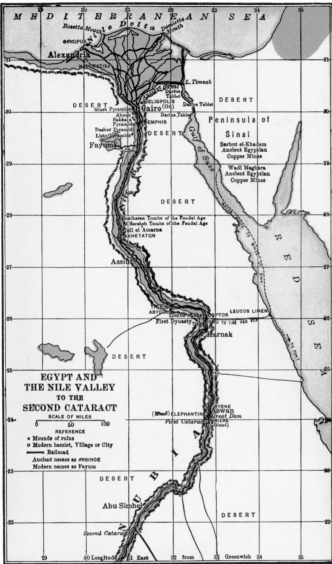

EGYPT AND
THE NILE VALLEY
TO THE
SECOND CATARACT

SCALE OF MILES
0   50   100

REFERENCE
• Mounds of ruins
○ Modern hamlet, Village or City
━━━ Railroad
Ancient names as ARSINOE
Modern names as Fayum

the greatest seaport of ancient times. And from there, nearly three thousand years before Alexander, Egyptian trade and civilization were to pass by ship to Crete and thence to Europe.

79. The consolidation of the North and South which we have called the First Union did not endure. In time the two kingdoms fell apart and for a period existed independently side by side. Then there arose a strong leader in Upper Egypt whose name was Menes. First he made himself king of the old kingdom of Upper Egypt. Then he invaded Lower Egypt and conquered it (about 3360 B.C.). This conquest brought about a new union, over which ruled a king of *Upper* Egypt. Menes inherited the civilization of the First Union. Just as the power and prosperity of the First Union was based on plow culture and the production of plentiful grain, so that of the Second Union grew out of the earliest mining on a large scale and the possession of plentiful copper.

Second Union founded by Menes (3360 B.C.)

80. The graves of the cemeteries of the First Union had contained many more tools and implements of copper than those of the Two Kingdoms. Copper axes and chisels were to be had in trade, and a few rare workmen possessed them. The First Union had therefore brought the Age of Metal much nearer. With the Second Union actually began the Age of Metal. The early kings of the Second Union were very proud of their ability to send mining expeditions into the mountains of the neighboring Peninsula of Sinai, and there we still find the long mining tunnels which they drove into the mountains. These are the earliest known copper mines, and the early successors of Menes had their people carve upon the neighboring rocks huge records of their presence there. These scenes are the oldest historical monuments known to us.

Age of Metal; beginning of royal mining expeditions

81. Not only did the early Pharaohs of the Second Union exploit the copper mines of Sinai, but they dispatched expeditions also northward by sea to Byblos, on the coast of

Fig. 37. *Oldest Known Royal* Monument: *Mining Inscription of a King of the* Second Union *Engraved on the Rocks of Sinai*

The king is represented twice wearing the tall white crown of Upper Egypt and once (center) wearing the curious crown of Lower Egypt, thus showing that this particular king ruled both of the old prehistoric divisions of the land. The earliest Egyptians told their story in this way by pictures instead of words. Another part of this picture-story is found in the arrangement of the first two figures at the left. The king, armed with stone mace and dagger (in his belt), grasps a kneeling captive by the hair and raises the mace for a fatal blow. The long-haired, bearded captive is a typical early Asiatic. The pictured story is that this king, by means of the military escort which protected his mining expedition, smote the Asiatics of Sinai and so established his right to mine copper in that region. Placed here as a record of the expedition, these gigantic figures of the Pharaoh, the earliest great historical monument, also served as a warning to any other Asiatics who might be tempted to molest later Egyptian mining expeditions in Sinai. The hieroglyphs in the two little rectangles at right and left give the name of the king. Expeditions, a few centuries later, were writing the whole story in hieroglyphs,— not forgetting even to complain of the heat in Sinai!

Syria. This port was very important because of the forests that lay behind it, and here the timber which Egypt needed **Egypt obtains wood** was cut and loaded upon the Pharaoh's fleet **from Syria** to be shipped back to the Nile. This commerce across the southeastern corner of the Mediterranean, the earliest known sea-borne trade, was carried in the earliest seagoing ships of which we have any record. The importation of plentiful wood into Egypt resulted in its common use in house-building, boat-building, and all kinds of carpentry and furniture-making.

82. For some four hundred years the early kings of the Second Union built their tombs of sun-dried mud brick. A group of these tombs was discovered in Upper Egypt. They are the earliest royal buildings ever found. Then, probably about 3000 B.C.. there was built in one of these brick tombs a burial chamber of *limestone blocks*. This was the beginning of architecture in stone, and the direct result of the possession of tools of copper by which the stone building blocks were cut and shaped.

Copper tools and beginning of stone architecture

83. Beginning thus about 3000 B.C., when the Second Union was about four hundred years old, its kings were able to erect stone tombs and stone temples. Such great stone buildings form records of the history of Egypt much fuller than the village cemeteries, with their pit-graves. We remember that these pit-graves are all that survive from the earlier stages of Egypt as a nation down through the Two Kingdoms and the First Union. In sharp contrast to the pit-graves the great stone buildings which began to rise after 3000 B.C. have made the Nile valley seem like a huge historical volume.

Stone buildings as historical records

SECTION 6. THE SECOND UNION OF EGYPT AND THE PYRAMID AGE (THIRTIETH TO TWENTY-FIFTH CENTURY B.C.)

84. In order to read the first chapter of this history in stone we must turn our attention to the royal cemetery at Gizeh. Here we find first the pyramids— the tombs of the kings — and then, clustering about the pyramids, great numbers of much smaller tombs of stone masonry. In these smaller tombs were buried the relatives of the king, and the great men of his court. As we shall see, these men, together with the king about whom they were grouped, formed the government of Egypt. Just as they formed a group around the king's palace in this life, so after death their tombs now cluster around the pyramid. The cemetery is thus a picture of the government of Egypt.

Royal cemetery

Such mighty buildings reveal many things about the men who built them. In the first place, the tombs tell us a great

FIG. 38. *Winged Sun-Disk, Symbol of the Sun-god*

The sun's disk is in the middle, and two serpents (cobras), one on each side of it, rear their heads. The wings are those of a falcon, for in this form the Sun-god was believed to be a falcon flying across the sky. We shall later see how the other nations of the Near East adopted this Egyptian symbol

deal in regard to the *religion* of these people. They show us that the Egyptians believed in a life after death, and that to obtain such a life it was necessary to preserve the body from perishing. They built these tombs to shelter and protect the body. From this belief came also the practice of embalming, by which the body was preserved as a mummy (Fig. 71). It was then placed in the great tomb, in a small room deep under the masonry.

85. The inscriptions in the tombs make known to us the many gods of the Egyptians, but there were two whom they **Egyptian gods and** worshiped above all others. The sun, which **their symbols** shines so gloriously in the cloudless Egyptian sky, was their greatest god, and their most splendid temples were erected for his worship. Indeed, the pyramid is a symbol sacred to the Sun-god. (See another symbol in Fig. 38.) They called him Re (pronounced *ray*). The other great power which they revered was the shining Nile. The great river and the fertile soil that he refreshes. and the green life that he brings forth,— all these the Egyptian thought of together as a single god, Osiris, the imperishable life of the earth which revives and fades every year with the change of the seasons. It was a beautiful and comforting thought to the Egyptian that this same life-giving power which furnished him his food in *this* world would care for him also in the *next*, when his body lay out in the cemetery on the edge of the desert. There were many Egyptian gods whose earthly symbols were *animals*, but the animal worship usually attributed to Egypt was a degeneration belonging to the last stage of the dying Egyptian religion. The animals were not gods in this early time, but only *symbols* of the divine beings, just as the winged sun-disk was a symbol of the Sun-god.

86. The great pyramid cemetery of Gizeh tells us about many other things besides the religion of the Egyptians. We have already learned that the Egyptian me- Advance in build- chanics now worked with copper tools. The ing pyramids of Gizeh are a measure of what they could do with those tools. It is difficult to believe that these colossal stone buildings were erected by men whose ancestors, only a few generations earlier, were buried, with their flint knives, in pits scooped out on the margin of the desert. Complete mastery of stone building was a step taken very quickly, but we have seen that it was preceded by a very slow and gradual change from stone tools to those of metal. That Egyptian in Sinai who noticed the first bit of copper must have lived about two thousand years before these pyramids were built, and for almost two thousand years the knowledge of metal had no effect upon building. Only a few generations, indeed less than a century, before the earliest of the great stone pyramids, the Egyptian masons were still building the tombs of their kings out of sun-baked brick. Such a royal tomb was at first merely a chamber in the ground, covered with a flat wooden roof. On this roof was raised a mound of sand and gravel as the king's monument. We recall (§ 82) that the first piece of stone masonry ever put together, so far as we know, was a lining of limestone blocks to form the underground burial chamber of a royal tomb. The structure can hardly be called a building, for, like a cellar wall, it was all below ground.

87. The next step, a real building aboveground, was still of brick. Then, in the Thirtieth Century B.C., the royal architect Imhotep created the first architecture in Imhotep, earliest stone. He built for his king, Zoser, a tomb architect in stone which is the oldest surviving building of building stone masonry in the world. Around this great tomb Imhotep erected a wonderful group of beautiful buildings, of the very

Fig. 39. *The Oldest Surviving* Building *of Stone Masonry* (*Thirtieth Century* b.c.)

This terraced building, often called the step pyramid, was the tomb of King Zoser. It is about 200 feet high and in outward form seems to be a series of buildings like No. 6 in Fig. 41, placed one on top of another. It thus formed a tapering building out of which developed the pyramid form

finest limestone masonry, including two more tombs of the royal family. The fronts of these two tombs were adorned with stone supports so gracefully fluted that they look like the slender Greek columns of 2500 years later. And the artist whose mind conceived this beauty deserves far greater fame and respect than do the early kings or conquerors themselves.

38. The erection of Imhotep's terraced building was an important step toward the construction of a pyramid. A generation later, so rapid was the progress, the king's architects were building the Great Pyramid of Gizeh (2885 b.c.). From the earliest piece of stone masonry to the construction of the Great Pyramid perhaps less than a century and a quarter elapsed. Most of this advance was made during the Thirtieth Century b.c., that is, between 3000 and 2900 b.c.

Century and a quarter from earliest stone masonry to Great Pyramid

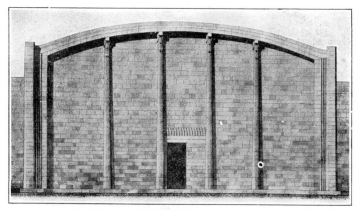

FIG. 40. *Front of Stone* TOMB-CHAPEL *erected by Imhotep*

Imhotep, the first great architect, was the originator of the pyramid tomb. He made his *stone* buildings with the forms and designs of the *wooden* buildings which were the only architecture of Egypt up to that time. The tall, slender, columnlike supports are not columns in the round, but are attached to ("engaged in") the masonry wall behind them. (After Lauer)

Such rapid progress in man's control of mechanical power can be found in no other period of the world's history until the Nineteenth Century of the Christian Era.

89. This progress becomes very real to us when we know that the Great Pyramid covers thirteen acres. It is a solid mass of masonry containing 2,300,000 blocks of limestone, each weighing on an average **Vast size of the Great Pyramid** two and a half tons; that is, each block is as heavy as a large wagonload of coal. The sides of the pyramid at the base are 756 feet long,[1] and the building was originally nearly 500 feet high. Herodotus tells us that a hundred thousand men were working on this royal tomb for twenty years, and we can well believe it.

90. To manage and to feed a hundred thousand workmen around this great building must have required a very skillful ruler and a great number of trained leaders who were in the

[1] It should be remembered that the pyramid is *solid*. Compare the length of the Colosseum (about 600 feet), which is built around a *hollow* inclosure.

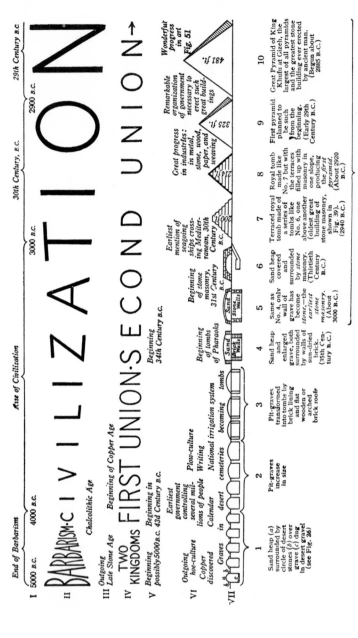

End of Barbarism   Rise of Civilization

I   5000 B.C.   4000 B.C.   30th Century, B.C.   3000 B.C.   2900 B.C.   29th Century B.C.

II   BARBARISM·CIVILIZATION   FIRST UNION·SECOND UNION→

III   Outgoing Late Stone Age | Beginning of Copper Age | Chalcolithic Age

IV   TWO KINGDOMS

V   Beginning possibly 5000 B.C. | Beginning in 43d Century B.C. | Beginning in 34th Century B.C.

VI   Outgoing hoe-culture   Copper discovered   Earliest government controlling several millions of people   Calendar   Plow-culture   Writing   National irrigation system

VII   Graves in desert cemeteries becoming tombs

Beginning of tombs of Pharaohs (34th Century B.C.)

Beginning of stone masonry, 31st Century B.C.

Earliest mention of seagoing ships crossing Mediterranean, 30th Century B.C.

Great progress in industries: in metal, stone, wood, paper, and weaving

Remarkable organization of government necessary to erect such great buildings

Wonderful progress in art Fig. 51

215 ft.   325 ft.   481 ft.   11,000 B.C.

1	Sand heap (a) surrounded by circle of desert stones (b) over grave (c) dug in desert gravel (see Fig. 26)
2	Pit-graves increase in size
3	Pit-graves transformed into tombs by brick lining and flat wooden or arched brick roof
4	Sand heap enlarged and grave, both surrounded by walls of sun-dried brick. (35th Century B.C.)
5	Same as No. 4, only wall of grave has become stone,—the earliest stone masonry. (About 3000 B.C.)
6	Sand heap covered and surrounded by stone masonry. (Thirtieth Century B.C.)
7	Terraced royal tomb made of a series of tombs like No. 6, one above another the oldest great building of stone masonry, shown in Fig. 39. (2940 B.C.)
8	Royal tomb made like No. 7 but with the terraces filled up with masonry in one slope, producing the first pyramid. (About 2920 B.C.)
9	First pyramid planned to be such from the beginning. (Early 29th Century B.C.)
10	Great Pyramid of King Khufu at Gizeh, the largest of all pyramids and the greatest stone building ever erected by ancient man. (Begun about 2885 B.C.)

Not more than 125 years
(from earliest stone masonry to the Great Pyramid)

FIG. 41. *Diagram of the* Progress of Egypt *from Late Stone Age Barbarism to Highly Developed Civilization*

Notice the dates in Row I, beginning possibly 5000 B.C. and extending into the Twenty-ninth Century. In that period of about 2000 years Row II suggests the gradual decline and disappearance of barbarism and the appearance and growth of civilization. Row III indicates this period as the one when stone implements were at first partially and then more largely displaced by copper. The political developments while this was going on are shown in Row IV, beginning with the Two Kingdoms and passing through the First Union to the Second Union. Row VI then lists the most important things which made possible the displacement of barbarism by civilization, and the progress of early civilization. Finally, Row VII shows us how this advance is revealed in ancient cemeteries of Egypt. The body of the Egyptian peasant in Fig. 26 lay at the bottom of a grave above which was a low heap of sand surrounded by a circle of rough desert stones to keep the sand in place. No. 1, above, shows this grave, cut down through the middle to expose the inside, with the sand-heap above it. In Nos. 2 and 3 we see these pit-graves becoming tombs of sun-dried brick masonry, with superstructures of such masonry appearing for the first time in No. 4. The series (Nos. 1 to 4) shows how the circle of stones around the sand-heap became real walls, first of brick (No. 4) and then of stone masonry (No. 6), enveloping the whole tomb, with the old

sand-heap still in the inside.¹ Tombs like No. 6 were then placed one above the other, producing a tapering terraced building (No. 7), which was soon improved until it became a pyramid (No. 8). Thus the sand-heap and its circle of stones were the germ out of which the mighty pyramids grew in the course of fifteen or twenty centuries. Notice how this wonderful growth in the art of building began with the sand-heap in the barbarism of the Late Stone Age, and carried the Egyptians out of barbarism and far into civilization in the thousand years from 4000 to 3000 B.C. It was itself one of the things which marked the early growth of civilization, and architecture passed from the earliest example of stone masonry (No. 5) to the Great Pyramid in less than a century and a quarter. The Pyramids and their predecessors thus stand like milestones marking the long road by which man passed from barbarism to a highly developed civilization. We learn thus what were the *visible* things that we must understand as making up civilization in the beginning. But there were some necessary things which also reached a high development at the same time and which were *not visible*. These were a belief in right living and kindness to others, and that a good life here was necessary to happiness in the next world. At the close of the Gizeh Period a wise man said, "Established is the man whose standard is righteousness, who walketh according to its way."

king's service. The king who was able to undertake such vast works was the most powerful human being that the world had ever seen. He was so reverenced

The Pharaohs

that the people did not mention him by name, but instead they spoke of the palace in which he lived, that is, Pharaoh, which means, in Egyptian, "Great House." Hence we may call the Second Union the "Age of the Pharaohs."

91. The Pharaoh had two kinds of officials to aid him in carrying on his government. There were the *local* officials

The Pharaoh's government

who were scattered about through all Egypt, and the *central* officials who lived at the capital near the king. It was the duty of the *local* officials to collect taxes all over Egypt. It was also their business to try the law cases which arose, and every judge had before him the *written law* [1] which bade him judge justly.

The taxes received from the people were not in coined money, which did not yet exist, but in produce, such as live stock, grain, wine, honey, linen, and the like. These were kept in cattle-yards, granaries, and storehouses, — a large group of buildings which formed the treasury and central offices of the king, where hundreds on hundreds of clerks, with their reed pens and their rolls of papyrus, were daily keeping the king's records and accounts. The clerks had lists of the taxpayers' names and how much they owed, and they issued receipts when the taxes were paid, just as at the present day. Such arrangements did not arise in Europe until far down in the Roman Empire.

92. Such government buildings made the capital a city of some size, — the largest which the life of man had yet pro-

The royal city

duced. The chief quarter of the royal city was formed by the palace of the Pharaoh and the beautiful gardens which surrounded it. The palace and its grounds, surrounded by the villas of the king's officials, and the offices of the government, especially the great group of treasury buildings, — all these together formed the capital of Egypt, the royal city. It extended far southward from

[1] This Egyptian code of laws has unfortunately been lost.

FIG. 42. *The Great* SPHINX *of Gizeh and the* PYRAMID *of Khafre*

A sphinx was the portrait head of a king attached to the body of a lion. The Great Sphinx was the portrait of King Khafre (Fig. 51), before whose pyramid it lies like a sentinel guarding the mighty cemetery of Gizeh. The body is 187 feet long, and the head is 66 feet high

Gizeh and was later called Memphis. But the city was built of sun-baked brick and wood, and it has therefore vanished.

93. The city of the dead (the pyramids and the tombs clustering around them), being built of stone, has fortunately proved more lasting. It is possible here at Gizeh to follow the history of the royal fam- Length and date of Pyramid Age ily and their relatives for about one hundred and ten years. And the other pyramid cemeteries carry us still farther. From the summit of the Great Pyramid there is a grand view southward, down a splendid line of pyramids rising dimly as far as one can see on the southern horizon. We must remember that if each pyramid was a royal tomb, then each tomb of this kind means that a king lived, ruled, and died. One after another for about five hundred years these kings were buried, each in his pyramid, until the pyramid line was over sixty

Fig. 43. *Relief Scene from the Chapel of a Nobleman's Tomb in the Pyramid Age*

The tall figure of the nobleman stands at the right. He is inspecting three lines of cattle and a line of fowl brought before him. Note the two scribes who head the two middle rows. Each is writing with pen on a sheet of papyrus, and one carries two pens behind his ear. Such reliefs, after being carved, were colored in bright hues by the painter

miles long and thus marks out for us today some five hundred years of time. This period, from the middle of the Thirtieth to the middle of the Twenty-fifth Century B.C., is the first great age of Egyptian civilization after the land was united under one king.

94. The Pyramid Age is the earliest period of human life which is very fully revealed to us in pictures produced at the time. These pictures are preserved in the tombs grouped around the pyramids. A stroll among these tombs is almost like a walk among the busy communities which flourished in this populous valley in the days of the pyramid-builders. Each tomb had its chapel, to which, it was thought, the dead nobleman who was buried beneath the tomb might return every day. Here, therefore, his relatives left food and drink for him. He

Tomb-chapels of Pyramid Age; life they reveal

would also find the stone walls of this room covered from floor to ceiling with carved pictures, beautifully painted, showing the daily life on the great farm or plantation which formed his estate.

Fig. 44. *Peasant* Milking *in the Pyramid Age*

The cow is restive and the ancient cowherd has tied her hind legs. Behind her another man is holding her calf, which rears and plunges in the effort to reach the milk

95. Let us examine some of the pictures carved on the chapel walls. Here we see the tall figure of the nobleman himself as he stands looking out over his fields and inspecting the work going on there. These scenes in the Egyptian tombs of the Pyramid Age are the oldest known pictures showing the work of planting and cultivating a field. Here, too, we see the herds, long lines of sleek, fat cattle, some of them milch cows led up and tied to be milked, others used as beasts of burden, for we notice the oxen drawing the plow. But we find no horses in these tombs of the Pyramid Age, for the horse was still unknown in Egypt. Pictured very often on the walls, however, we see the donkeys with loads of grain on their backs, for it would have been impossible to harvest the fields without them.

96. On the next wall we find again the tall figure of the nobleman overseeing the booths and yards where the craftsmen of his estate are working. Yonder is the coppersmith. He had never heard of his ancestor who picked up the first bead of copper, perhaps two thousand years earlier. Much progress had been made since that day. This man could make excellent copper tools of all sorts, but the tool which demanded the greatest skill was the long, flat ripsaw, which the smith knew how to hammer into shape out of a broad strip of copper five or six feet long. Such a saw may be seen in use in Fig. 46. Besides this he knew how to make one that would saw great blocks of stone for the

pyramids. Moreover, this coppersmith was already able to
deliver orders of surprising size, such as thirteen hundred
feet (about a quarter of a mile) of copper drainpiping for
a pyramid temple (Fig. 55).

97. On the same wall we see a craftsman who can cut very
hard semiprecious stones. We call him a *lapidary*. He holds
Lapidary, gold-   up for the nobleman's admiration splendid
smith, and jeweler stone bowls cut from diorite. Although this
kind of stone is as hard as steel, the bowl is ground to such
thinness that the sunlight glows through its dark-gray sides.
Other workmen are cutting and grinding tiny pieces of beautiful blue turquoise. These pieces they set together with
wonderful accuracy, so that they form a pattern on the surface of a magnificent golden vase just made ready by the
goldsmith. The booth of the goldsmith is filled with workmen
and apprentices. They hammer and cast, solder and fit together, richly wrought jewelry which can hardly be improved
upon by the work of the best goldsmiths and jewelers of
today.

98. In the next space on this wall we find the potter no
longer building up his jars and bowls with his fingers alone,
Potter's wheel and as in the Stone Age. He now sits before a
furnace; earliest   small horizontal *wheel*, upon which he deftly
glass   shapes the whirling vessel. When the soft
clay vessels are ready, they are no longer unevenly burned
in an *open* fire, as among the Late Stone Age potters in the
Swiss lake-villages, but here in the Egyptian potter's yard
are long rows of *closed* furnaces of hard clay as tall as a man.
When the pots are packed into these furnaces they are
burned evenly, because they are protected from the wind.
Here also the craftsmen are making glass in the form of
glaze. This art the Egyptians had discovered centuries before. They made brilliant tiles covered with gorgeous glazes
for beautifying house and palace walls. Later the Egyptian
craftsmen learned how to make glass objects, that is, not
merely spread as a glaze on other substances but shaped into
many-colored bottles and vases, which were widely exported.

FIG. 45. *Potter's* WHEEL *and* FURNACE

The potter squats before his horizontal wheel, which is like a flat, round plate
on which the jar revolves while it is being shaped. He keeps the wheel turning with
one hand, and with the other he shapes the soft clay jar as it whirls on the wheel.
This wheel is the ancestor of our lathe. The completed pots are stacked in the
brick furnace at the left. The furnace is already very hot, for the man tending
the fire holds up his hand to shield his face from the heat. The man in the center
places the pots in rows. The three men at the right are smoothing off the rough
places which the wheel cannot take care of. Perhaps one of them is polishing
the outside of the burned pot with a shell,— a custom of the ancient Egyptian
as well as of his present-day descendant

99. The scenes on the wall show us also women weaving
linen cloth. The picture, of course, gives no idea of the fine-
ness of the fabric, but fortunately pieces of **Weavers and tap-**
royal linen, wrapped around the mummy of **estry-makers**
a king of this age, have survived. This product of the
ancient Egyptian *hand* loom is so finely woven that it can
scarcely be distinguished from silk, and the best work of the
modern *machine* loom is coarse in comparison. With such a
hand loom these weavers of Egypt furnished the earliest
known specimens of tapestry, to be hung on the walls of the
Pharaoh's palace or stretched out to shade the roof garden
of the nobleman's villa.

100. On the next wall we find huge bundles of papyrus
reeds, which bare-legged men are gathering along the edge
of the Nile marsh. These reeds are split into **Paper-makers**
long, thin strips, which are then laid overlapping and pasted together. The resulting long, narrow
sheets are again pasted together "two-ply," one on the
other, forming tough whitish or pale-yellow paper. Egyptian
ships on the Mediterranean (Fig. 56) added bales of this Nile
paper to their cargoes and carried it to Syria and Europe.
Egypt thus came to be the world's paper mill for 3000 years.

FIG. 46. CABINETMAKERS *in the Pyramid Age*

At the left a man is cutting with a chisel which he taps with a mallet; next, a
man "rips" a board with a copper saw; next, two men are finishing off a couch,
and at the right a man is drilling a hole with a bow-drill. See the carrying-chair
of Queen Hetep-heres (Fig. 47) as an example of the Egyptian craftsman's skill

101. We seem almost to hear the hubbub of hammers and
mallets as we approach the next section of wall, where we
find the cabinetmakers and shipbuilders at
work. Here are the busy cabinetmakers, fash-
ioning luxurious furniture for the nobleman's
villa. The finished chairs and couches for the king or the
rich are overlaid with gold and silver, inlaid with ebony and
ivory, and upholstered with soft leather cushions. Close by
the furniture workshops is a long line of curving hulls, with
workmen swarming over them like ants, fitting together the
earliest seagoing ships as well as river boats.

*Carpenters, cabi-
netmakers, and
shipbuilders*

102. The river shipping which had already begun under the
First Union increased now very rapidly as the manufacture of
so many different things encouraged exchange
among the towns. Indeed, the river must have
been fairly alive with boats and barges (often
depicted on the tomb walls) bearing goods to
be carried either to the treasury of the Pharaoh for taxes or
to market. Here on the wall is a picture of the market-place
itself. We can watch the shoemaker offering the baker a
pair of sandals as payment for a cake, or the carpenter's
wife giving the fisherman a little wooden box to pay for a
fish, while the potter's wife is willing to give the apothecary
two bowls fresh from the potter's furnace in exchange for

*River commerce;
exchange of goods
before the exist-
ence of money*

FIG. 47. *The* CARRYING-CHAIR *of Queen Hetep-heres, the Mother of Khufu,*
Builder of the Great Pyramid of Gizeh (*Thirtieth Century* B.C.)

After the mother of the great Khufu had been buried, her tomb was entered and
partially plundered by tomb-robbers. Thereupon the Pharaoh ordered that her
sarcophagus and beautiful furniture be taken from her tomb and placed in a deep
shaft just east of the site of the Great Pyramid. Here it was so well hidden that
it was never again disturbed. When discovered by the Harvard-Boston expedition, the wooden framework of the furniture had decayed or shrunken almost
beyond recognition. But the sheet gold with which the furniture had been overlaid still survived and made it possible to restore each piece by building a new
framework of modern wood, which could then be re-covered with the ancient gold
overlay. Thus we are today able to see among other things the very chair in
which the queen rode when her bearers carried her out to take the air. (Courtesy
of the Museum of Fine Arts, Boston)

a jar of fragrant ointment. We see, therefore, that these
people had *no coined money* to use, and that in the market-
place trade was exchange of actual goods. Such was the
business of the common people. If we could see the large
dealings in the palace and its offices, we should find there
heavy rings of gold of a standard weight, which circulated
like money. Rings of copper also served the same purpose.
Such rings were the forerunners of coined money.

103. These people in the picture of the market-place on
the chapel wall were the common folk of Egypt in the Pyramid Age. Some of them were free men, following their own
business or industry; others were slaves, working the fields

on the great estates. Neither of these lower classes owned any land. Over them were the landowners, the Pharaoh and

Society in the Pyramid Age his great lords and officials. Many of them are known to us by name from their tombs. If we could take a walk through the cemetery of Gizeh we could copy a list of them, which would be like a "directory" of the great men of Egypt whose houses formed the wealthy quarter of the royal city when the pyramids of Gizeh were being built nearly five thousand years ago. We might even visit the tomb of the architect who built the Great Pyramid of Gizeh, and we have portrait statues of

FIG. 48. *The Golden* HIEROGLYPHS *spelling the Name and Titles of Queen Hetep-heres*

Each of these signs is an individual piece, wrought in solid gold by the ancient goldsmith and then applied to the ebony strips which form the back of the carrying-chair (Fig. 47). These human figures, birds, animals, trees, tools, weapons, etc. are among the most exquisite examples of the goldsmith's skill produced by ancient men. They are of about the same date as the marvelous gold work from the early tombs at Ur (p. 155). (Courtesy of the Museum of Fine Arts, Boston)

many other noblemen. Here are also the tombs of the royal family, and excavation has even revealed the magnificent tomb furnishings of King Khufu's mother, Queen Hetep-heres (Figs. 47–49). These gifts to the queen from her husband and her son Khufu furnish us almost our only vision of the royal splendor of the Pyramid Age,[1] revealing to us the art and the life of the royal court fifteen hundred years before the glimpses of royal luxury which we gain from the furniture of Tutenkhamon.

[1] See Reisner, *Bulletin of the Boston Museum of Fine Arts*, May, 1927, Supplement to Vol. XXV; Vol. XXVI (1928), pp. 76–88: Vol. XXX (1932). pp. 55–60.

104. While the rich furnishings of Queen Hetep-heres reveal to us the luxuries surrounding Egyptian royalty in the Pyramid Age, the tomb walls give us charming pictures from the actual life of the courtiers. There we may see the owner of the tomb seated at ease in his carrying-chair, a kind of wheelless carriage borne upon the shoulders of slaves. After his inspection of his estate where we have been following him, his bearers carry him into the shady garden before his house, where they set down the palanquin and cease their song.[1] His wife advances at once to greet him. Her place is always at his side; she is his sole wife, held in all honor, and enjoys every right which belongs to her husband. This garden is the nobleman's paradise. Here he may recline for an hour of leisure with his family and friends, playing at a game of draughts, listening to the music of the harp played by his wife, or to a three-piece orchestra of harp, pipe, and lute; or watching women entertainers in the slow and stately dances of the time. Meanwhile his children are sporting about among the arbors, splashing in the pool as they chase the fish, playing with ball, doll, and jumping jack, or teasing the tame monkey, which takes refuge under their father's ivory-legged stool. From these pictures we learn for the first time that, after several hundred thousand years of Stone Age savagery and barbarism, family life was beginning to bring a kindly spirit into the lives of men.

Nobleman of the Pyramid Age in his home

SECTION 7. ART AND ARCHITECTURE IN THE PYRAMID AGE

105. The nobleman drops one hand idly upon the head of his favorite hound, and with the other beckons to the chief gardener and gives directions regarding the fresh romaine lettuce which he wishes to try for dinner. The house where this dinner awaits him is large and commodious, built of sun-dried brick and wood. Light and airy, as suits the climate, we find that it has many lat-

The nobleman's house

---

[1] This song is recorded, with other songs, on the tomb-chapel walls.

ticed windows on all sides. The walls of the living rooms are scarcely more than a frame to support gayly colored hangings which can be let down as a protection against winds and sand storms when necessary. These give the dwelling a very bright and cheerful aspect. The house is a work of art, and we discern in it how naturally the Egyptians demanded beauty in their surroundings. This they secured by making all their *useful* things *beautiful*.

FIG. 49. *The* JEWELS *of Queen Hetep-heres*

These magnificent rings are of silver adorned with dragon flies separated by disks. The designs are recessed, or let into the surface of the silver. The rings are in two sets of eight each, and are graduated in size from small to large as if to fit the swell of the leg above the ankle, or of the arm above the wrist. One of the sets has partially perished; the other is in much better condition. The rings are mounted here upon two cones of wood, restored from a study of the original jewel box in which they were lying when discovered. (Courtesy of the Museum of Fine Arts, Boston)

106. Beauty surrounds us on every hand as we follow **Art of its furniture and decoration** the nobleman in to his dinner. The lotus blossoms on the handle of his carved spoon, and his wine sparkles in the deep blue calyx of the same flower, which forms the bowl of his wineglass. The muscular limbs of the lion or the ox, beautifully carved in ivory, support the chair in which he sits or the couch where he reclines. The painted ceiling over his head is a blue and starry heaven resting upon palm-trunk columns (Fig. 55), each crowned with its graceful tuft of drooping foliage carved in wood and colored in the dark green of the living tree; or columns in the form of lotus stalks rise from the floor as if to support the azure ceiling upon their swaying blossoms. Doves and butterflies, exquisitely painted, flit across this indoor sky. Beneath our feet we find the pavement of the dining-hall carpeted in paintings picturing everywhere the deep green of disheveled

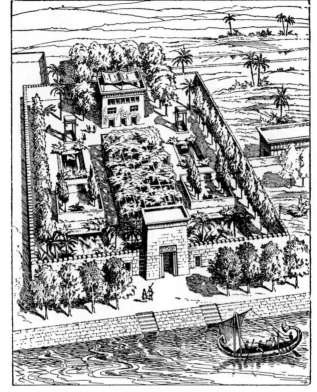

FIG. 50. VILLA *of an Egyptian Nobleman*

The garden is inclosed with a high wall. There are pools on either side as one enters, and a long arbor extends down the middle. The house at the rear, embowered in trees, is crowned by a roof garden shaded with awnings of tapestry

marsh grasses, with gleaming water between and fish gliding among the swaying reeds. Around the margin, leaping among the rushes, we see the wild ox tossing his head at the birds twittering on the nodding rush tops, as they vainly strive to frighten away the stealthy weasel creeping up to plunder their nests. Numbers of huge grasshoppers are perched securely on the reed stems, while here and there portly frogs wink demurely from below.

Fig. 51. *Portrait of* King Khafre, *Builder of the Second Pyramid of Gizeh*

Found in his valley temple (Fig. 54). It is carved in excessively hard stone, called diorite. The falcon with protecting wings outstretched is a symbol of the great god Horus (Twenty-ninth Century B.C.)

Fig. 52. Head *of a Royal* Statue *of Copper in the Pyramid Age*

This is a statue of King Pepi I (nearly 2600 B.C.). It was hammered into shape over a wooden form. The metal is incrusted with rust, but owing to the eyes, of inlaid rock crystal, the portrait is very lifelike (cf. Fig. 215)

107. It was only because they possessed trained artists that the Egyptians were able to leave the beautifully painted reliefs in their tomb-chapels. Indeed, we can find, in one of the chapels, painted in one corner of the wall, a portrait of the artist himself. Here he has represented himself enjoying a plentiful feast among other people of the estate. His drawings all around us show that he has not been able to overcome all the difficulties of drawing, on a flat surface, objects having thickness and roundness. Animal figures are drawn, however, with great lifelikeness. Perspective is almost entirely unknown to him, and objects in the background or distance are depicted of the same size as those in front. Insects and small animals are carved with attention to detail.

Painting and relief in tombs and temples

108. The portrait sculptor was the greatest artist of this age. His statues were carved in stone or wood and painted in the colors of real life; the eyes, inlaid with rock crystal, still continue to shine with the gleam of life. The result is that more lifelike portraits have never been produced by any age, although these are the earliest known portraits in the history of art. Such statues of the kings are often superb. They were set up in the Pharaoh's pyramid temple. In size the most extraordinary statue of the Pyramid Age is the Great Sphinx, which stands here in this cemetery of Gizeh. The head is a portrait of King Khafre, the Pharaoh who built the second pyramid of Gizeh, and was sculptured from a promontory of rock which rose high above the royal city. It is the largest portrait ever wrought.

Fig. 53. *Statuette of an Egyptian* POTTER *at Work at his Wheel*

This wizened little potter has in his face a wistful expression and shows individual characterization which suggests that we have here a portrait and not a statue of just any potter. Yet this man was the humble servant of an obscure cemetery official. (From the collection of the Oriental Institute, University of Chicago)

109. We have already mentioned the beauty of the earliest architecture in stone, produced by Imhotep (§ 87), the first architect. A second stage of architecture in stone is revealed to us in the massive granite piers and walls of Khafre's valley temple be- side the Sphinx. This splendid hall was lighted by a series of oblique slits, which are really low roof windows. They occupied the difference in level between a higher roof over the middle aisle of the hall and a lower roof on each side of the middle. Such an arrangement of roof windows, called a clerestory (*clearstory*), passed from Egypt over to Greece and Rome, where the Christian architects finally found it and used it for the roof and windows of the nave in the basilica churches and cathedrals. The weight and massiveness of the piers in Khafre's hall make it a place of grandeur. Less than a century later (Twenty-eighth Century B.C.) it was gracefulness rather than grandeur which the Egyptian architects desired. Instead of these heavy *square* piers or pillars the architects then began to erect slender and graceful *round* columns with beautiful capitals. These shafts, when ranged in rows, formed the earliest known colonnades in the history of architecture (Fig. 55).

Fig. 54. *Restoration of the* Clerestory Hall *in the Valley Temple of Khafre*

The roof of this hall was supported on two rows of huge stone piers, each a single block of polished granite weighing 22 tons. This view shows only one row of the piers, the other being out of sight at the right. At the left, above, the light streams in obliquely from the very low clerestory windows. Compare the cross section in Fig. 266. The statues shown here had been thrown by unknown enemies into a well in an adjacent hall, where they were found about eighty years ago. See head of the finest in Fig. 51. (After Hoelscher)

110. The useful and beautiful things which Egypt was now making began to be carried across the Mediterranean to Europe, and by land to Western Asia. These things

Fig. 55. Colonnades *in the* Court *of a Pyramid Temple*

Notice the pyramid rising behind the temple. The door in the middle leads to the holy place built against the side of the pyramid. The center of the court is open to the sky; the roof of the porch all around is supported on round columns, the earliest known in the history of architecture. Contrast the square piers, without any capital, which the architect of Khafre put into his temple hall (Fig. 54) two generations earlier than these columns. Each column represents a palm tree, the capital being the crown of foliage. The whole place was colored in the bright hues of nature, including the painting on the walls behind the columns. Among these paintings was the ship in Fig. 56. Thirteen hundred feet of copper piping, the earliest known plumbing, was installed in this building. (After Borchardt)

were a part of the earliest civilization which commerce was thus bringing to Europe and Asia. At the same time, as we shall see, Western Asia also had been making the most surprising advances in civilization. These advances began to exert an influence in Egypt, showing that there was active commerce between Egypt and Asia. This commerce also connected the western Delta and Crete. We have already learned, however, that the Pharaoh had been carrying on some oversea commerce for centuries (§ 81).

Earliest seagoing ships; northward spread of Egyptian civilization

111. Besides continuing the work on their copper mines in Sinai (see map, p. 66) the Pharaohs were also sending caravans of donkeys far up the Nile into the Sudan, to traffic

FIG. 56. *Earliest* REPRESENTATION *of a Seagoing Ship* (*Twenty-eighth Century* B.C.)

The scene is carved on the wall of a temple (Fig. 55). The people are all bowing to the king whose figure (now lost) stood on shore (at the left), and they salute him with the words written in a line of hieroglyphs above, meaning, "Hail to thee! O Sahure [the king's name], thou god of the living! We behold thy beauty." Some of these men are bearded Phœnician prisoners brought by this Egyptian ship, which, with seven others, had therefore crossed the eastern end of the Mediterranean and returned. The big double mast is unshipped and lies on supports in the stern. The model and ornaments of these earliest known ships spread in later times to ships found in all waters from Italy to India

with the people of the south and to bring back ebony, ivory, ostrich feathers, and fragrant gums. The officials who con-

Southern commerce; earliest navigation on the Red Sea

ducted these caravans were the earliest explorers of inner Africa, and in their tombs at the First Cataract they have left interesting records of their exciting adventures among the wild tribes of the south, — adventures in which some of them lost their lives.[1] The royal fleet was also sent on expeditions to a far-away coastland of the south called Punt, at the southern end of the Red Sea (see map, p. 146), where they found the same products and brought them back by water.

112. We have seen the grandeur and beauty of the civilization gained by the Egyptians of the Pyramid Age. We

End of Pyramid Age

now realize how many more things the men of the Nile could make than the men of Europe, who were still living in the Stone Age towns at the very time the Egyptian tomb-chapels were built. It was the appearance of all these new things which made the life of Egypt

[1] The teacher will find it of interest to read these records to the class. See the author's *Ancient Records of Egypt*, Vol. I, §§ 325–336, 350–374.

civilized, especially after 3000 B.C. But the noblemen finally became so powerful that the Pharaohs could no longer control them. Then, in struggles among themselves, they destroyed the Pharaoh's government, soon after 2450 B.C. Thus ended the Pyramid Age, which had lasted some five hundred years,— the age in which men for the first time advanced far into civilization and left barbarism behind (see Fig. 41).

113. We have found that the two things which finally made possible the development of civilization were, first, *agriculture on a large scale* and, second, *plen-* Stages of emerg-*tiful metal*. Now a plentiful supply of metal ing civilization required extensive mining operations in distant localities. Such enterprises could be carried out only by powerful kings, and these rulers gained the necessary power and wealth from the enlargement of the grain fields made possible by the invention of the plow. This invention went far toward completing the development of *food-production*, but the resulting enlargement of the grain fields would have been impossible without a great *national* system of *irrigation canals*. These canals could never have been dug, or, when dug, could never have been kept in constant operation, without a *government* with a king at its head. Such a government could not carry on its work without *writing* and a *calendar*.

114. Back of all these things which we have just listed lies the fact that the Stone Age hunters could not have taken possession of the Nile valley if they had not Conditions of shift been able to draw on the wild animals as a from savagery to, source of food. The domestication of the wild civilization animals began the development of *food-production*. The increased control of the wild creatures and final possession of them as domesticated animals were closely connected with the drying of the Sahara, which drove the wild animals into the Nile gorge, where the hunters could much more easily imprison them in stockades. As we continue backward we reach the stage of *food-gathering*, and eventually the Early Stone Age savagery which surrounded the entire Mediterranean until the combination of favorable circumstances enabled the inhabitants of the Nile valley to advance far beyond all other peoples of that time. The Age of the Pharaohs was not ended with the fall of the Pyramid-builders. There were two more great ages in the long story of human life on the Nile: the Feudal Age and the Empire. The monuments which these later ages left lie farther up the river, and we must now turn our attention to them.

QUESTIONS

Section 5. Explain the necessity of irrigation in Egypt. What led to the rise of government? Discuss the civilization of the earliest two nations known in human history. Explain the importance of the invention of the plow. Trace the steps by which phonetic writing arose. Where did the first alphabet arise? Discuss the importance of the invention of writing. To what country were the earliest mining expeditions sent, and who sent them? Describe the effect of the use of metal on architecture.

Section 6. What do the tombs of Egypt tell us of the religious beliefs of the people? Study Fig. 41 and tell how the Egyptian tombs reveal the transition from barbarism to civilization. Describe the government of the Pyramid Age. Make a list of the industries revealed in the tomb-chapel pictures. Discuss trade and commerce.

Section 7. Describe the house and garden of a nobleman in the Pyramid Age. Discuss painting and portrait sculpture. Describe the roof windows called clerestory windows (Figs. 54 and 266) and what they finally came to be. Compare the earliest piers (Fig. 54) with the piers (columns) built a hundred years later (Fig. 55). Describe the earliest seagoing ships. Give the date of the Pyramid Age and tell why it was important.

BIBLIOGRAPHY FOR TOPICAL STUDIES

The Pyramid-builders: BREASTED, *Ancient Egyptians*, §§ 94–102; *Bulletin of the Boston Museum of Fine Arts*, April, 1911, pp. 13–20, April, 1915, pp. 29–35, and Supplement to Vol. XXV; QUIBELL, *Egyptian History and Art*, pp. 34–39.

Early explorations: BAIKIE, *Ancient Egypt*, chaps. ix–x; BREASTED, *Ancient Egyptians*, §§ 116–122; QUIBELL, pp. 45–49.

Burial customs: BREASTED, *Religion and Thought*, pp. 62–69; *Bulletin of the Metropolitan Museum of Art*, December, 1920, Part I, pp. 14–32; MASPERO, *Art in Egypt*, pp. 6–21, 28–38, 88–90.

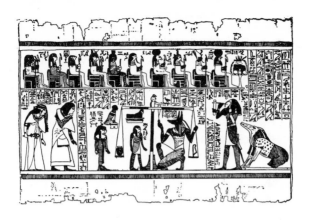

Chapter IV · The Story of Egypt: The Feudal Age and the Empire

Section 8. The Feudal Age

115. After the Pyramid Age the leadership of Egypt passed from the north to the south. If we should voyage upriver by steamer from Gizeh we should discover that after a time the great stone pyramids would disappear altogether, but far away in the south we should find other buildings, tombs, and monuments which tell us of two more great ages on the Nile, — the Feudal Age and the Empire. We have seen how the growth in power of the noblemen caused the downfall of the government in the

Meaning of Feudal Age in Egypt

NOTE. A picture from the BOOK OF THE DEAD. At the left we see entering, in white robes, the DECEASED, a man named ANI, and his WIFE. Before them are the balances of judgment for weighing the human heart, to determine whether it is just or not. A jackal-headed god adjusts the scales, while an ibis-headed god stands behind him, pen in hand, prepared to record the verdict of the balances. Behind him is a monster ready to devour the unjust soul as his heart (looking like a tiny jar) in the left-hand scalepan, is weighed over against right and truth (symbolized by a feather) in the right-hand scalepan. The scene is painted in water colors on papyrus. Such a roll is sometimes as much as 90 feet long and filled from beginning to end with magical charms for the use of the dead in the next world. Hence the modern name for the whole roll, the "Book of the Dead."

Pyramid Age. The Pharaoh had been forced to make grants of lands to these men under arrangements which in later Europe we call feudal. They were thus powerful barons, living like little kings on their broad estates. This Feudal Age of Egypt lasted for several centuries and was flourishing by 2000 B.C.

116. In the cliffs back of the fertile valley estates the noblemen excavated their tombs. Here again from the scenes
Tombs and libra- painted on the tomb walls we may reconstruct
ries of Feudal Age the life of the times. Fragments from the libraries of these feudal barons — the oldest libraries in the world — have also been found, and from these papyrus rolls we actually learn what these people *thought*, as well as how they lived! These oldest of all surviving books are in the form of rolls of papyrus, which were once packed in jars, neatly labeled, and ranged in rows on the nobleman's library shelves. Here are the most ancient story-books in the world, — tales of wanderings and adventures in Asia, tales of shipwreck at the gate of the unknown ocean beyond the Red Sea, the earliest "Sindbad the Sailor," and tales of wonders wrought by ancient wise men and magicians.

117. Some of the stories tell about the sufferings of the poor and the humble, in the hope of stirring up the rulers of
Books on kindness the people to be just and kind in their treat-
and justice ment of the weaker classes. Some describe the wickedness of men and the hopelessness of the future. Others tell of a righteous ruler who was yet to come, a "good shepherd" they called him, meaning a good king. Thus arose the earliest dream of a Messiah. It was believed that he would bring in justice and happiness for all. We notice here a contrast with the Pyramid Age. With the incoming of the Pyramid-builders we saw a tremendous growth in power, in building, and in art; but in the Feudal Age there were men who tried to advance also in still higher things. These things were character and right conduct (see also the explanation under Fig. 57). For the first time, men began to believe that only a good man could hope for a blessed life hereafter.

FIG. 57. CLIFF-TOMB *of an Egyptian Nobleman of the Feudal Age*

This tomb is not a masonry building, like the tombs of the Pyramid Age, but is cut into the face of the cliff and is therefore of solid rock. The chapel entered through this front door contains painted relief pictures, like those of the Pyramid Age, and also many written records. In this chapel the nobleman tells of his kind treatment of his people; he says: "There was no citizen's daughter whom I misused; there was no widow whom I oppressed; there was no peasant whom I evicted; there was no shepherd whom I expelled; . . . there was none wretched in my community, there was none hungry in my time. When years of famine came I plowed all the fields of the Oryx barony [his estate] . . . preserving its people alive and furnishing its food so that there was none hungry therein. I gave to the widow as to her who had a husband; I did not exalt the great above the humble in anything that I gave." All this we can read inscribed in this tomb

118. Probably a number of papyrus rolls were required to contain the drama of Osiris, — a great play in which the life, death, burial, and resurrection of Osiris were pictured. This play was performed at an annual feast in which all the people loved to join. It is our earliest known drama, — a kind of Passion Play; but the rolls on which it was written have perished. Excavation has uncovered fragments of another book roll which sets forth a similar drama in the form of a pageant. In this earliest

Drama and poetry

Fig. 58. A *Page from the* Story *of the* Shipwrecked Sailor, *the Earliest "Sindbad," as read by the Boys and Girls of Egypt Four Thousand Years Ago (One Third of Size of Original)*

This page reads: "Those who were on board perished, and not one of them escaped. Then I was cast upon an island by a wave of the great sea. I passed three days alone, with (only) my heart as my companion, sleeping in the midst of a shelter of trees, till daylight enveloped me. Then I crept out for aught to fill my mouth. I found figs and grapes there and all fine vegetables, etc. . . ." The tale then tells of his seizure by an enormous serpent with a long beard, who proves to be the king of this distant island in the Red Sea, at the entrance of the Indian Ocean. He keeps the sailor three months, treats him kindly, and returns him with much treasure to Egypt. The island then seems to have sunk and vanished forever. In form such a book was a single strip of papyrus paper, 5 or 6 to 10 or 12 inches wide, and often 15 to 30 or 40 feet long. When not in use this strip was kept rolled up, and thus the earliest books were rolls, looking when small, like a high-school diploma or, when large, like a roll of wall paper

preserved play we find parts of the dialogue, with stage directions accompanied by pictures of the action. This papyrus dates from the Eighteenth or Nineteenth Century B.C. and is probably the oldest illustrated book in the world. There were also rolls containing songs and poems, like the beautiful hymn sung by the nobles of the Pharaoh's court as a greeting to the sovereign every morning when he came out of his apartment.

119. It is a surprising fact that even at this early date a number of rolls were needed to deal with the beginnings of science. The most valuable of all contained what had been learned about surgery and the organs of the human body. This earliest known book on surgery is a papyrus roll now

preserved in the library of the New York Historical Society. It is the oldest surviving book in which a man tried to discover new facts by careful study of the objects around him, just as Sir Isaac Newton is said to have watched a falling apple and to have received from it a hint of the law of gravitation. This book of surgery is therefore the earliest book of science. Its subject is the human body, and what happens when its parts are injured. It contains the earliest known mention of the human brain, the earliest notice of the fact that the brain controls the limbs and that an injury to it paralyzes them.

Earliest books of science: surgery

120. There are also rolls containing many of the recognized rules of arithmetic, based on the decimal system which we still use; others treat the beginnings of algebra and geometry. In *plane* geometry it is surprising to find that these earliest known mathematicians already had rules for computing correctly the area of a triangle, of a trapezium, and even of a circle, which was figured as the square of eight ninths of the diameter. The value of π which results from this computation is 3.1605, a result surprisingly near the correct value. This led to a rule for the calculation of the area of a hemisphere. It was a method rediscovered by the Greeks 1600 years later. Finally, in dealing with *solid* geometry these mathematical rolls show methods of calculating how many bushels of grain there are in cylinder-shaped granaries of varying depths and diameters. They also explain how to calculate the content of a frustum of a square pyramid, and even the cubical content of a hemisphere could be computed. The formula for solving this problem was not discovered in Europe until 3000 years later. Observations of the heavenly bodies with simple instruments were made; but these records, like those in engineering and geography have been lost.

Books of science: mathematics

121. Along with this higher progress the Pharaohs of the Feudal Age much improved the government. Every few years they made census lists to be used in taxation, and a few of these, the earliest census sheets in the world, have

Fig. 59. *Restoration of the* Fortifications *which* GUARDED THE NILE *at the Southern Entrance to Feudal-Age Egypt*

At either end of the granite barrier obstructing the Nile at the Second Cataract still stand the Feudal Age fortresses erected about four thousand years ago. The two fortresses completely commanded the narrow gap in the barrier, and no boat could descend without the consent of the garrisons. The walls, with towers projecting far beyond them, show full knowledge of the strategics of defense. Cut in the surrounding rocks are records of the greatest yearly height of the Nile during the Feudal Age, when the Pharaohs were much interested in engineering and the control of irrigation. By observing the rise of the river here, word could be sent down the river when plenty of water for irrigation was assured, and thus the king's treasurer knew in advance that he could collect the usual amount of taxes. (After Borchardt)

survived. These kings erected huge earthen dikes and made large basins for storing up the Nile waters needed for irriga-

Administration and irrigation projects in the Feudal Age tion, thus greatly increasing the yield of the feudal lands and estates. They measured the height of the river from year to year, and their marks of the Nile levels are still to be found cut on the rocks at the Second Cataract. Thus nearly four thousand years ago they were already doing on a large scale what our government has only recently begun to do by its irrigation projects among our own arid lands.

122. At the same time these rulers of the Feudal Age tried to reach the wealth of other lands by sea. Their fleets sailed

Commerce by sea; a Suez Canal four thousand years ago over among the Ægean islands and probably controlled the large island of Crete. They dug a canal from the north end of the Red Sea westward to the nearest branch of the Nile in the eastern Delta, where the river divides into a number of mouths (see map, p. 66). This canal made it possible for the Pharaoh's Mediterranean ships to sail up the easternmost mouth

FIG. 60. *Model of a* TRAVELING BOAT *which belonged to a Nobleman of the Early Feudal Age*

The sail is just being hauled up, showing that the boat is to travel with the wind. As the prevailing wind blows from the north in Egypt, we know that the boat is about to voyage southward. We see the sailors making fast the backstays and hauling on the halyards. The most interesting feature of this boat is the cabin, the interior of which we see in Fig. 61. (Courtesy of Metropolitan Museum of Art)

FIG. 61. FURNITURE *in the Cabin of the Model Traveling Boat* (Fig. 60)

This little cabin is detachable and has here been removed, exposing the furniture. The steward sits watchfully beside the bed under which the trunks of his master have been placed, just as in a modern steamship cabin. (Courtesy of Metropolitan Museum of Art)

of the Nile, then to enter the new canal and, passing east-ward through it, reach the Red Sea. Thus the Mediterra-nean Sea and the Red Sea were first connected by a real Suez Canal four thousand years ago. Such a connection was as important to the Egyptians as the Panama Canal is to the United States or the Suez Canal to England. By go-ing through this canal, Nile ships could sail from the eastern Delta directly to the land of Punt and to the straits leading to the Indian Ocean. These waters seemed to the sailors of the Feudal Age the end of the world, and their stories of wonderful adventures in these far-away regions must have delighted many a circle of villagers on the feudal estates.

123. In this age the Pharaoh had organized a small stand-ing army. He could now make his power felt in both north and south, in Palestine and in Nubia. He conquered the territory of Nubia as far south as the Second Cataract (see map, p. 66), and thus added two hundred miles of river to the kingdom of Egypt. Here he erected strong frontier fortresses against the Nubian tribes. The wise rule of the Pharaohs of the Feudal Age did much to prepare the way for Egyptian lead-ership in the early world. Three of these kings bore the name "Sesostris," which became one of the great and il-lustrious names in Egyptian history. But not long after 1800 B.C. the power of the Pharaohs of the Feudal Age sud-denly declined. Their final fall was due to an invasion of a foreign people called Hyksos, who entered Egypt from Asia.

Military expansion north and south; end of Feudal Age

SECTION 9. THE FOUNDING OF THE EMPIRE

124. The monuments along the river banks have thus far told us the story of two of the three periods[1] into which the career of this great Nile people falls. After the modern Nile traveler has passed the tombs of the Feudal Age and has

[1] These three ages are:
1. The Pyramid Age, about 30th to 25th Century B.C. (Sections 6-7).
2. The Feudal Age, flourishing 2000 B.C. (Section 8).
3. The Empire, about 1580 to 1150 B.C. (Sections 9-11).

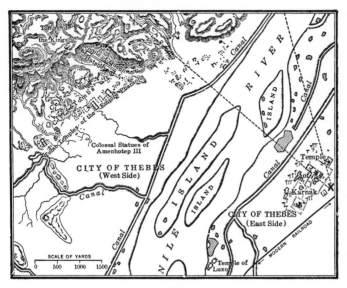

Map of THEBES

This map may be compared with the air view of Karnak (Fig. 66), taken over the point marked X. In the upper left corner are shown the western cliffs, in and along which lie the tombs of the vast cemetery (Fig. 4). In front of these west-ern cliffs, and parallel with them, stretched a long line of temples facing the great temples of Luxor and Karnak on the east side of the river. The houses of the ancient city have passed away

continued his journey over four hundred miles southward from Cairo, he sees mighty masses of stone masonry and lines of tall columns rising among the palms on the **Thebes and the his-** east side of the river. They are the ruins of **tory of the Empire** the once great city of Thebes, which tell us the story of the third period, the Empire.

125. Here we find not only an enormous cemetery but also a series of great temples on both sides of the river (see map, above). The walls of these immense temples **Temple reliefs;** are covered with enormous pictures sculp- **arrival of the** tured in relief, depicting the victorious wars **horse in Egypt** of the Egyptians in all directions, but especially in Asia, to which they drove back the Hyksos. In these pictures we

FIG. 62. A PHARAOH *of the Empire fighting in his* CHARIOT

This relief shows the Pharaoh (Ramses II) after he has overcome the bearded
defenders of two Asiatic strongholds shown at the left. The reins of the horses
are fastened around the Pharaoh's waist, leaving both his hands free, and with
uplifted spear he is on the point of stabbing the Asiatic chieftain, who is helplessly
falling out of the smaller chariot in the foreground. This is one of an enormous
series of such scenes, 170 feet long, carved in relief on the outside of the Great Hall
of Karnak. Such sculpture was brightly colored and served to enhance the archi-
tectural effect of the building, as well as to impress the people with the heroism
of the Pharaoh. The color has now disappeared, and the sculpture is battered and
weatherworn. (After Wreszinski)

see the giant figure of the Pharaoh as he stands in his war
chariot, scattering the enemy before his plunging horses.
The Pharaohs of the Pyramid Age had never seen a horse,
and this is the first time that we have met horses on the
ancient monuments. After the close of the Feudal Age
horses began to be imported from Asia, where we shall find
them in use at a much earlier time (see § 174). Chariots
came with them, and Egypt, having learned warfare on a
scale unknown before, became a military empire.

126. The Pharaohs thus became great generals, with a well-
organized standing army made up chiefly of archers and
Egypt a military em- heavy masses of chariots. With these forces
pire   the Pharaohs conquered an empire which extended from the Euphrates in Asia to the Fourth Cataract
of the Nile in Africa (see map I, p. 266). By an empire we

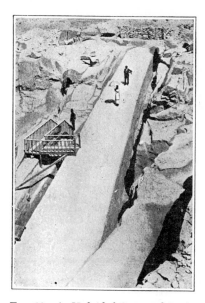

FIG. 63. *An Unfinished* OBELISK *lying in the Granite Quarry at the First Cataract of the Nile*

The top surface of this long shaft of granite was made flat by hammering with ball-shaped "pounders" made of a very hard stone called *dolerite*. The exact shape of the obelisk was then outlined on this flat surface. When hammered with the dolerite pounders along these outlines the granite crumbled and could be removed as dust. As the hammers ground their way downward the workmen thus eventually found themselves hammering at the bottom of long trenches ten to fifteen feet deep. Three faces of the obelisk — that is, the top and two sides — were thus detached from the quarry, but how the

mean a group of nations subdued and ruled over by the most powerful among them. In much earlier times human government had begun with tiny city-states, which gradually merged together into nations such as Upper and Lower Egypt; but the organization of men had now reached the point where *many nations* were combined into an empire including a large part of the Ancient Near East. This world power of the Pharaohs lasted from the Sixteenth to the Twelfth Century B.C., — a period of somewhat over four hundred years.

127. The Karnak Temple, which stood in the enormous city of Thebes, now serves as a

Queen Hatshepsut, the first great woman in history

great historical volume telling us much of the story of the Egyptian Empire. Behind the great hall there towers a huge obelisk, a

fourth side, the bottom, was undercut without cracking the mighty shaft is uncertain. This obelisk is still attached to the quarry along the bottom. After an obelisk was extracted from the quarry, it was dragged along a causeway to the river and then transported by Nile boat to its destination. Our obelisk was left lying here in the quarry because the engineers discovered flaws in the stone. The shaft is 137 feet long and, if extracted, would have weighed over 1100 tons, the largest single block of stone ever quarried by engineers ancient or modern.

(Photograph by the Oriental Institute of the University of Chicago)

FIG. 64. *Part of the* FLEET *of Queen Hatshepsut loading in the Land of Punt*

Only two of Hatshepsut's fleet of five ships are shown. The sails on the long spars are furled, and the vessels are moored. The sailors are carrying the cargo up the gangplanks, and one of them is teasing an ape on the roof of the cabin. The inscriptions above the ships read: "The loading of the ships very heavily with marvels of the country of Punt: all goodly fragrant woods of God's-Land [the East], heaps of myrrh-resin, with fresh myrrh trees, with ebony and pure ivory, with green gold of Emu, with cinnamon wood, *khesyt* wood, with two kinds of incense, eye-cosmetic, with apes, monkeys, dogs, and with skins of the southern panther, with natives and their children. Never was brought the like of this for any king who has been since the beginning." The scene is carved on the wall of the queen's temple at Thebes, in the garden of which she planted the myrrh trees

shaft of granite in a single piece nearly a hundred feet high. It was erected early in the Empire by Queen Hatshepsut, who is regarded as the first great woman in history. There were once two of these enormous monuments, and it was no small task for the queen's engineers to cut out and transport them, and then erect them in this temple. But the queen did not stop with this achievement. She even dispatched an expedition of five ships through the Red Sea to Punt, to bring back the luxuries of tropical Africa for another beautiful terraced temple which she was erecting against the western cliffs at Thebes (map, p. 103). Such deeds reveal quite clearly the ability of this first great woman as a ruler.

128. If we examine the Karnak obelisk of Hatshepsut, we find around the base the remains of stone masonry with which it was once walled in and covered almost up to the top. This was done by the queen's successor, the great soldier Thutmose III, in order to cover up the records which proclaimed

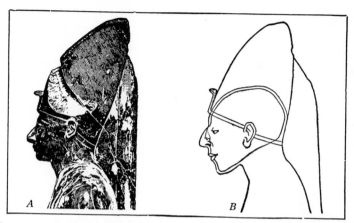

FIG. 65. *Portrait of* THUTMOSE III, *the* Napoleon *of Ancient Egypt* (A), *compared with his Mummy* (B)

This portrait (A), carved in granite, can be compared with the actual face of the great conqueror as we have it in his mummy. Such a comparison is shown in B, where the profile of this granite portrait (outside lines) is placed over the profile of Thutmose III's mummy (inside lines). The correspondence is very close, showing great accuracy in the portrait art of this age

to the world the hated rule of a woman. In her great temple he commanded his people to take hammers and smash to pieces over a hundred stone statues of the queen. Everywhere he had the names of Hatshepsut and all the men who aided her cut out and obliterated, including the name of the skillful architect and engineer who had erected the Karnak obelisk and its companion. But the masonry covering the obelisk has since fallen down, thus revealing inscriptions which still proclaim the fame of Hatshepsut.

End of Hatshepsut and triumph of Thutmose III

129. Thutmose III was the first great general in history, the Napoleon of Egypt, the greatest of the Egyptian conquerors. He ruled for over fifty years, beginning about 1500 B.C. On the temple walls at Karnak we can read the story of nearly twenty years of warfare, during which Thutmose crushed the cities and kingdoms of Western Asia and welded them

Campaigns of Thutmose III (1501–1447 B.C.)

into an enduring empire. At the same time he built the earliest known fleet of warships, and with this fleet he was able to carry his power even to the Ægean Sea, where one of his generals became governor of the Ægean islands (map I, p. 266). A series of great Pharaohs, whom we may call Egyptian emperors, followed Thutmose III, and their power did not begin to decline for a century or more after his death.

SECTION 10. THE HIGHER LIFE OF THE EMPIRE

130. The wealth which these Egyptian emperors captured in Asia and Nubia brought them power and magnificence un-

Temple architecture

known to the world before, especially as shown in their vast and splendid buildings. A new and impressive chapter in the history of art and architecture was begun. The temple of Karnak (§ 127) contains the greatest colonnaded hall ever erected by man (Fig. 67). The vast capital forming the summit of *each* column is large enough to contain a group of a hundred men standing crowded upon it at the same time. The clerestory windows on each side of these giant columns are no longer low, depressed openings, as in the Pyramid Age, but they have now become fine, tall windows, showing us the Egyptian clerestory hall on its way to become the basilica church of much later times (Fig. 266).

131. Such temples as these at Thebes were seen through the deep green of clustering palms, among towering obelisks and colossal statues of the Pharaohs. The whole was bright with color, and flashing at many a point with bands of sheet gold and silver. Mirrored in the unruffled surface of the

* This point of view is behind (east of) the great Karnak Temple at the point marked X in the map (p. 103). We look northwestward across the temple and the river to the western cliffs. From the rear gate below us (lower right-hand corner of view) to the tall front wall nearest the river the temple is nearly a quarter of a mile long and was nearly two thousand years in course of construction. The oldest portions were built by the kings of the Feudal Age, and the latest, the front wall, by the Greek kings (the Ptolemies, Section 63). The standing obelisk of Queen Hatshepsut can be seen rising in the middle of the temple. Beyond it is the vast colonnaded Hall of Karnak, on the outside wall of which are the great war reliefs (Fig. 62). On the left we see the pool, — all that remains of the sacred lake.

FIG. 66. *The Great* TEMPLE OF KARNAK *and the Nile Valley at Thebes seen from an Airplane* *

The area included in this view will be found bounded by two diverging dotted lines on the map of Thebes (p. 103). It will be seen that our view includes only a portion of the ancient city, which extended up and down both sides of the river. (For description of Karnak see note on opposite page)

Fig. 67. *Restoration of the* Great Hall of Karnak, *Ancient Thebes,— Largest Building of the Egyptian Empire*

It is 338 feet wide and 170 feet deep, furnishing a floor area about equal to that of the cathedral of Notre Dame in Paris, although this is only a single room of the temple. There are one hundred and thirty-four columns in sixteen rows. The nave (three central aisles) is 79 feet high and contains twelve columns in two rows, which the architects have made much higher than the rest in order to insert lofty clerestory windows on each side. Compare the very low windows of the earliest clerestory (Fig. 54). In this higher form the clerestory passed over to Europe

temple lake, it made a picture of such splendor as the ancient world had never seen before. As the visitor entered he found himself in a spacious and sunlit court, surrounded by splendid colonnaded porches. Beyond, all was mystery as he looked into the somber forest of towering columns in the hall behind the court. These temples were connected by long avenues of sphinxes sculptured in stone, forming parkways which united the temples in an impressive group. They thus transformed Thebes into the first great "monumental city" ever built by man, — a city which, as a whole, was itself a vast and imposing monument.[1]

Surroundings of Empire temples at Thebes

132. Much of the grandeur of Egyptian architecture was due to the sculptor and the painter. The colonnades, with flower capitals, were colored to suggest the plants they represented. The enormous battle scenes carved on the temple

[1] City plans which treat a whole city as a symmetrical and harmonious unit are now beginning to be made in America.

Fig. 68. *The Colossal* Columns *of the* Nave *in the* Great
Hall of Karnak

These are the columns of the middle two rows in Fig. 67. On the top of the
capital of each one of these columns a hundred men can stand at once.
These great columns may be seen in the air view (Fig. 66) just at the left
of the two obelisks

wall were painted in bright colors. The portrait statues of the Pharaohs, set up before these temples, were often so large

Painting and sculp-
ture in temples

that they rose above the towers of the temple front itself (the tallest part of the building), and they could be seen for miles around. The sculptors could cut these colossal figures from a single block, although they were sometimes eighty or ninety feet high and weighed as much as a thousand tons. This is equal to the load drawn by a modern freight train of twenty-five cars, but, unlike the trainload, it was not cut up into small units of weight light enough for convenient handling and loading. Nevertheless the engineers of the Empire moved many such vast figures for hundreds of miles, using the same methods employed in moving obelisks. It was in works of this massive, monumental character that the art of Egypt excelled (Fig. 77).

133. Two enormous portraits of Amenhotep III, the most luxurious and splendid of the Egyptian emperors, still stand

Tombs of great
men of the Empire

on the western plain of Thebes, across the river from Karnak. As we approach them we see rising behind them the majestic western cliffs, in which are cut hundreds of tomb-chapels belonging to the great men of the Empire. Here were buried the able generals who marched with the Pharaohs on their campaigns in Asia and in Nubia. Here lay the gifted artists and architects who built the vast monuments we have just visited. Here in these tomb-chapels we may read their names and often long accounts of their lives. Here is the story of the general who saved Thutmose III's life, during a great elephant hunt in Asia, by rushing in at the critical moment and cutting off the trunk of an enraged elephant which was pursuing the king. Here also was the tomb of the general, Thutiy, who took the city of Joppa in Palestine by concealing his men in panniers loaded on the backs of donkeys, and thus bringing them into the city as merchandise, — an adventure which afterward furnished part of the story of "Ali Baba and the Forty Thieves." The tomb of this general is now covered by rubbish, and we do not even know where it is located; but a

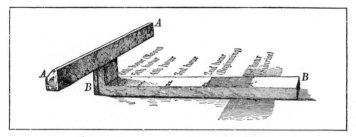

FIG. 69. *The Oldest Clock in the World,— an Egyptian Shadow Clock*

In sunny Egypt a shadow clock was a very practical instrument. In the morning the crosspiece (*AA*) was turned toward the east, and its shadow fell on the long arm (*BB*), where we see it at the first hour. As the sun rose higher the shadow shortened, and its place on the scale showed the hour, which could be read in figures for six hours until noon. At noon the head (*AA*) was turned around to the west and the *lengthening* afternoon shadow on the long arm (*BB*) was measured in the same way. It was from the introduction of such Egyptian clocks that the twelve-hour day reached Europe. This clock bears the name of Thutmose III and is therefore about thirty-four hundred years old. Nearly a thousand years later such clocks were adopted by the Greeks. It is now in the Berlin Museum. The headpiece (*AA*) is restored after Borchardt

golden dish which came out of it is preserved in the Museum of the Louvre in Paris (see Fig. 145).

134. When it has not been plundered by tomb-robbers, such a tomb is a storehouse of ancient household life; for when a wealthy Egyptian died, his family de- Furniture and sired to supply him with everything that had equipment placed made life pleasant in this world, and that in Empire tombs they believed might serve to do the same in the life after death (cf. § 94). In the same way the royal family furnished the tomb of a dead Pharaoh with the greatest splendor and gave the departed king a magnificent array of royal furniture and personal ornaments taken from his palace. Such royal tombs, because of the great value of their contents, were plundered and entirely emptied long ago by the ancient Egyptians themselves. The sole exception is the now famous tomb of Tutenkhamon, which was saved by a curious acci- dent. Workmen who were tunneling into the cliff higher up to make the tomb of a later king threw out a great quantity of stone chips, which then slipped down over the face of

FIG. 70. *Portrait* HEAD *thought to be* IKHNATON, *the Earliest Monotheist*

Discovered by Borchardt in the studio of an ancient Egyptian sculptor at Amarna. The head is carved in limestone and conveys a wonderful impression of dreamy beauty. The resemblance to Ikhnaton's son-in-law, Tutenkhamon, is striking, and it may be his portrait

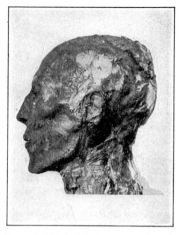

FIG. 71. *Head of the Mummy of* SETI I, *Father of Ramses II*

One of the royal bodies discovered at Thebes (§ 146). The head of Seti is the best-preserved of the entire group, but the royal mummies are all beginning to show evidences of decay. The Egyptian government has accordingly had them removed to a modern tomb at Cairo

Tutenkhamon's tomb and covered it completely. It was so entirely forgotten that, after the fall of the Empire, when the other royal tombs were robbed, no one remembered it.

135. These tombs show us also how much farther the Egyptians had advanced in religion since the days of the

Religion in the Empire

pyramids of Gizeh. Each of these great men buried in the Theban cemetery looked forward to a judgment in the next world, where Osiris was the great judge and king. Every good man might rise from the dead as Osiris had done, but in the presence of Osiris he would be obliged to see his soul weighed in the balances over against a feather, the symbol of truth and justice. The dead man's friends put into his coffin a roll of the "Book of the Dead" (headpiece, p. 95), to aid him in the hereafter.

FIG. 72. *King* IKHNATON *sitting at* DINNER *with his Family*

Old Egyptian custom regarded it as unfitting that a Pharaoh should be portrayed as taking part in the everyday affairs of life with his family. On the earlier Egyptian monuments we are given glimpses of only the most formal family groups until we come to study the cliff-tombs of Ikhnaton's followers at Amarna. In violation of all good old custom these noblemen took delight in picturing on the inner walls of their tombs intimate and charming scenes from the life of their beloved young king. In the left center of the above relief he sits at a well-stocked table eating heartily of a huge haunch of meat held in his right hand. The queen, behind him, is demolishing a *whole* roasted fowl and is not in the least ashamed to "eat with her fingers." Seated on smaller chairs beside her, two little princesses follow the example of their parents. The king's mother and her daughter (at right) dine with the royal family. Four serving men, in the center foreground, busy themselves in passing the food, and an orchestra of stringed instruments furnishes the music at the royal dinner

While their ideas about the *next* world were thus growing they were also gaining ideas about *this* world. They had al‑ ways believed in many gods; but they had thought of the gods (even such an important one as Re, the Sun-god) as ruling only in Egypt, for no one had ever heard of a god who ruled the whole world. The kings of Egypt for two thousand years or more had been ruling only Egypt, and the Egyptians had never thought of any rule that included both Egypt and the larger world outside of it. They had never dreamed of a *whole world* as the kingdom of either a single king or a single god. In the Empire, however, they saw the Pharaoh ruling far beyond the limits of Egypt, and they began to grow accustomed to the idea of a larger rule which included a great part of the world they knew. Thus the question arose in their minds: perhaps the Sun-god ruled more than Egypt, — perhaps he was god of all the world.

136. When the Empire was some two hundred years old, Amenhotep III's youthful son Amenhotep IV became king, about 1375 B.C. He was convinced that the Sun-god was the god of the whole world, and also that he was the *only* god. There was an old Egyptian word "aton" which meant "sun," and Amenhotep IV took this word as the name for his new god. He commanded that all the people of the Empire should worship only Aton and forget all the old gods. In order that they might do this he closed all the temples and cast out their priests. Everywhere he had the names of the gods erased and cut out, especially on all temple walls. He particularly hated Amon, or Amen, the great Theban god of the Empire to whom was dedicated the great temple at Karnak. His own royal name, Amen-hotep (meaning "Amen is satisfied"), contained this god *Amen's* name, and he therefore changed his name Amenhotep to Ikhnaton, which means "Profitable to Aton."

Religious revolution of Amenhotep IV (Ikhnaton)

137. Ikhnaton, as we must now call him, finally forsook Thebes, the magnificent capital, where there were so many temples of the old gods, and built a new city farther down the river, which he named "Horizon of Aton." It is now called Amarna (see map, p. 66). This city furnishes very valuable information about Ikhnaton and his new religion; for the place was forsaken a few years after Ikhnaton's death, and beneath the rubbish of its ruins today we find the lower portions of the

Ikhnaton's new capital, now called Amarna

walls of the houses and palaces which the king and his followers built. In the ruins of a sculptor's studio the excavators found many beautiful works, which have greatly increased our knowledge of the wonderful sculpture of the age (Frontispiece). The cliffs behind the city still contain the cliff-tombs of the followers whom the young king was able to convert to the new faith. and in them we find engraved on the walls beautifully sculptured scenes picturing the life of the now forgotten city (Fig. 72).

138. In these Amarna tomb-chapels we may still read on the walls the hymns of praise to the Sun-god, which Ikhnaton himself wrote. They show us the simplicity and beauty of the young king's faith in the sole God. He had gained the belief that one *Ikhnaton's hymns to Aton, the sole God* God created not only all the lower creatures but also all races of men, both Egyptians and foreigners. Moreover, the king saw in his God a kindly Father, who maintained all his creatures by his goodness, so that even the birds in the marshes were aware of his kindness and uplifted their wings like arms to praise him, as a beautiful line in one of the hymns tells us. In all the progress of men which we have followed through thousands of years, no one had ever before caught such a vision of the great Father of all. Such a belief in one god is called *monotheism*, which means literally "one-god-ism."

SECTION 11. THE DECLINE AND FALL OF THE EGYPTIAN EMPIRE

139. A new faith like this could not be understood by the common people in such an early age of the world. The discontented priests of the old gods and the equally dissatisfied soldiers of the neglected army secretly plotted together against the *Ikhnaton's troubles at home and abroad* king. Confusion and disturbance arose in Egypt. The consequences in Asia have been revealed to us by a remarkable group of over three hundred letters, found by native diggers in one of Ikhnaton's government offices at Amarna, where

they had lain for over three thousand years. Most of these
letters, written on clay tablets in Babylonian writing, proved
to be from the kings of Western Asia to the Pharaoh. They
form the oldest international correspondence in the world,
and show us how these kings were gradually shaking off the
rule of the Pharaoh.

140. The Pharaoh's *northern* territory in Syria (see map I,
p. 266) was being taken by the Hittites, who came in from
Loss of Asiatic em- Asia Minor (§ 324), while his *southern* terri-
pire and death of tory in Palestine was being invaded by the
Ikhnaton Hebrews, who were drifting in from the desert. In the midst of these troubles at home and abroad the
young Ikhnaton died, leaving no son behind him. Although
a visionary and an idealist, he was the most remarkable religious genius of the early world before the Hebrews; but
the faith in one god which he attempted to introduce perished
with him.

141. Ikhnaton lacked a son; but he had gained two sons-
in-law by marrying two of his daughters to young nobles
Feeble reign of of the court. The first son-in-law died, and
Tutenkhamon the second, although he was only ten or
eleven years old, was then appointed joint king to rule in
company with Ikhnaton. His name was Tutenkhaton (or
"Living-Image-of-Aton"). When Ikhnaton died, this lad
was possibly twelve years old; nevertheless he became sole
king. The revengeful priests of Amon were now in power.
They forced the boy-king to leave the new capital at Amarna
and to return to Amon's great city of Thebes, where they
obliged him to change his name by cutting out the word
"Aton" at the end of it and inserting "Amon" in its place.
Thus the name "Tutenkhaton" became "Tutenkh*amon*"
("Living-Image-of-Amon"). The worship of Amon and of
the other gods of Egypt was restored, and the beautiful Aton
faith of Ikhnaton disappeared. After a rule of little more
than six years, when not much over eighteen years of age,
Tutenkhamon died, having perhaps been put to death by
the ambitious priests and soldiers who surrounded him. He

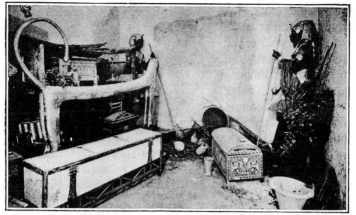

A

B

FIG. 73. *Tomb of* TUTENKHAMON: *North End of Antechamber*

In *A* we see furniture, funeral bouquets, and the sentinel statues of the king standing as if guarding the sealed doorway, the outlines of which may be distinguished by a color darker than the surrounding wall. When the photograph *B* was taken, everything had been removed except the royal statues. The archæologists had also cut out enough of the masonry filling of the sealed door to permit them to enter the burial chamber. The *outer* burial shrine, gold-covered and inlaid with blue glaze, is partially revealed in the background and seen through the doorway. (Courtesy of Howard Carter)

was buried among the emperors, the great ancestors of his wife, Ikhnaton's third daughter. There was no longer a prince of the old Theban family strong enough to maintain its rights. Thus passed away the most powerful family of Pharaohs that Egypt had ever seen. We call them the Eighteenth Dynasty, and they must be remembered as the founders of the first great empire of the early East. They had ruled for some two hundred and thirty years when their line disappeared (about 1350 B.C.).

142. The reign of Tutenkhamon thus ended

Destruction of monuments of Ikhnaton

before he had reached the years of manhood. It could not be expected that any ruler in his situation could carry on to success such a remarkable effort to transform the religion of Egypt and her empire. As one might tear up the roots

Fig. 74. *Unbroken* Seal *on Doorway of Second* Shrine *in the* Tomb of Tutenkhamon *just as it was Found*

Shortly after Tutenkhamon was buried his tomb was entered by robbers, but they were caught in the midst of their plundering. The tomb was then reclosed and resealed, and was not opened again for over 3270 years, that is, until the autumn of 1922 (cf. § 143). The outer doors of the burial shrine had been broken open, but on the inner doors the seal remained intact. The photograph shows it as the author saw it on the day when the burial chamber was reopened by Howard Carter. The seal here shown on the knotted rope fastening the double doors of the burial shrine still retained not only the impression of the king's name but also the thumb-print of the ancient official who put it there. (Courtesy of Howard Carter)

Fig. 75. *Scene at the* Entrance *to the* Tomb of Tutenkhamon

The native workmen, under the direction of the excavators, are carrying from the tomb a chest which once contained part of Tutenkhamon's royal clothing. The work of preservative treatment, packing, and transportation of these objects from this tomb was going on from its discovery in 1922 until 1931

FIG. 76. TUTENKHAMON *and his* QUEEN *in their Palace*

The beautiful scene above is from the back of a chair found in the tomb of Tutenkhamon. The workmanship on the piece of furniture here shown is remarkable. The background is of heavy sheet gold, the white garments are of silver, the flesh is of reddish glass, and the ornamental details are incrustations of brightly colored, costly stones. The pleasantly informal picture of the young king and his wife is entirely unknown in earlier Egyptian art, and illustrates the disregard of tradition which was characteristic of Ikhnaton's reign. (Courtesy of Howard Carter)

of a plant, so Ikhnaton's movement attempted to tear out of the hearts of the Egyptian people their long-cherished beliefs, customs, habits, and especially those religious hopes of protection and happiness in the realm of Osiris after death. Very naturally, after Ikhnaton was gone, the people, particularly the priests, made a savage effort to destroy everything that Ikhnaton's artists and craftsmen had produced.

They succeeded so well in this work of destruction that not a great deal has survived to reveal to us the marvelous art and religion of Ikhnaton's revolutionary reign.

143. When discovered in 1922, the tomb of Tutenkhamon proved to be of the greatest importance not only because it was a storehouse of works of art and craftsmanship from the age of Ikhnaton but also because it was — as it still remains — the only royal tomb yet found in Egypt practically intact. It was a never-to-be-forgotten experience to enter the antechamber of Tutenkhamon's tomb a short time after its discovery, when nothing had yet been removed from the place. There stood the magnificent furniture of a Pharaoh's palace just as it had been placed in this tomb some three thousand two hundred and seventy years ago. The most splendid piece was a marvelous chair bearing the name of Tutenkhamon on one of its arms. I shall never forget my feelings when I read on the other arm the name "Tutenkh*aton*," the *earlier* form of the young ruler's name. This older form of the name proved that this exquisite chair was the work of *Ikhnaton's* craftsmen, for it had been used in his Amarna palace before Tutenkhamon had been forced to change his name. It thus showed that this wonderful tomb was a treasury of art and life reaching back into the revolution of Ikhnaton, when the human mind had for the first time freed itself from old habits and limitations and had caught a new vision of beauty and of life.

Tomb of Tutenkhamon

144. When Ikhnaton's revolution thus brought to an end the power of his great family, they were followed by a new line of kings, the greatest of whom were Seti I (Fig. 71) and his son Ramses II (Fig. 77). After desperate efforts these two kings, father and son, were able to restore to some extent the Egyptian Empire. But they were unable to drive the Hittites out of Syria; for these powerful invaders from Asia Minor possessed iron, which they could use for weapons, while the declining Egyptian Empire was the last great power of the Age of Bronze.

A new line of Pharaohs and beginning of Iron Age

FIG. 77. *Colossal* PORTRAIT FIGURE *of* RAMSES II *at Abu Simbel, in Egyptian Nubia*

Four such statues, 75 feet high, adorn the front of this temple, which, like the statues, is hewn from the sandstone cliffs. The faces are better preserved than that of the Great Sphinx (Fig. 42), and we can here see that such vast figures were portraits. The face of Ramses II here closely resembles that of his mummy (Fig. 117). (From a photograph taken from the top of the crown of one of the statues by a University of Chicago expedition)

145. At Thebes the symptoms of the coming fall may be seen even at the present day. If we examine the great war
Mercenary troops; pictures on the Theban temples, we find in
foreign invaders; the battle scenes of the later Empire numbers
fall of the Empire of foreigners serving in the Egyptian army.
This shows that the Egyptians had finally lost their temporary interest in war and were calling in foreigners to fight their battles. Among these strangers are the peoples of the northern Mediterranean whom we left there in the Late Stone Age. Here on the Egyptian monuments we find them pictured after they had learned from Eastern peoples the art of using metal. With huge bronze swords in their hands we see them serving as hired soldiers (Fig. 152) in the Egyptian army. Their kindred at home and other Mediterranean foreigners finally invaded Egypt in such numbers that the weakened Egyptian Empire fell, in the middle of the Twelfth Century B.C.

146. The great emperors were buried at Thebes in a wild and desolate valley in the western desert (Fig. 4). Here, in
Bodies of the over forty rock-hewn galleries, some reaching
emperors hundreds of feet into the mountain, the bodies
of the Empire Pharaohs were laid to rest. But we recall that it was only the tomb of Tutenkhamon (§ 134) which escaped pillage and robbery after the fall of the Empire. Ruling as feeble kings at Thebes, the weak successors of the emperors hurried the royal bodies from one hiding place to another, and finally concealed them in a secret chamber hewn for this purpose in the western cliffs. Here they lay undisturbed until, in 1881, they were discovered and removed to the National Museum at Cairo (Fig. 71). Until recently we were able to look into the very faces of these lords of Egypt and Western Asia who lived and ruled from thirty-five to thirty-one hundred years ago.[1]

147. Thus ends the story of the Empire at Thebes. The pyramids, tombs, and temples along the Nile have told us

[1] The Egyptian government has now removed these royal bodies to a modern tomb at Cairo.

FIG. 78. RAMSES III *hunting Wild Bulls in the Marshes*

The king stands in his swiftly moving chariot, and, leaning far forward with one foot planted outside on the pole of the chariot, thrusts his long spear into the great bulls plunging through the jungle only to sink down mortally wounded at the water's edge. The dashing horses and the vigorous movement of the body-guard below make this scene probably the most powerful and impressive relief sculpture surviving from ancient Egypt. In its original colors (the water blue, the jungle green), with the pathetic figures of the dying bulls and the gorgeous trappings of the Pharaoh, his chariot, his horses, and his bodyguard, it must have been a scene of rare beauty and brilliance

the history of early Egypt in three epochs: the pyramids of Gizeh and the neighboring cemeteries have disclosed to us the Pyramid Age; the cliff-tombs and the papyrus-roll libraries have revealed the history and civilization of the Feudal Age; and the temples and cliff-tombs of Thebes have given us the story of the Empire. The Nile has thus become for us a great volume of history. Let us remember, however, that, preceding these three great chapters of civilization on the Nile, we also found here the earlier story of how man passed from Stone Age barbarism to a civilization possessed of metal, writing, and government. On the other hand, as we look forward we

Significance of Egyptian history and civilization

should remember also that the three great chapters did not
end the story; for Egyptian institutions and civilization continued far down into the Christian Age and greatly influenced
later history in Europe.

148. In this summary of the story of ancient Egypt we
have gained our knowledge from the monuments and the
Knowledge of   written records. However, only a little over
meaning of hiero-   a hundred years ago no one knew what these
glyphs lost   written records meant; for the last men who
could read Egyptian hieroglyphs had been dead for over a
thousand years, and after their time there was no one who
understood the curious writing which travelers found covering the great monuments along the Nile.

149. For a long time scholars puzzled over the strange Nile
records, but made little progress in reading them. Then a
Champollion deci-   young Frenchman named Champollion took
phers Egyptian   up the problem, and after years of discourag-
hieroglyphs   ing failure he began to make progress. He
discovered the names of Ptolemy and Cleopatra written both
in hieroglyphs and in Greek letters on the same monument.
He was thus able to determine the sounds of twelve hieroglyphic signs used in these two names, and he proved them
to be alphabetic. Champollion was then able to read several
other royal names, and in 1822, in a famous letter to the
French Academy, he announced his discovery and explained
the steps he had taken. It was not until this point was
reached that he was able to make use of the well-known
Rosetta Stone (Fig. 203), which enabled him to increase his
list of known hieroglyphic signs and to learn the meanings
of words. When he died, in 1832, he had written a little
grammar and prepared a small dictionary of hieroglyphic.
Others took up the work, and thus the monuments of the
Nile have gained a voice to tell us the wonderful story of the
early advance of men after they had gained civilization.

150. In a similar way the monuments discovered along the
Tigris and Euphrates rivers in Asia have been deciphered
and have been made to tell their story. They show us that,

following the Egyptians, the peoples of Asia emerged from barbarism, developed industries, learned the use of metals, devised a system of writing, and finally rose to the leading position of power in the ancient world. We must now turn, in the next chapter, to the story of the early Near East in Asia, especially the Babylonians.

Transition to Asia

QUESTIONS

Section 8. Describe the civilization of the Feudal Age barons. Discuss the policies of the Pharaohs of the Feudal Age. What great commercial link between two seas was created?

Section 9. How did the Pharaohs who built the Temple of Karnak at Thebes differ from those who built the pyramids? Discuss the first great woman in history. Tell about the reign of the greatest Egyptian general. What was the extent of the Egyptian Empire?

Section 10. What did the Egyptian emperors do with the wealth gained from subject peoples? Describe the great Karnak hall, and tell how the clerestory was improved. Give an account of the Theban cemetery and what it contains. Discuss the earliest belief in one god.

Section 11. What were the consequences of Ikhnaton's movement? Tell about the Amarna letters. Discuss the importance of the discovery of the tomb of Tutenkhamon. What northerners held Syria, and what new weapons did they have? What foreigners invaded Egypt and aided in destroying the Empire? What happened to the bodies of the emperors? Why were our great-grandfathers unable to read hieroglyphic? Discuss its decipherment. Describe the Rosetta Stone and tell how it helped in the reading of Egyptian hieroglyphs (Fig. 203).

BIBLIOGRAPHY FOR TOPICAL STUDIES

Civilization of Feudal Age: BREASTED, *Ancient Egyptians*, §§ 155–166, and *Dawn of Conscience*, pp. 182–206; MASPERO. *Art in Egypt*, pp. 95–122.

Conquests of the emperors: BLACKMAN, *Luxor and its Temples*, pp. 84–110; BREASTED, *Ancient Egyptians*, §§ 214–234, 237–243, 285–310.

Painting and drawing: *Bulletin of the Metropolitan Museum of Art*, July, 1920, Part II, pp. 24–33, and December, 1920, Part II, pp. 33–40; MASPERO pp. 161–166; PETRIE, *Art and Crafts*, chap. v

Chapter V · Western Asia: Babylonia

Section 12. The Quarter of the Globe where Civilization Grew Up and Developed

151. Thus far we have watched the developing life of early men in the regions on both sides of the Mediterranean Sea. In doing so we have found that the lands where these early men lived entirely surrounded the great sea. Together with this fringe of inhabited lands around it, the Mediterranean formed the center of advancing human life, beginning with the earliest appearance of man. While bearing this fact in mind, let us examine as a whole the quarter of the globe in which the Mediterranean Sea occupies such an important part. As we all know, the Mediterranean is surrounded by three continents: Europe on the north, Africa on the south, and Asia on both the east

Mediterranean world

Note. The above scene shows us the Semitic Nomads on the Fertile Crescent along the Sea of Galilee. In spring the region is richly overgrown, but the vegetation soon fades. The dark camel's-hair tents of these wandering shepherds are easily carried from place to place as they seek new pasturage. They live on the milk and flesh of the flocks.

and the north. The only early *civilized* life on the African side of the Mediterranean was limited to a narrow strip along the shore (because of the Sahara Desert lying behind) and a narrow line extending southward along the Nile. On the European side of the Mediterranean civilized men moved gradually northward and in time reached the Baltic, the North Sea, and the British Isles. At the Asiatic end of the great sea civilized life developed far inland, and eventually eastward to India and China, although these two countries will concern us very little, as we shall see.

152. Beginning with the Mediterranean, then, we find that its three coast lines, southern, northern, and eastern, together with the lands back of them, formed a great **Great Northwest** world where the life of early men was devel- **Quadrant** oping on three continents, — a narrow belt along the northern end of Africa, the western part of Asia, and a large portion of Europe, only its most northerly parts being omitted. Viewed as one whole, these regions form a great triangle (see diagram, p. 130), including a large part of the northwestern quarter of the Eastern Hemisphere. This triangle, which has been called the Great Northwest Quadrant, has as its base line the southern borders of the desert in Africa and Asia. Its eastern boundary is a north-and-south line roughly coinciding with the Ural Mountains, while on the west and north it extends to the Atlantic and Arctic oceans. In this enormous triangle developed the civilization which Europe and America of today have inherited.

153. In the geography of the Great Northwest Quadrant we at once notice two outstanding features: first, the Mediterranean Sea, and, second, the mountain **Three geographic** ranges on the north of this sea. The moun- **zones** tain ranges divide the land into three zones, lying likewise in east-and-west lines. There is, first, the long *Highland Zone,* to which the mountains belong, stretching along the northern side of the Mediterranean and then far eastward into the heart of Asia beyond the eastern boundary of our triangle. On the northern side of the Highland Zone there are *Northern*

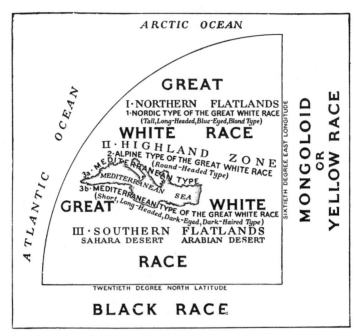

FIG. 79. *Racial Diagram of the Great* NORTHWEST QUADRANT

The diagram is intended to show the three important geographical zones, numbered from north to south, I, II, and III, and to indicate in general the position of the subdivisions of the Great White Race on these three geographical zones (see Fig. 80). At the bottom, below the twentieth degree of north latitude, the general position of the black race is noted; and, similarly, at the right of the sixtieth degree of longitude, it places the Mongoloid, or yellow, race. It should be observed that the above is a rough diagram, not a geographically accurate map. A rough indication of the Mediterranean Sea is inserted to show that it separates the Europeans of the Mediterranean type from those of North Africa. On the south of the Mediterranean the people of the Great White Race are darker-skinned than elsewhere. For more accurate geographical relations the map of the Northwest Quadrant on page 13 should be carefully compared

Flatlands, which likewise stretch far eastward and deep into Asia. On the south side of the Highland Zone there are *Southern Flatlands,* which are largely occupied at the west end by the basin of the Mediterranean. It is important to observe that much of the Southern Flatlands is desert, extending from North Africa eastward across the Red Sea and far into Asia.

154. The peoples of the Great Northwest Quadrant, as far back as we know anything about prehistoric man, have all been members of a race of white men, who have been well called the Great White Race (see Fig. 80). The men of this race created the civilization which we have inherited. If we look outside of the Great Northwest Quadrant, we find in the neighboring territory only two other clearly distinguished races, — the Mongoloids on the east and the Negroes on the south. These peoples occupy an important place in the modern world, but they played no part in the rise of civilization.

Three races

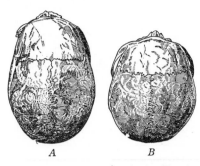

A   B

Fig. 80. *Comparison of an Ancient Egyptian* Long Skull *(A) and the* Short Skull *(B) of an Ancient Highland Zone Man*

The people of the Great White Race differ markedly in certain physical characteristics. Scientists have found, for instance, that there is a striking variation in the shape of the skull. Based on this difference a rough subdivision of the white race in the Great Northwest Quadrant is sometimes made. On the Northern Flatlands we find fair-haired, *long-headed* people, such as the Scandinavians, who are sometimes called Nordics, and among whom we are familiar with the Swedes and Norwegians. Their neighbors on the south are *round-headed* men dwelling in the Highland Zone, and hence are often called Alpine or Armenoid peoples, such as the Tyrolese, Swiss, and Armenians. On the Southern Flatlands, finally, live dark-haired peoples with *long heads*, now commonly known as the Mediterranean race because they are found on nearly all the shores of the Mediterranean and practically surround it. These three types peopled the whole of the Great Northwest Quadrant, and the ancestors of the population now living there were the creators of the civilization we have inherited. The skull *A* is typical of the Mediterranean race, while *B* illustrates the shortness and greater width of the skull of the Highland Zone man. The scientific term for the long heads is *dolichocephalic*, and for the round heads *brachycephalic*

155. On the *east* of the Northwest Quadrant the isolated plateaus of inner Asia, commonly called High Asia, were early inhabited by the Mongols, or Mongoloids, a race of men with straight, black, wiry hair, round head, almost beardless face, and yellow skin. Among these Mongoloids, civilization did not arise until long after it was far advanced

Mongoloids

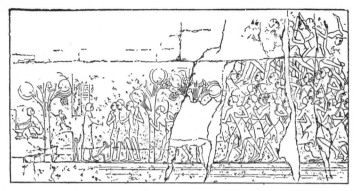

FIG. 81. *The Earliest Known* REPRESENTATION *of* NEGRO LIFE *(Thirteenth Century* B.C.*)*

Under a palm at the left a Negro woman sits stirring an earthen pot over a fire, preparing food. Meanwhile a great commotion has arisen. A large group of defeated soldiers (on the right), fleeing before the wrath of the Egyptian king, have burst into camp. At the left, somewhat in advance of the main group, a wounded soldier is supported by two comrades who lead him to the arms of his wife and two children approaching from the left. In the palm tree beside them a monkey hops up and down and chatters frenziedly at the confusion, and an excited child rushes past to tell the cook of the misfortune which has befallen them. This relief is found in a temple of Ramses II, thus dating to the Thirteenth Century B.C. The gaps in the above picture are due to the breakages in the ancient original relief

in the Northwest Quadrant.[1] The migrations of these yellow men out of High Asia finally carried them in all directions, but they did not reach the Northwest Quadrant until long after civilization there was already highly developed. Groups of Asiatic wanderers related to the Mongoloids finally migrated to the far northeast of Asia, and perhaps about ten thousand years ago they crossed to Alaska. As they wandered farther into America they became the ancestors of the North American Indians, whose bodies, especially their faces, continue to show their Asiatic origin.

[1] Chinese civilization is much later than that of Western Asia and Egypt. The popular impression that it is older is wholly incorrect. No piece of metal as yet found in China can be dated earlier than about 1200 B.C., that is, at least three thousand years later than in Egypt and very much later than in Western Asia. As for writing, there is no surviving document written in Chinese which may be dated any earlier than about the Eleventh, or at the earliest the Twelfth, Century B.C., that is, over two thousand years later than in Egypt and Western Asia.

156. On the *south* of the Northwest Quadrant lay the teeming black world of Africa, as it does today. It was separated from the Great White Race by the broad stretch of the Sahara Desert. The valley of **Negroes** the Nile was the only road leading across the Sahara from south to north. Sometimes the blacks of inner Africa did wander along this road into Egypt, but they came only in small groups. Thus cut off by the desert barrier and living by themselves, they remained uninfluenced by civilization from the north. The Negro peoples of Africa were therefore without any influence on the development of early civilization.

SECTION 13. THE LANDS AND RACES OF WESTERN ASIA

157. We have followed the rise and progress of civilization in Egypt on the Southern Flatlands in North Africa, and we must now trace the rise and spread of civili- **Post-glacial condi-** zation in Western Asia. In prehistoric times **tions in Western** the topography of Western Asia was quite **Asia** different from what it is at present. At the close of the Ice Age the Persian Gulf extended probably over five hundred miles farther northwest than it does now. Living along the shores of the great gulf, the Stone Age hunters have left their lost flint implements where we now find them still lying. Some of these hunters probably lived also on small islands at that time dotting the great gulf, and at the present day excavation uncovers their stone tools and weapons buried deep in some ruined Babylonian city on a spot which was once an island. For in the Stone Age the Persian Gulf covered all of the area which later became the Plain of Babylonia, and some of Assyria as well. Its northern shores at that time were probably the highlands along the south side of the Highland Zone. In strong contrast with Egypt, therefore, the earliest dwellers along these shores felt the cold of the glaciers on the southern slopes of the Highland Zone. Furthermore, at the end of the glacial period the violent torrents formed by the melting snows and ice in the Highland Zone poured

FIG. 82. *Typical View of the* MIDDLE EUPHRATES VALLEY

The Euphrates never succeeded in eroding a valley of continuous breadth. It is in some stretches a narrow defile, or cañon; again the valley expands to a width of some miles. Throughout all the desert course of the river, however, its valley never widens so as to create an alluvial floor of sufficient extent to sustain a large population. Although several miles long, the cultivated strip shown here is so narrow that the whole of it would not exceed the area of a good-sized farm in the upper Mississippi valley. (Oriental Institute photograph)

down through this region between the mountains and the Southern Flatlands and cut its cultivable land to pieces, so that it was for a long time unsuited to the settled life that leads to civilization.

158. The Babylonian Plain did not yet exist, and it was not until long after the Ice Age that it began to be slowly created as the drainage of the Highland Zone carried down the upland soil and spread it in a growing fringe along the northern shores of the Persian Gulf. This soil at last formed a low, level plain, later called Babylonia. This kind of land formation, being dependent on the disappearance of the glaciers, was later than that which took place in Egypt, which never suffered from an invasion of the ice. The Nile brought the soil of Egypt from the tropics, but the soil of the Babylonian Plain was brought by the Two Rivers from the glacial north.

159. The most important early home of men in Western Asia is the borderland between the mountains, or Highland Zone, on the north and the desert of the South- The Fertile ern Flatlands. This borderland between the Crescent desert and the mountains is a kind of cultivable fringe of the desert, — a Fertile Crescent[1] having the mountains on one side and the desert on the other (see map, p. 146). It forms roughly a semicircle with the open side toward the south. Its western end is at the southeastern corner of the Mediterranean, the center lies directly north of Arabia, and the eastern end is at the northern end of the Persian Gulf. It lies like a horseshoe opening southward, with one side stretching along the eastern shore of the Mediterranean and the other reaching out to the Persian Gulf, while the center has its back against the northern mountains. The end of the western side is Palestine, Assyria makes up a large part of the center, while the end of the eastern side is Babylonia.

160. This great semicircle, the Fertile Crescent, may also be likened to the shores of a desert bay, upon which the mountains behind look down, — a bay not The desert bay of water but of sandy waste, some five hundred miles across, forming a northern extension of the Arabian Desert. This desert bay, a part of the Southern Flatlands, is a limestone plateau of some height, — too high, indeed, to be watered by the Tigris and Euphrates, which have cut cañons obliquely across it. Nevertheless, after the meager winter rains, wide tracts of the northern desert bay are clothed with scanty grass, and spring thus turns the region for a short time into grasslands. The history of Western Asia may be described as an age-long struggle between the mountain peoples of the north and the desert wanderers of these grasslands — a struggle which is still going on — for the possession of the Fertile Crescent, the shores of the desert bay.

[1] There is no name, either geographical or political, which includes all of this great semicircle. Hence in the first edition of this book (1916) the author was obliged to coin a term. It was called, therefore, the Fertile Crescent. **The term** has since become current and is now widely used.

161. Arabia is totally lacking in rivers and enjoys but a few weeks of rain in midwinter; hence it is largely desert

Arabian Desert and Semitic nomads

very little of which is habitable. Its people are and have been from the remotest ages a branch of the Great White Race called Semites. The Semites have always been divided into many tribes and groups, just as were the American Indians, whom we call Sioux or Seminoles or Iroquois. So we shall find many tribal or group names among the Semites. With two of these peoples we are familiar, — the Arabs, and the Hebrews whose descendants dwell among us. They all spoke and still speak dialects of the same tongue, of which Hebrew was one. For ages they have moved up and down the habitable portions of the Arabian world, seeking pasturage for their flocks and herds. Such wandering shepherds are called nomads, and we remember how their manner of life arose after the domestication of cattle, sheep, and goats (see § 45).

162. From the earliest times, when the spring grass of the border wilderness is gone these nomads have been constantly

Shift of the nomads from the desert to the Fertile Crescent

drifting in from the sandy sea upon the shores of the northern desert bay. If they can secure a footing there, they slowly make the transition from the *wandering* life of the desert nomad to the *settled* life of the agricultural peasant. There have been times when this slow shift swelled into a great tidal wave of migration. Then the wild hordes of the wilderness rolled in upon the fertile shores of the desert bay, — a human tide from the desert to the towns, which they gradually overwhelmed. We can see this process going on for thousands of years. Among such movements we are familiar with the passage of the Hebrews from the desert into Palestine, as described in the Bible, and some readers will recall the invasions of the Arab hosts, who, when converted to Mohammedanism, even reached Europe and threatened to girdle the Mediterranean. After they had adopted a settled town life the colonies of the Semites stretched far westward along the Mediterranean, especially in northern Africa, even to southern Spain and the

Atlantic (see Fig. 123, and map, p. 346). But it took many centuries for the long line of their settlements to creep westward until it reached the Atlantic, and we must begin with the Semites in the desert.

163. Out on the wide reaches of the desert there are no boundaries; the pasturage is free as air to the first comer. No man of the tribe owns land; there are no landholding rich and no landless poor. The men of the desert know no law. The keen-eyed desert marauder looks with envy across the hills dotted with the flocks of the neighboring tribe, which may be his when he has slain the solitary shepherd at the well. But if he does so, he knows that his own family will suffer death or heavy damages, not at the hands of the state but at the hands of the slain shepherd's family. This custom, known as "blood revenge," has a restraining influence like that of law. Under such conditions there is no state or government. Writing and records are unknown, industries are practically nonexistent, and the desert tribesmen lead a life of complete freedom. The governments holding Arabia today are as powerless to control the wandering Arabs of the wilderness as were formerly the American authorities in suppressing the lawlessness of their cowboy herdsmen.

Lack of institutions and industries among Semitic nomads

164. The tribesmen drift with their flocks along the margin of the Fertile Crescent till they discern a town among the palm groves. Objects of picturesque interest to the curious eyes of the townsmen, they appear in the market place to traffic for the weapons, utensils, and raiment which the nomads cannot dispense with (headpiece, p. 217). They early learned to carry goods from place to place and thus became not only the common carriers of the settled communities but also traders on their own account, fearlessly leading their caravans across the wastes of the desert bay, lying between Syria-Palestine and Babylonia. They were the greatest merchants of the ancient world, as their Hebrew descendants among us still are at the present day.

Traffic and caravan

165. The wilderness is the nomad's home. Its vast solitudes tinged his soul with solemnity. His imagination peopled
Religion of the   the far reaches of the desert with invisible
nomad   and uncanny beings, and he believed that
they inhabited every rock and tree, hilltop and spring. These
creatures were his gods, whom he fancied he could control
by the utterance of magic charms, — the earliest prayers.
He believed that such charms would render these mysterious
gods powerless to do him injury and would also compel them
to grant him aid.

166. The nomad pictured each one of these beings as
controlling only a little corner of the great world, perhaps
Tribal god of the   only a well and its surrounding pastures. At
nomad   the next well, only a day's march away, there
was thought to be another god, belonging to the next tribe,
for each tribe had a favorite or tribal god, who, as they believed, journeyed with them from pasture to pasture, sharing
their food and their feasts and receiving as his due from the
tribesmen the firstborn of their flocks and herds.

167. The thoughts of the desert wanderer about the character of such a god were crude and barbarous, and his
Nomad's thoughts   religious customs were often savage, even
about his tribal   leading him to sacrifice his children to appease
god; his ideas   the angry god. On the other hand, the nomad
of right   had a dawning sense of justice and of right,
and he felt some obligations of kindness to his fellows which
he believed were the compelling voice of his god. In Palestine
such feelings, much influenced by the moral teachings of the
Egyptian wise men, at last became lofty moral vision, which
made the Semites the religious teachers of the civilized world.

168. As early as 3000 B.C. the Semites were drifting in
from the desert and settling in Palestine, on the *western* end
Semites on the   of the Fertile Crescent, where we find them
Fertile Crescent   in possession of walled towns by 2500 B.C.
These earliest Semitic dwellers in Palestine were the predecessors of the Hebrews there. They were a people called
Canaanites; farther north settled a powerful tribe known as

Amorites; while along the shores of north Syria some of these one-time desert wanderers, the Phœnicians, had taken to the sea. The earliest city or the Phœnicians was a flourishing harbor town called Byblos. In the mountains behind it were the great cedar forests furnishing valuable timber, which long before 3000 B.C. had led the Pharaohs to take possession of the city and harbor. Here they built a temple to the Lady of Byblos, the goddess of the town. The Phœnician lords of Byblos were subject to the Pharaoh and paid him tribute, — a kind of foreign taxes. They wrote their first inscriptions in Egyptian hieroglyphs, they used Egyptian furniture and utensils, and they wore Egyptian jewelry. Thus all these settled communities of the western Semites gradually learned civilization, drawn at first from Egypt, but later from Babylonia also. Their lands along the eastern end of the Mediterranean were like a corridor forming the highway between these two countries, and they were in constant contact with both (see map, p. 146). We shall take up the story of the Phœnicians later in discussing the history of the Eastern Mediterranean.

169. While the Semites thus invaded the Fertile Crescent from the *inside* of the semicircle, the peoples on the *outside*, that is, the peoples of the Highland Zone, very early entered the Fertile Crescent and established homes there. These people were not Semites, but seem to have belonged to different groups of the Great White Race. The most important of them were the Hittites, who occupied the western region of the Highland Zone, especially central Asia Minor (Anatolia). For centuries the Hittites and other Highland peoples all along the Fertile Crescent fought with the Semites for its possession.

Non-Semites of the mountains on the Fertile Crescent

170. The earliest civilization of Western Asia, and likewise the most important, arose on the eastern end of the Fertile Crescent along the lower courses of the Two Rivers. These two important streams, the Tigris and the Euphrates, rise in the northern mountains, whence they issue to cross the

Fertile Crescent and to cut obliquely southeastward through
the northern bay of the desert. Here, on these two great
Two Rivers and
three great chap-
ters in their history rivers of Western Asia, we can follow through
several thousand years the earliest civiliza-
tion known in Asia. Just as on the Nile, so
here on the Two Rivers, we shall find three great chapters
in the story.

171. As on the Nile, so also the earliest of the three chapters of Tigris-Euphrates history will be found in the lower
Earliest chapter of
history of the Two
Rivers in the Plain
of Shinar valley near the rivers' mouths. This earliest
chapter is the story of Babylonia.[1] As the
Two Rivers approached most closely to each
other, about one hundred and sixty or seventy
miles from the Persian Gulf,[2] they emerged from the desert
and entered a low plain of fertile soil, formerly brought down
by the rivers. This plain was Babylonia, the eastern end
of the Fertile Crescent. But during the first thousand
years of the known history of this plain the later city of
Babylon had not yet arisen, or was a mere village playing
little or no part in the history of the region. The plain was
then called Shinar, and "Babylonia" is a name that properly
should not be applied to it until the Twenty-first Century B.C.
(see § 211).

172. Rarely more than forty miles wide, the Plain of Shinar
contained probably less than eight thousand square miles of
Area and fertility
of Plain of Shinar cultivable soil, — roughly equal to the state
of New Jersey or the area of Wales. It lies in
the Mediterranean belt of rainy winter and dry summer, but
the rainfall is so scanty (less than seven inches a year)[3] that
irrigation of the fields is necessary in order to ripen the grain.

---

[1] The other two chapters of the Tigris-Euphrates history are Assyria and the
Chaldean Empire (Chapter VI).

[2] This distance applies only to ancient Babylonian and Assyrian days. The
rivers have since then filled up the Persian Gulf for from one hundred and fifty to
one hundred and sixty miles, and the gulf is that much shorter at the present day
(see note under scale on map, p. 146).

[3] Based on British reports for the thirty-seven years from 1887 to 1924. In
the United States a rainfall of less than 30 inches per year is considered almost
too scanty for successful agriculture.

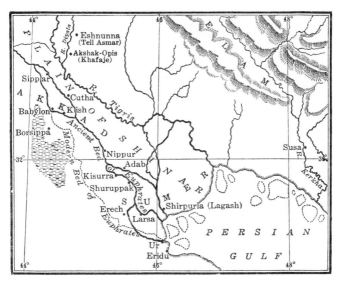

Sketch Map of SUMER *and* AKKAD

When properly irrigated the Plain of Shinar is prodigiously fertile, and the chief source of wealth in ancient Shinar was agriculture. This plain was the scene of the most important and long-continued of those frequent struggles between mountaineer and nomad. We are now to follow the story of the first series of those struggles, lasting well over a thousand years and subsiding after 1900 B.C.

SECTION 14. RISE OF SUMERIAN CIVILIZATION IN THE AGE OF THE CITY-KINGDOMS, AND THE EARLY STRUGGLE OF SUMERIAN AND SEMITE

173. At a very early period, possibly before 4000 B.C., some of the Highland peoples migrated and settled on the Fertile Crescent. Among them the earliest Unknown race of people clearly revealed to us by the excava- early Sumerians tions in the Plain of Shinar were called Sumerians. We are still in ignorance of their race. As shown in relief pictures on the most ancient monuments of Shinar they were a round-headed people (cf. Fig. 80). Some of them appear on the monuments with shaven heads and without beards, but the monuments show that there were other Sumerians who wore beards and did not shave their heads. Long before 3500 B.C. they had begun to reclaim the marshes around the mouths of the Two Rivers. They finally held the southern portion of the Plain of Shinar, and this region at length came to be called Sumer.

174. Their settlements of low huts, at first of plaited reeds (wattle) and then of mud brick, crept gradually northward, Material civiliza- especially along the Euphrates, for the banks tion of Sumerians of the Tigris were too high for convenient irrigation. These people learned to control the spring freshets with dikes, to distribute the waters in irrigation trenches, and to reap large harvests of grain. They were already cultivating barley and wheat, which were the two chief grains in Western Asia as they were in Egypt. The Sumerians called the wheat by its Egyptian name. They already possessed cattle, as well as sheep and goats. These animals played such an important part in the life of the Sumerians that one of their important goddesses had the form of a cow, and they believed that she protected the flocks and herds. Recently discovered sculptures in her temple near Ur show us interesting pictures of the dairy industry among the Sumerians of nearly 3000 B.C. Oxen drew the plow, and horses and donkeys pulled *wheeled* carts and chariots. These Sumerian chariots are the earliest known wheeled vehicles, and the wheel as a burden-bearing device appeared here for the first time. Not long after 3000 B.C. horses from the northeastern mountains were already known, although they continued to be rare for nearly a thousand years. At the same time metal had also been introduced, and the smith had learned to fashion utensils of copper, but he had not yet learned to harden the copper into bronze by admixture of tin. Meantime, as in Egypt, stone implements continued to be used for a long time side by side with copper.

Fig. 83. A Dairy *near Ancient Ur* (*about* 3000 b.c.)

This frieze formed part of the decoration on the front of the little temple of the cow-goddess. It was originally mounted on a plank, edged above and below with a strip of copper. The figures themselves, however, are carved from pieces of shell or limestone and mounted in a thin layer of black bitumen which filled the space between the strips of copper. *Above* is part of a frieze of marching bulls, while *below* is the dairy scene. At the right we see two cows, each with her calf before her. According to Sumerian custom the milking was done from behind, and we see the dairyman, therefore, seated *behind* the cow he is milking. This milking is going on in a cow-yard, of which the gate is seen near the middle, behind the left-hand cow. At this gate two calves are represented with only the fore quarters showing, to indicate that they are coming out of the gate and are only halfway out. At the extreme left four dairymen are at work with the milk. The man at the left plunges his arm deep into a tall pointed jar in order to dip out the last of the milk it contains. Two men in the middle are engaged in pouring the milk through a strainer into a jar on the ground. With his back to the gate the last man sits on a small, square stool while he rolls about on the ground a large jar which serves as a churn and is placed on its side in order that it may more easily be rolled about to produce the agitation of the cream which results in butter.

(Courtesy of the University Museum of Philadelphia)

175. Agriculture and cattle-breeding produced most of the wealth which formed the basis of Sumerian life, but there were other important sources of wealth. Be-   **Rise of Sumerian** sides the metal which we have just mentioned,   **trade** the wool from the flocks made possible the development of weaving and the production of plentiful woolen cloth. Metal work, woolen goods, and some native products, like dates and grain, developed active trade with other countries of Western Asia. We now know that this trade extended far into Asia, even reaching the mouth of the Indus and the

FIG. 84. *Ancient Babylonian* SEEDER, *or Machine Planter*

The seeder is drawn by a yoke of oxen, with their driver beside them. Behind the seeder follows a man holding it by two handles. It is very pointed and evidently makes a shallow trench in the soil as it moves. Rising from the frame of the seeder is a vertical tube (*a*) on the top of which is a funnel (*b*). A third man walking beside the seeder is shown dropping the grain into this funnel with one hand; with the other he holds what is probably a sack of seed grain suspended from his shoulders. The grain drops down through the tube and falls into the trench made by the seeder. The scene was carved on a small stone seal. (After Clay)

lower valley of that river. At the same time the discovery in Sumer of a seal from the Indus[1] makes the fact of such trade quite certain. There is every indication that this trade passed between the Tigris and the Indus *by land*. It is not yet clear whether the Sumerians had been able to develop seagoing ships for traffic on the Persian Gulf and beyond it. The region of the Two Rivers, of which Sumer formed the southern part, lay between the Eastern Mediterranean world on the west and remoter Asia on the east. Between these two widely separated regions the people of the Two Rivers began very early to carry on extensive commerce, which later spread

[1] Recent excavations in northwestern India, in the lower valley of the Indus River, have uncovered remains of a civilization reaching back to at least 2500 B.C. The discovery by the Oriental Institute of The University of Chicago of the seal shown in Fig. 85 has established this date. In the Indus valley were early towns with houses of burnt brick. The men who built them were already cultivating fields of grain and raising cattle. They had tamed the horse, had learned to harness the bullock to two-wheeled carts, and had taught the elephant to serve as a burden-bearer. Tools of copper and bronze were in use, and craftsmen worked in silver and understood the art of glazing. A form of picture writing had been developed. There are evidences that they had in very early times established trade connections with the Sumerians, from whom, no doubt, they had received their civilization.

FIG. 85. A CYLINDER SEAL (*above*) *discovered in the Ruins of the Ancient Babylonian City of Eshnunna* (*cf. Fig. 89*) *compared with* STAMP SEALS (*below*) *found in the Lower Indus Valley*

When compared with objects recently excavated in the Indus valley this seal is shown to be of East Indian origin rather than Babylonian. That it was imported is indicated not only by the style of carving but also by the animal subjects chosen for decorating the seal, for the elephant does not appear in the art of the Tigris-Euphrates valley, and the rhinoceros was unknown there. As this seal was found with other objects dating to the Twenty-fifth Century B.C., it is evident that we may date the Indus valley civilization at least as far back as about 2500 B.C.

in a great network of roads and sea routes. These communications not only connected the countries of the Near East with each other but likewise linked the Near East as a whole with the Asiatic world on one side and the Mediterranean world on the other. This commerce from the Two Rivers overlapped with that of Egypt in the Eastern Mediterranean and must have extended to Egypt itself. It was such intercourse between the Two Rivers and Egypt which already in prehistoric times gave these two regions a number of things in common, like the use of the cylinder seal, the pear-shaped war mace, and the use of balanced animal figures in decorative art (see Fig. 94).

176. Trade and government very early led the Sumerians to make records, scratched in rude pictures with the tip of a reed on a flat oval or disk of soft clay. When dried in the sun such a clay record became very hard, and if well baked in an oven it became an almost imperishable pottery

Rise of Sumerian pictorial writing on clay

tablet. On the earliest surviving specimens of these tablets the writing still employs the old pictures, much as in the beginning. This picture stage was perhaps in use as early as 3500 B.C.

177. The instrument with which these signs were traced on the clay we call a *stylus*. An example recently discovered

Sumerian picture signs become cuneiform signs

by the excavators is made of bone. Others are known to have been made of a strip split from a hard, reedlike bamboo. The end used was triangular in shape (see a scribe holding a stylus in Fig. 105). The writer did not scratch the lines of his picture, but in making a single line he impressed one corner of the tip of the stylus into the soft clay, and then raised it again to impress another line in the same way. Owing to the oblique tilt of the stylus, as well as its shape, each line thus made was wider at one end than at the other, and hence appeared triangular or wedge-shaped, thus ▻— or ⟨. Finally every picture or sign written with such a stylus came to be made up of a group of wedge-shaped lines like ⟨⟨, which was once a stalk of grain, or ⟩—⟨⟨, once a foot (Fig. 86, *6*, *10*). We therefore call the system *cuneiform* (from Latin *cuneus*, meaning "wedge"), or wedge-form, writing. Pictures made up of these wedge lines became more and more difficult to recognize, especially as speed in writing increased. All resemblance to the earlier pictures finally disappeared.

178. The transition from the picture stage to the phonetic stage was early made. Sumerian writing finally possessed

Rise of phonetic cuneiform signs; no alphabetic signs

over five hundred and sixty signs, but each of these signs represented a syllable [1] or a word, that is, a *group* of sounds; the Sumerian system never developed an alphabet of the letters which made up the syllables. That is, there were signs for syllables,

---

[1] The only exceptions were later the vowels and some surviving pictorial signs which served as graphic hints, like the Egyptian determinatives (Fig. 34).

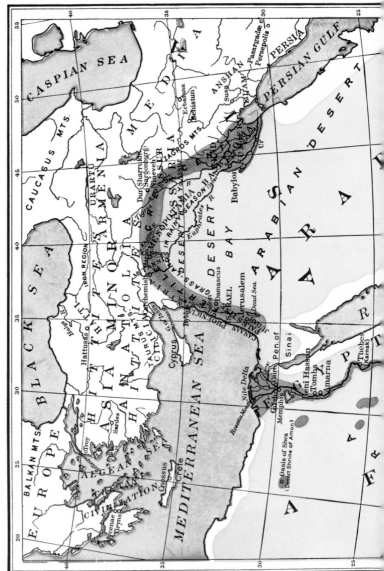

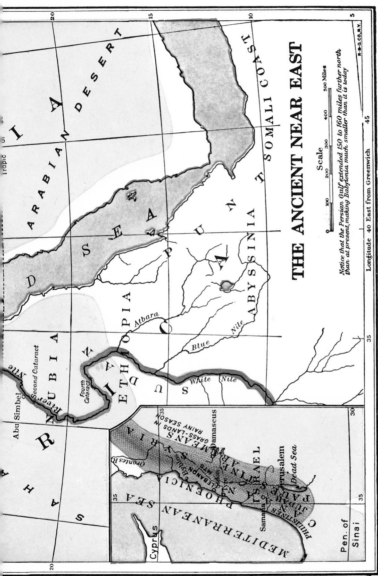

THE ANCIENT NEAR EAST

Scale

0 100 200 300 400 500 Miles

Notice that the Persian Gulf extended 150 to 160 miles further north than, at present, making Babylonia much smaller than it is today

Longitude 40 East from Greenwich 45

ARABIAN   DESERT

Tropic

RED   SEA

NUBIA

Abu Simbel

Second Cataract

Fourth Cataract

SAHARA

Nile

Atbara

Blue   Nile

White   Nile

ETHIOPIA

SUDAN

ABYSSINIA

PUNT

SOMALI COAST

MEDITERRANEAN   SEA

Cyprus

PHOENICIA

SYRIA

ARAMEANS
GRASS-LANDS
RAINY SEASON

Damascus

Orontes R.

Lebanon

Anti-Lebanon

PALESTINE

ISRAEL

Samaria

Jerusalem

Dead Sea

PHILISTINES

CANAAN

Pen. of
Sinai

20

15

10

5

45

35

30

35

35

20

R-M-CO. N.Y.

9371]

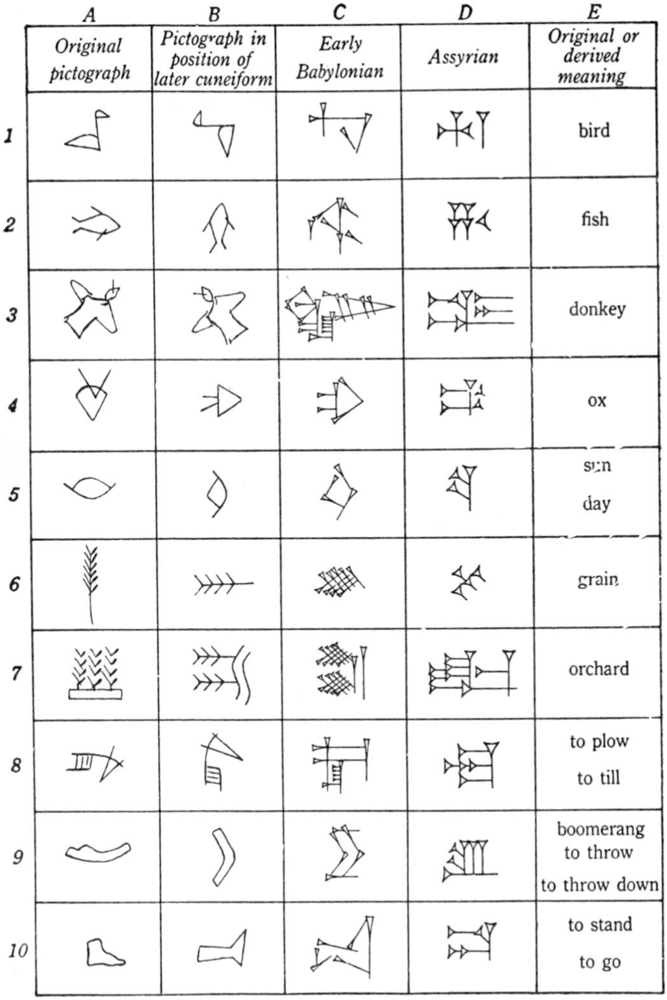

	A	B	C	D	E
	Original pictograph	Pictograph in position of later cuneiform	Early Babylonian	Assyrian	Original or derived meaning
1					bird
2					fish
3					donkey
4					ox
5					sun day
6					grain
7					orchard
8					to plow to till
9					boomerang to throw to throw down
10					to stand to go

FIG. 86. *Diagram showing Pictorial Origin of* TEN CUNEIFORM SIGNS

The development of 3 is particularly interesting. In *A* and *B* a short line was inserted in the donkey's right ear to indicate that the open side was turned toward the reader, while the left ear was turned away. In the early cuneiform sign (*C*) this line has survived as a single wedge inside the square which stands for the right ear, and below the square are three horizontal wedges, — all that remains of the left ear. The muzzle is still quite distinct, crossed by two pairs of oblique wedges, once the right eye and nostril. (Compiled and drawn by Professor Arno Poebel)

like *kar* or *ban*, but no signs for the letters *k* or *r*, *b* or *n*, which made up such syllables. Hence we cannot insert here an alphabet, as we did in discussing Egyptian writing.

179. These clay records show us that in measuring time the Sumerian scribe began a new month with every new

Sumerian moon calendar; year-names

moon, and he made his year of twelve of these moon-months. We remember that twelve such months fall far short of making up a year. The scribe therefore slipped in an extra month whenever he found that he had reached the end of his calendar year a month or so ahead of the seasons. This inconvenient and inaccurate calendar was inherited by the Jews and Persians, and is still used by the Oriental Jews and the Mohammedans. As in Egypt, the years themselves were not numbered, but each year was named after some important event occurring in the course of the year.

180. The Sumerian system of numerals was not based on tens, but had the unit sixty as a basis. A large number was

Sumerian numerals and weights

given as so many sixties, just as we employ a score (fourscore, fivescore). From this unit of sixty has descended our division of the hour and minute, and perhaps also our division of the circle (six sixties); but this last is not at all certain. The leading unit of weight which they used was a *mina*, divided into sixty shekels. The mina had the weight of our pound, and traffic with the East at last brought this measure of weight to us, though under another name (see also § 495).

181. The most important portion of the Sumerian town, and indeed the nucleus of its civilization, was the temple

Temple inclosure and its management

inclosure. Here were places of worship, storehouses, and business offices, surrounded and protected by a massive wall. Here ruled a wealthy priesthood. Assisted by scribes, they rented and cared for temple property. The ruler of the town was also the chief priest, and his temple duties kept him about as busy as did the task of ruling the community outside of the temple walls.

FIG. 87. *Early Babylonian* CYLINDER SEAL *(about* Twenty-fifth *Century* B.C.)

Instead of signing his *name* to a clay-tablet document the early Sumerian rolled over the soft clay a little stone roller, or cylinder, engraved with beautiful pictures and sometimes also bearing the owner's name, as here. The impression left by the roller in the soft clay served as a signature. They have been found in great numbers, showing the growth and decline of Babylonian art for some three thousand years, beginning 3000 B.C. This picture shows side view (right) and impression made by rolling (left). The subject of the seal above is the story of Gilgamesh, the Sumerian ancestor of Hercules. He is seen slaying a wild bull (center). His friend Engidu, half man, half bull, wrestles with a lion (at left and right). We can appreciate the excellence of the carving when we realize that this seal is only a little over one inch high

182. Rising high above the other buildings in the temple inclosure was the tower-temple, which was in general shape almost a cube, though it tapered slightly in a series of steps toward the top. In front were *The temples* three lofty flights of stairs rising nearly a hundred and fifty feet and converging on a door almost halfway up the front of the building. In the upper part of the tower was a square temple, with a court open to the sky, and a holy place behind it. Probably the first of such tower-temples was built at Nippur as a sanctuary to Enlil, the Sumerian god of the air. Alongside the tower-temple was a low building serving as the temple proper. Here the arrangement was very simple, consisting of a court and the sanctuary. Indeed, it is clear that this lower temple was considered merely as a dwelling of the god, like the dwelling houses of the people in the town.

183. To this sanctuary under the shadow of the tower-temple the peasant brought his offering, — a goat and a jar of water containing a few green palm branches *Sumerian religion* intended to symbolize the vegetable life of the *and worship* land, which the god maintained by the annual rise of the river. The worshiper's jar with the green palm branches in it later became "the tree of life," a symbol often depicted on the monuments of the land. These gifts the worshiper laid before the gods of earth and its green life, of the air, the sky, or the sea, praying that there might be plentiful waters and generous harvests, but praying also for deliverance from the destroying flood which the god had once sent to overwhelm the land. Of this catastrophe the peasant's fathers had told him, and the tradition of this flood finally passed over to the Hebrews.

184. In one important matter of religion the Sumerians were very different from the Egyptians. The dead were often buried in the town, under the court of a house or the floor of a room, although cemeteries outside a town were not unknown. Of the next world they had only vague and somber impressions, as a gloomy place of darkness and dust beneath the earth, to which all men, both good and bad, descended. However, they shared in a widespread belief that when a man died he would need his household in the next world. Provisions were made, therefore, that the dead man might not be obliged to live without his servants and animals in the life beyond the grave. Very early tombs recently found at Ur have disclosed the dead man's bodyguard, his servants, male and female, his draft oxen still yoked to the chariot, all lying slain at the door of the burial chamber, that they might accompany their master and continue to serve him after death.

Sumerian burials and beliefs about the hereafter

185. In the middle of the Sumerian town was usually the temple inclosure, and around it extended the houses of the citizens, — bare rectangular structures of sun-dried brick, each with a court on the north side, and on the south side of the court a main chamber from which the other rooms were entered. At first only a few hundred feet across, the town slowly spread out, although it always remained of very limited extent. Such a town usually stood upon an artificial mound, which it is important for us to examine; for each such mound is a great storehouse of ancient monuments and records.

Sumerian house and town

© *The Illustrated London News*

FIG. 88. HOUSEHOLD *of a Prince of* UR AWAITING DEATH *at the Door of his* Tomb

The Anglo-American Expedition under C. L. Woolley, excavating at Ur, discovered the bodies of these men women, and animals, with their equipment, lying there at the door of the burial chamber. Directed by the archæologists, the modern artist has here raised the dead by depicting them in the positions which they occupied at the last fatal moment before they were slain. This slaughter was made in order that these people might pass on into the next world with their ruler and continue to serve him there

186. The ordinary building material of the entire ancient world was sun-baked brick. The houses of the common people in the Near East even at the present day are still built of these bricks. The walls of such houses in course of time are slowly eaten away by the rains, till after a heavy rain an old house sometimes falls down. When this happens at the present day the rubbish is leveled off and the house is rebuilt on top of it. This practice has been going on for thousands of years. It was the fall of such a house that Jesus had in mind in his parable (Matt. vii, 27). As this process went on for many centuries, it produced a high mound of rubbish, on which the town stood. Many a surviving Oriental town still stands on such an ancient mound; but there are other mounds which

The formation of ancient city mounds

FIG. 89. EXCAVATIONS *at Eshnunna*

These ruins, only fifty miles northeast of Baghdad, mark the site of the ancient city of Eshnunna, now being excavated by the Oriental Institute of The University of Chicago. We see the work of excavation actually going on. The earth is carefully loosened with hand picks, and the loosened débris is taken out in baskets. These baskets are carried away by the laborers to steel dump-cars (see background at right), which run on tracks over ever-growing banks of excavated earth at some distance beyond the limits of the ruins. Down to about 1840 the monuments and records of Babylonia and Assyria preserved in Europe could all be contained in a show case only a few feet square. Since that time, however, such excavations have recovered great quantities of antiquities and records. At Persepolis the Oriental Institute found over 30,000 cuneiform tablets

were long ago abandoned. Mounds so formed are to be found in all the lands of the Ancient Near East (Figs. 89 and 116).

187. The clay tablets containing the household records, letters, bills, receipts, notes, accounts, etc., which were in the houses when they fell, were often covered by the falling walls, and they still lie in the mounds. In the temples and public buildings the documents covered up were frequently important government records, while in the dwelling or offices of the ruler they were often narratives of wars and conquests. Sometimes the ruler placed accounts of his erection of temples or palaces, records of his victories and other great deeds, deep

Contents pre-
served in these
ancient mounds

in the foundations of his buildings, in order that later rulers might find them. Besides all these written records many articles of household use or sculptured works of art still lie buried in such mounds.

188. We are thus able to understand how these ruins of the ancient Sumerian cities reveal to us the life which filled the once busy streets, now sleeping under the silent mounds. We see that the most impor- *Age of Sumerian city-kingdoms* tant class of citizens in the town were the free *(about 2900-2500 B.C.)* landowners who worked their lands with numerous slaves and carried on trade by caravans and in small boats up and down the river. Over these free middle-class folk were the officials and priests, the aristocrats of the town. Such a community, owning the lands for a few miles round about the town, formed the political unit, or the state, which we call a city-kingdom. The earliest monuments of Babylonia show us that these little city-kingdoms were already in existence throughout a large part of the Plain of Shinar by 3000 B.C. Beginning at about 2900 B.C. the written documents and other monuments enable us to follow the life and the history of these early Sumerian cities for some four centuries. This period forms the first chapter of history in ancient Babylonia. We may call it the Age of the Sumerian City-Kingdoms.

189. In spite of oppressive and dishonest taxation such a community owed much to its ruler, or *patesi* (pronounced *pa-tay'see*). He was useful in a number of *Sumerian city-kingdoms and their patesis* matters, but chiefly in two ways: in war and in irrigation. The irrigation canals and dikes required constant repairs. The planting and the harvesting of the fields would have stopped and the whole community would have starved if the ruler had ceased his constant over-sight of the dikes and canals and the water supply had been cut off.

190. As to war, we can watch more than one of these city rulers marching out at the head of heavily armed troops marshaled in massive phalanx (Fig. 90) or charging the

Fig. 90. *A Sumerian* City-King *leading a* Phalanx *of his* Troops

The king himself, whose face is broken off from the stone, marches at the right, heading his troops, who follow in a compact group. This is the earliest example of grouping men together in a mass, forming a single fighting unit, called a phalanx. This must have required long drill and discipline, after many centuries of loose, irregular, scattered fighting. This was the first chapter in the long history of the art of war, and it took place in Asia. Such discipline was unknown at this time in Egypt. These Sumerian troops have their spears set for the charge, but they carry no bows. Tall shields cover their entire bodies, and they wear close-fitting helmets, probably of leather. They are marching over dead bodies (symbolical of the overthrow of the enemy). The scene is carved in stone and is a good example of the rude Sumerian sculpture in Babylonia in the days of the Gizeh pyramids

enemy in heavy chariots. These war chariots are the earliest known wheeled vehicles; they were mounted on either two or four wheels and drawn by teams of four horses, the oldest known domesticated horses.

Wars among Sumerian city-kingdoms

We found on the Nile the earliest highly developed arts of peace; we find here among the Sumerians the earliest highly developed art of war. When the towns-people heard that a neighboring city-kingdom was trying to take possession of a strip of their land, they were glad to follow the patesi's leadership in order to drive out the invaders. As such occurrences were common, the early history of Sumer was largely made up of the ever-changing fortunes of these city-kingdoms in war.

191. The earliest city to gain the leadership of Sumer was Ur, a city of the extreme south, situated on the Euphrates not far Leadership of Ur from its mouth, as shown on the map (p. 141) drawn with the coast line in its ancient position. The earliest known king in Western Asia was Mes-anni-padda, who ruled at Ur about 2900 B. C. It was his son who built the little temple to the cow-goddess in a suburb of Ur (see § 174). Four of Mes-anni-padda's descendants ruled in Ur, and this line of five kings is called the First Dynasty (or family) of Ur.

FIG. 91. *Two-Wheeled* CHARIOT *drawn by Earliest Known* DOMESTICATED HORSES

The three fragments forming all but the lower left corner of this plaque were discovered by the Oriental Institute of The University of Chicago in the ruins of Opis (see map, p. 141), fifty miles east of modern Baghdad. An Anglo-American expedition at Ur had earlier found the lower left corner of a similar plaque which completed the chariot and the bodies of the animals (probably wild asses, possibly horses). The complete restoration made from these various fragments is very important, for we have here not only one of the earliest representations of a two-wheeled chariot but also possibly the domesticated horse in Babylonia nearly three thousand years before the Christian Era

192. Recent excavations at the ancient city have resulted in the Civilization of Ur: goldsmiths' work; sculpture most surprising discoveries. Far down beneath the accumulated rubbish of fallen buildings were found the tombs of the princes and nobles who were buried there at the time of the First Dynasty. The magnificent equipment of these very early burials rivals that of the tombs of Egypt, and has revealed a new and earlier chapter of Sumerian civilization. The works of the goldsmith disclose remarkable skill and craftsmanship, as well as refinement of design (Fig. 92), showing how far the life of Western Asia had risen above the Stone Age savagery which had once filled all this region. These kings of the First Dynasty were already able to adorn the little temple of the cow-goddess with impressive works of sculpture in copper. On the platform before the building stood vigorous figures of bulls cast in copper, while the front entrance itself was guarded by a splendid lion-headed eagle with outspread wings hovering over a pair of stags, the whole fashioned of copper. Along the face of the building ran a line of bull figures cut out of heavy sheet copper. Another decorative band crossing the front of the temple was made up of dairy scenes with the figures carved in shell or limestone (Fig. 83).

193. The works of the Sumerian sculptors in stone **Sumerian lapidaries** were in the beginning very rough and crude, but the demand for personal seals cut in stone soon developed a beautiful art of engraving tiny figures on a hard

FIG. 92. HELMET OF GOLD *from the Tomb of an Early Noble or Prince of Ur*

The helmet is wrought of heavy sheet gold, on which the goldsmith has engraved the details of the waved and curling hair or wig, and the elaborate headdress. This work is one of the most magnificent examples of the goldsmith's art that have survived from the ancient world. It belonged to a man named Mes-kalam-shar, a prince or noble of Ur. (Courtesy of the University Museum of Philadelphia)

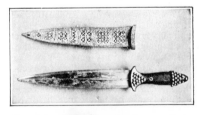

FIG. 93. *Golden* DAGGER *from an Early Tomb at Ur*

The handle is of lapis lazuli mounted in gold, while the sheath has been wrought in openwork of unusually rich and beautiful detail, all likewise done in gold. (Courtesy of the University Museum of Philadelphia)

FIG. 94. SCULPTURE *once adorning the Entrance of the* TEMPLE *of the*
Cow-GODDESS *near* Ur

In the middle is a lion-headed eagle hovering over the figures of two stags. This balanced arrangement of animal figures is one of the great creations of Sumerian art. The entire monument is seven feet nine inches long. It was probably mounted over the door of the temple, although it had long since fallen down when found by the excavator, Dr. H. R. Hall. It is the largest sculpture in copper of so early a date ever yet found in Western Asia. The eagle is the divine bird which the Sumerians called "Im-dugud," a malicious creature perhaps placed over the door of the temple to frighten away evil powers and protect the place. Such symbols, made up of balanced pairs of animal figures, later passed over into Europe, where they are still used in decorative art and in the heraldic symbols or arms of kings and nations. The eagle still appears in the arms of Austria, Prussia, and other European nations, and finally reached the West as the "American" eagle, — really the Sumerian eagle of five thousand years ago. (Courtesy of the British Museum)

stone surface. We remember that craftsmen who do such work are called lapidaries. The early Sumerian lapidaries soon became the finest craftsmen of the kind in the ancient Oriental world, and their influence has not yet disappeared from our own decorative art.

194. Sumerian history really begins with this brilliant chapter of early civilization at Ur, which opened with the reign of Mes-anni-padda. Several rival city-kingdoms of Sumer contended with Ur for the leadership. The rival best known to us was Lagash (see map, p. 141), where excavation has uncovered many important monuments similar to those of Ur. The king of Lagash finally overthrew the king of Ur and captured his city. From this defeat Ur was long unable to recover.

Ur falls before its rivals

195. While the city-kingdoms of Sumer were thus

The earliest
Semitic city-
kingdoms

often fighting
among them-
selves they
were also called upon to
meet an enemy from the
outside. The Semitic nom-
ads of the desert, proba-
bly coming from the northwest and moving down the
Euphrates, reached the narrow region where the Two
Rivers are hardly twenty
miles apart. Here they
early began to settle north
of Sumer, where they first
seized the city of Opis, discovered and identified by
the Oriental Institute in
1934. At Opis (see map,
p. 141) these desert invaders became the earliest
Semitic city-kings in an-
cient Shinar. Other Se-
mitic leaders later did the
same at Kish, a city not far
from Opis. This region first
occupied by the Semites in
the northern part of Shinar
was finally called Akkad
(see map, p. 141), and the
leading Semitic settlers
there bore the name of
Akkadians. Akkad occu-
pied a very strong com-
mercial position on the

Fig. 95. Sewer Main *through the An-*
cient Babylonian City of Eshnunna *in the*
Age of Sargon I

A break in the rear portion of the sewer
nearly below the dog shows that the sewer
was vaulted at the top. The ancient masons leaned their arch against a thick,
heavy wall visible on the right. The top
of the arch, leaning against this thick
wall, may be seen for some distance beyond the man in the foreground. In the
immediate foreground is a branch of the
sewer which extends toward the left into a
house lying under the rubbish at the left
and not yet excavated. There is a long
series of such branches connecting the
water-closets inside the houses on either
side with this sewer and serving to carry
away the household sewage. The construction is of burned brick, for sun-dried
brick would have collapsed if used for a
sewer. This is the oldest such town sewage
system ever yet found. Compare **Fig. 89**

main road from the Two Rivers to the eastern mountains, and its trade always brought it prosperity.

196. Unlike the Sumerians, these Semitic wanderers of the desert had never learned discipline and drill in war. They depended on their skill as archers, and they therefore gave battle at a distance. Or, if they came to close quarters, they fought single-handed, in open order. Their thin and open line was evidently at first no match for the heavy phalanx of the Sumerians. Thus two hostile races faced each other on the Plain of Shinar : in the north, the half-settled Semitic nomads of Akkad ; and in the south, the settled agricultural Sumerians.

Earliest wars of the Sumerians and the Semites

Section 15. The First Semitic Triumph : the Age of Sargon

197. Late in the Twenty-sixth Century B.C., that is, about 2500 B.C., there arose in Akkad a Semitic Chieftain named Sargon. So skillful in war was he that he succeeded in scattering the compact Sumerian spearmen and making himself lord of all the Plain of Shinar. The old Sumerian city-kings were defeated, and the Sumerian towns down to the mouths of the Two Rivers submitted to him. He even embarked his troops on the Persian Gulf in his attack on Elam. He led his swift Akkadian archers from the eastern mountains of Elam westward up the Euphrates to the shores of the Mediterranean. From the Mediterranean Sargon seems to have pushed northward into eastern Asia Minor in order to protect the trade which was already active between the silver-bearing regions of southeastern Asia Minor and the merchants of the Two Rivers. Sargon was the first great Semitic leader in history, and he was the first ruler to build up a powerful nation in Western Asia, reaching from Elam on the east to the Mediterranean and far up the Two Rivers toward the west and north (see map, p. 146). His splendid conquests made an impression upon the Tigris-Euphrates world which never

Sargon and the first Semitic triumph (ca. 2500-2300 B.C.)

faded, in spite of the fact that a serious revolt brought his reign to an end. His conquests were resumed by his grandson Naram-Sin, who even extended them and left his monuments on the upper Tigris.

198. Sargon's conquests forced his nomad tribesmen (the Akkadians) to make a complete change in their manner of life. We may best picture the change if we say that they forsook their tents and built houses of sun-dried brick which could not be picked up every morning and pitched somewhere else at night. At first they did not even know how to write, and they had no industries. Some of them now learned to write their Semitic tongue by using the Sumerian wedge-form signs for the purpose. It was in this age, therefore, that a Semitic language began to be written for the first time. These former nomads had never before attempted to manage the affairs of settled communities,— such business as we call government administration. All this too they were now obliged to learn from the Sumerians. The Semitic Akkadians therefore adopted the Sumerian calendar, weights and measures, system of numerals, and business methods. With the arts of peace the Akkadians gained also those of war. They learned to make helmets of leather and copper weighing over two pounds. These are the earliest-known examples of the use of metal as a protection in war. From such beginnings as these were to come the steel-clad battleships and gun turrets of modern times.

Semitic Akkadians adopt Sumerian civilization

199. Among other things the Akkadians learned also the art of sculpture, but they soon far surpassed their Sumerian teachers. The relief of Naram-Sin (Fig. 96) belongs among the real triumphs of art in the early world, and is especially interesting as the first great work of art produced by the Semitic race. The beautiful Sumerian art of seal-cutting the Akkadians now carried to a wonderful degree of perfection. The ability of these artists to depict men and animals in violent action marked great progress in art.

Great Semitic art of Age of Sargon

FIG. 96. A King of Akkad STORMING A FORTRESS,— the Earliest Great
Semitic Work of Art (Twenty-fifth Century B.C.)

King Naram-Sin of Akkad (grandson of Sargon) has pursued the enemy
into a mountain stronghold in Elam. His heroic figure towers above his enemies, each one of whom has fixed his eyes on the conqueror, awaiting his sig-
nal of mercy. The sculptor, with fine insight, has depicted the dramatic
instant when the king lowers his weapon as the sign that he grants the conquered their lives. The king's enemies are made much smaller than he, to
indicate their inferiority. Compare the superiority of this *Semitic* sculpture
of Akkad over the *Sumerian* sculpture of two centuries earlier (Fig. 90)

Fig. 97. *A Semitic* Prince *and his Sumerian* Secretary

The third figure (wearing a cap) is that of the prince Ubil-Ishtar, who is brother of the king. He is a Semite, as his features show. Three of his four attendants are probably also Semites, with beards and long hair as usual; but one of them (just behind the prince) is beardless and shaven-headed. He is the noble's secretary, for, being a Sumerian, he is skilled in writing. His name, "Kalki," we learn from the inscription in the corner, which reads, "Ubil-Ishtar, brother of the king; Kalki the scribe, thy servant." This inscription is in the Semitic (Akkadian) tongue of the time and illustrates how the Semites have learned the Sumerian signs for writing. The scene is engraved on Kalki's personal seal (cf. Fig. 87), and the above drawing shows the impression left on the soft clay when the seal was rolled over it. It is a fine example of the Babylonian art of seal-cutting in hard stone. The original is in the British Museum

200. Thus the life of the desert Semites mingled with that of the non-Semitic townsmen on the Babylonian Plain, much as Normans and English mingled in England. On the streets and in the market places of the Euphrates towns, where once the round-headed and often smoothly shaven Sumerian townsmen were the only people to be seen, there was now a plentiful sprinkling of the swarthy, always heavily bearded, long-headed Semites of Akkad. In war the Sumerians continued to serve in the army with shield and spear, along with their Semitic lords carrying only the bow, and in peace the Semitic noblemen could not do without their deft Sumerian clerks.

Commingling of Sumerians and Akkadians (Semites)

SECTION 16. UNION OF SUMERIANS AND SEMITES: THE
REVIVAL OF UR AND THE KINGS OF SUMER AND AKKAD

201. When at last the Semites of Akkad had been en-
feebled by the town life which they had adopted, the line of
Sargon declined and fell, having ruled less
than two centuries. As a result the Sumerian   Sumerians and
Semites unite in
cities of the south were able to recover control   kingdom of Sumer
and Akkad
of the country not long after 2300 B.C.
Headed by the ancient city of Ur, three of the old Sumerian
cities gained the leadership one after another. But the
Semites had now been a part of the population of the Babylonian Plain for centuries, and many of them were living in
the old Sumerian towns. Henceforth they were therefore
recognized as part of the unified nation of the ancient Plain
of Shinar, which now for the first time gained a national
name. The new nation was called Sumer and Akkad. The
kings of this age were both Sumerians and Semites. The
period of the kings of Sumer and Akkad (beginning about
2300 B.C.) may be summed up as more than a century of
prosperity under the leadership of Ur, followed by two centuries of decline under the successors of Ur. There were
conquests northward up the Tigris, including even Assyria,
which appears in this connection *for the first time in history*.
These conquests also extended eastward into Elam and westward up the Euphrates, where the barbarous western Semites,
known as Amorites (see § 168), were dangerous invaders.

202. These conquests brought a large area of Western
Asia under a more effective political control than ever before.
One of the important results was the greatest
development of trade that Western Asia had   Expansion of trade
and use of silver
thus far seen. In the Stone Age we know that   as a medium
of exchange
men traded in amber and flint and other natural products. With the development of agriculture, measures of barley or wheat served as a convenient scale of values.
If A bought from B a river boat worth twenty measures of
barley, he might offer in payment an ox worth fifteen meas-

ures, and he would then pay in actual grain besides the ox
only five more measures of barley. Gradually the increase in
the amount of precious metals, however, made them a more
convenient medium of exchange. The Babylonians early
began to use pieces of silver each weighing a shekel, or the
sixtieth part of a pound (mina). When a silver shekel was
shaped into a disk, it might be no larger than a dime. It was
now possible to give prices and values in weights of silver. The
value of silver was about four of silver to one of gold, but as
it became more plentiful it decreased greatly in value (§ 224).

203. This trade has left an enormous body of bookkeeping
records in the form of clay tablets found by excavation in
Business usages   the ancient cities of the age. It was at this
and rise of law   time that many of the business forms which
we still use and which make business transactions a matter
of record arose for the first time. Thus grew up business and
social customs, especially business credit. These practices
gradually came to be regarded as the only ones to be followed,
and thus finally became laws controlling the life of the people.

204. Thus able to bring a wide region under orderly laws
and enjoying far-reaching trade connections, Ur rapidly
Prosperity, build-   gained wealth and power, as revealed to us
ing, and literature   by its impressive tower-temple and the tombs
of three of the greatest kings of Ur, discovered in 1930.
Unfortunately these tombs had been plundered by the
Elamites and therefore were empty when the modern excavators entered them. The tablets containing the literature
of this age have been lost, but some of the schoolbooks and
exercise tablets of the boys, who were already studying this
literature at school, have survived and are often our only
copies of valuable works of literature which have otherwise
perished. In such a school there were already clay-tablet
treatises on grammar, dictionaries, and lists of signs. The
lads could study tablets on arithmetic and geometry, and they
might even find on the shelves of the tablet library discussions on medicine and healing. In these the only known
cause of disease was evil spirits, which the Babylonians be-

lieved could enter the human body. There were also religious
hymns, but the greater part of the *real* literature of the age
was a series of stories and mythical tales.

205. In simple stories these men of Sumer and Akkad had
now begun to answer those natural questions regarding life
and death which always rise in the minds of
early men. They told of the wonderful adventures of the shepherd Etana when his flocks
Thought and myth.
Source of life: the
Etana story
were stricken with unfruitfulness and no more lambs were
born. Etana then mounted on the back of an eagle and rose
to the skies in search of the herb in which was the source of
life. But as he neared his goal he was hurled to the earth
again. This is the earliest tale of flying by man.

206. The dark mystery of death led to the story of the
fisherman Adapa. When the south-wind goddess overturned
his boat, Adapa flew into a rage and broke her
wing. Thereupon he was summoned to the
throne of the Sky-god, whose wrath was at
Death and eternal
life: the Adapa
story
length appeased so that he offered to Adapa the bread and
water of life. This would have made him immortal and
destroyed death, but, suspicious and forewarned of danger,
the unhappy Adapa refused the food and thus lost, both for
himself and for mankind, the treasure of immortal life.

207. In the same way they told how the gigantic hero
Gilgamesh, after many mighty deeds and strange adventures,
failed to gain immortal life. Among all these
heroes, indeed, there was but one who was
granted endless life. Of him there was a
Immortality: the
Gilgamesh story;
the deluge story
strange tale, telling how, together with his wife, he survived
the great deluge in a large ship. Then the gods carried them
both away to blessedness. But not even the *kings* of Sumer
and Akkad were supposed to enter a blessed hereafter, much
less the common people. Many of these stories of creation
and flood were afterwards known to the Hebrews.

208. Mingled with touches from the life of both Sumerian
and Semite, these tales now circulated in both the Semitic
and the Sumerian language. Most of them, however, were

Fig. 98. *The* Flight *of Etana to the* Skies

At the right Etana sits on the back of the flying eagle, with his arm around the bird's neck. Above him is the moon, while, below, two dogs look up after him, barking. At the left approaches a goatherd driving three goats; before them walks a man with hand upraised in wonder. All, including the goats, are looking up in amazement at the flight of Etana. Over the goatherd a potter is making jars, and at the right of his jars a squatting baker is making round loaves. The scene is carved on a cylinder seal, and our drawing shows the impression on the soft clay when the seal is rolled over it

written in Sumerian, and it was this old Sumerian tongue which was regarded as the more sacred. It later continued in use as a kind of sacred language, like Latin in the Roman Catholic church today. The old Sumerian towns were now rapidly declining (Twenty-second Century B.C.), but religious stories were written in Sumerian, centuries after it was no longer spoken.

Decline of Sumerian language; survival as a sacred tongue

209. The period of the kings of Sumer and Akkad represents the highest level of the mixed Sumerian and Akkadian civilization,— that civilization which we now call Babylonian. The power and splendor of Ur in this age were never forgotten, and later, when Hebrew civilization had arisen in Palestine, the Hebrews were very proud to trace back their ancestry to Abraham, believed by them to have been a citizen of Ur toward the close of the great period with which we have been dealing.

Enduring glory of the civilization of Sumer and Akkad

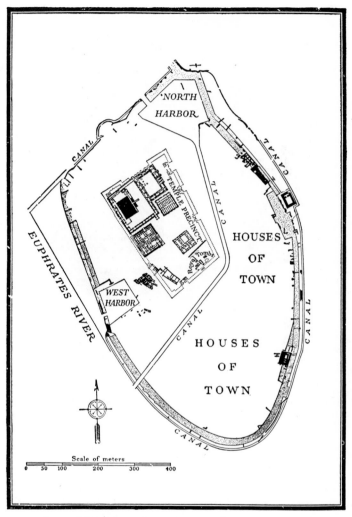

PLAN of the CITY of UR, *according to the Latest Excavations*

Showing that it was a river port lying on the Euphrates, with two harbors and a canal crossing the town. (Drawing after Woolley)

FIG. 99. A *Seal-Cutter's* PORTRAIT *of the* LAST KING *of* Ur

The king, Ibi-Sin, seated at the right, gives audience to a priest of Enlil, standing at the left, and presents to him a small jar containing perhaps some costly oil or ointment. This scene is found on a clay tablet in the University Museum of Philadelphia. Thousands of years ago, when the document on the clay tablet had been written, a stone cylinder seal, into which had been cut this representation of Ibi-Sin and the priest, was rolled across the soft clay. Thus was preserved for us one of the rare memorials of this unfortunate king who fought so valiantly yet vainly to retain his dominion. (Courtesy of the University Museum of Philadelphia)

SECTION 17. THE SECOND SEMITIC TRIUMPH: THE AGE OF HAMMURAPI AND AFTER

210. Before 2000 B.C. the united kingdom of Sumer and Akkad had fallen, and never again did the old Sumerian cities hold political leadership. This final fall was due not only to wars among the city-kingdoms themselves but also to foreign invasion, which broke through the frontier defenses in both east and west at the same time. In the east the Elamites seized the Sumerian

End of Sumero-Akkadian power

cities, led captive the last king of Ur, and plundered the royal tombs of the city. In the west a new tribe of Semites, called Amorites, began an invasion of Akkad. Between these two invasions the old Sumero-Akkadian power was slowly but completely crushed.

211. In the time of the Kings of Sumer and Akkad the Amorites (§ 168) began descending the Euphrates valley, just as the Akkadians had done long before Amorite seizure of under Sargon. In the middle of the Twenty- Babylon first Century B.C. (2050 B.C.) they seized the little town of Babylon, which was at that time still an obscure village on the Euphrates. These Amorite chiefs of Babylon held the place for three hundred years (about 2050 to 1750 B.C.) and made the city finally such an outstanding center of power and civilization that it gave its name to the old Plain of Shinar, which we may thenceforth properly call Babylonia.

212. The earlier Amorite kings of Babylon were not able at once to take possession of all Sumer and Akkad, and the struggle against the Elamites coming in from Triumph of Ham-the east went on for a long time without a murapi decisive victory. Following a century of such warfare, there came to the throne a king named Hammurapi (1948–1905 B.C.). He was the sixth in the Amorite line of kings at Babylon. Hammurapi at once took up the war against the invading Elamites with great vigor. For over thirty years he fought them, before he was able to drive them back into the eastern mountains from which they had come. Then Hammurapi made his city of Babylon for the first time supreme throughout the ancient Babylonian Plain. This long war is an instructive example of the age-long struggle between the mountaineers and the plainsmen for possession of the Fertile Crescent.

213. Hammurapi survived his triumph twelve years. While fighting and conquest did not wholly cease, nevertheless these years gave him opportunity to devote himself Hammurapi the to peaceful administration, in which he proved organizer himself, as he had done in war, the ablest of his line. He was the second great Semitic ruler, as Sargon had been the first.

Only a few generations earlier his ancestors, like those of Sargon, had been drifting about the desert, without any organization. But he now put forth his powerful hand upon the teeming life of the Babylonian towns, and with a touch he brought in order and system such as Babylonia had never seen before. Two chief sources of information have survived nearly four thousand years to reveal to us the deeds and the character of this great king : these are a large group of his letters and the splendid monument bearing his laws.

214. Hammurapi's letters afford us for the first time in history a glimpse into the busy life of a powerful Oriental

Hammurapi's letters: their dictation and preparation

ruler in Asia. They disclose him to us sitting in the executive office of his palace at Babylon, with his secretary at his side. In short, clear sentences the king begins dictating his brief letters, conveying his commands to the local governors of the old Sumerian cities which he now rules. The secretary draws a reed stylus from a leather holder at his girdle and quickly covers the small clay tablet with its lines of wedge-groups. The writer then sprinkles over the soft, wet tablet a handful of dry powdered clay. This is to prevent the clay envelope, which he now deftly wraps about the letter, from adhering to the written surface. On this soft clay envelope he writes the address and sends the letter out to be put into the furnace and baked.

215. Messengers constantly hand him similarly inclosed letters. This secretary of Hammurapi is a trusted confidential

Hammurapi's letters: navigation

secretary. He therefore breaks to pieces the hard clay envelopes in the king's presence and reads aloud to him letters from his officials all over the kingdom. The king quickly dictates his replies. The flood has obstructed the Euphrates between Ur and Larsa, delaying a long string of boats which have been tied up and are waiting until the government takes action. The king therefore dictates a letter ordering the governor of Larsa to clear the channel at the earliest moment and make it navigable again.

216. The king is much interested in his vast flocks of sheep, as if the nomad instinct had not altogether vanished from the blood of his line. He orders the offi- Hammurapi's let-cials to appear in Babylon to celebrate the ters: feasts and spring sheep-shearing like a great feast. The the calendar calendar has slipped forward a whole month in advance of the proper season, and the king sends out a circular letter to all the governors, saying "Since the year hath a deficiency, let the month which is now beginning be registered as a second [month of] Elul."

217. But he warns the governor that all taxes otherwise falling due within the next month are not to be deferred by this insertion. Delinquent tax-gatherers are Hammurapi's let-firmly reminded of their obligations and called ters: delinquents upon to settle without delay. Prompt punishment of an official guilty of bribery is authorized, and we can see the king's face darken as he dictates the order for the arrest of three officials of the palace gate who have fallen under his displeasure. More than once the governor of Larsa is sharply reminded of the king's orders and bidden to see that they are carried out immediately.

218. Many a petitioner who has not been able to secure justice before the board of judges in his home city is led in before the king, confident of just treatment; Hammurapi's let-and none is disappointed. The chief of the ters: justice and temple bakers finds that royal orders to look religion after a religious feast at Ur will call him away from the capital city just at the time when he has an important lawsuit coming on. He easily obtains an order from the king postponing the lawsuit. The king's interest in the religious feast is here as much concerned as his sense of justice, for many of the letters which he dictates have to do with temple property and temple administration.

219. With his eye thus upon every corner of the land, alert, vigorous, and full of decision, the great king finally saw how necessary it was to bring into uniformity all the various and sometimes conflicting laws and business customs of the land.

He therefore collected all the older written laws and usages of

Hammurapi's Code of Laws business and social life, going back to old Sumerian times. These he arranged systematically. He improved them or added new laws where his own judgment deemed wise, and then he combined them into a great code, or body, of laws. It was written, not in Sumerian, as some of the old laws were, but in the Semitic speech of the Akkadians and Amorites. He had it engraved upon a splendid shaft of stone. The new code was set up in the temple of the great god Marduk in Babylon. This shaft has survived to our day, the oldest preserved code of ancient law. Fragments of other copies on clay tablets, the copies used by the local courts, have also been found.

220. Hammurapi's code insists on justice to the widow, the or-

Spirit of Hammurapi's code; position of women phan, and the poor; but it also allows many of the old and simple ideas of justice to stand. Especially prominent is the principle that the punishment for an injury should require the infliction of the same injury on the culprit, —the principle of "an eye for an eye, a tooth for a tooth." Injustice often resulted. For example,

FIG. 100. *The* LAWS *of* HAMMURAPI, *the Oldest Surviving Code of Laws*

A diorite shaft nearly 8 feet high, bearing the laws, extending entirely around the shaft and occupying over 3600 lines. Above stands Hammurapi, at the left, receiving the laws from the Sungod, seated at the right, an impressive work of Semitic art, some 500 years later than Fig. 96

when a house fell (§ 186) and killed the son of the house-holder, the guilty builder must also suffer the loss of *his* son, and the innocent son was therefore condemned to die. Marriage was already a relation requiring legal agreements between the man and his wife, and these are carefully regulated in Hammurapi's code. Indeed, the position of woman in this early Babylonian world, as in Egypt, was a high one. Women engaged in business on their own account and even became professional scribes. They must have attended such a school as that described below in Fig. 101.

221. Thus regulated, the busy Babylonian communities prospered as never before. Their products were chiefly agricultural, especially grain and dates, but they Industries of Hammurapi's time had also flocks and herds, from which they obtained wool and leather. The weaving of wool was a great industry, for woolen clothing was commonly worn in Western Asia. Copper had been displaced by bronze, and one document refers to iron, but this metal was still much too rare to play any part in industry. Iron for common use was still nearly a thousand years in the future in Hammurapi's time.

222. A standing army kept the frontiers safe and quiet, and the slow donkey caravans of the Babylonian merchants, plodding from town to town, were able to Babylonian commerce in Hammurapi's time penetrate far into the surrounding communities. They were so common on the upper Euphrates that a town there was called Haran (or Kharan), from the Babylonian word *kharanu*, meaning "journey." Many a courtyard was piled high with bales, each bearing a clay seal with the impression of the merchant's name. These clay seals, broken away as the bales were opened, are found today lying in the rubbish of the Babylonian towns, where the modern excavator picks them up, still displaying on one side the merchant's name and on the other the impression of the cord which bound the bale.

223. Such seals and the clay-tablet bills which accompanied the bales had to be read by many a local merchant in the towns of Syria and beyond the passes of the northern moun-

tains. Thus Babylonian cuneiform writing slowly made its way through Western Asia, and the merchants of Syria and

Spread of cunei-
form writing
through Western
Asia

the Hittite country in Asia Minor began to write bills and letters of their own on clay tablets. Hammurapi's commercial influence was widely felt in the West. The memory of his name had not wholly died out in Syria-Palestine in Hebrew days a thousand years after his death.

224. While the Babylonian merchants were a powerful class and were even called the rulers in some communities,

Temples the cen-
ters of business

it was the temples, with their large possessions, which were the center of business life. They dealt in merchandise, controlled extensive lands, and loaned money (silver shekels; see § 202) like banks. The rate of interest on loans was high, — twenty per cent a year, payable in monthly installments. Silver had become so plentiful that it had decreased greatly in value. Gold was used sparingly, for it was from twelve to fifteen times as valuable as silver.

225. Commercial interests were therefore the leading influences in Babylonian life, even in religion. The temples,

Babylonian reli-
gion in Age of
Hammurapi

as we have said, had a large place in business life, and religion never proclaimed the rights of the poor and the humble or championed their cause against the rich and powerful. To be sure, the ritual of the temple contained some prayers which indicated a sense of sin and fear of divine displeasure. But the advantages of religion consisted in being able to obtain substantial benefits from the gods and to avoid their displeasure.

226. The people still worshiped the old Sumerian gods, but the political leadership of Babylon had enabled the men of

Marduk and Ishtar

that city to put their Semitic god Marduk at the head of all the gods, and in the old mythical stories they inserted the name "Marduk" where once the ancient Sumerian god Enlil had played the leading part. At the same time the great Asiatic goddess of love, Ishtar, rose to be the leading goddess of Babylon. She was later to

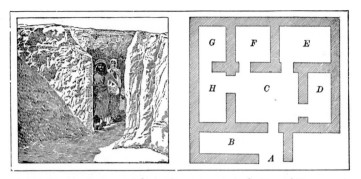

FIG. 101. *An Ancient Babylonian Schoolhouse in the Days of Hammurapi*

On the right is the ground plan of the schoolhouse, which was about 55 feet square. The children went in at the door (*A*), across the end of the long room (*B*), where the doorkeeper sat and perhaps kept a clay-tablet tardy-list of the pupils who came late. Then the children entered a court (*C*), which was open to the sky, and we may suppose that they separated here, the big boys and girls going into their own rooms, while the little ones went into others. Somewhere in the schoolhouse, and probably in the court (*C*), was a pile or box of soft clay, where a boy who had already filled his clay-tablet slate with wedge-marks could quickly make himself a new slate by flattening a ball of soft clay. On the left we look through one of the doors of this oldest schoolhouse in the world as it appeared on the day when it was uncovered by the French in 1894. The native Arab workmen who uncovered it stand in the doorway. The walls of sun-dried brick are still 8 or 9 feet high. (Drawing after Scheil)

pass over to the Mediterranean, there finally to become the Aphrodite of the Greeks and the Venus of the Romans.

227. Among the benefits granted by the gods was the ability to foretell the future. This art we call divination, and the priest who practiced it was a diviner. Already under the kings of Sumer and Akkad the skilled diviner could interpret the mysterious signs on the liver of the sheep slain in

Babylonian methods of reading the future, or divination

sacrifice, and his anxious inquirers believed that he could thus reveal the unknown future. He could note the positions of the stars and the planets, and in this manner he could discern the decrees of the gods for the future. These practices later spread westward. Under the Chaldeans star-reading developed into the art of astrology, and then later into the science of astronomy. We shall find the reading of the liver a common practice in Rome.

228. To train such men and to furnish clerks for business and government, schools were necessary. These were usually
Education: in or connected with the temple. A school-
a Babylonian house of the time of Hammurapi has actually
schoolhouse been uncovered, with the clay-tablet exercises
of the boys and girls of four thousand years ago still lying on the floor. They show how the child began his long and difficult task of learning to understand and to write over five hundred different signs.

229. The pupil's slate was a soft-clay tablet, on which he could rub out his exercises at any time by smoothing off the
Education: learn- surface with a flat piece of wood or stone.
ing to write With his reed stylus in his hand he made long
rows of single wedges in three positions, horizontal, vertical and oblique. When he could make the single wedges neatly enough, the master set him to work on the wedge-groups forming the signs themselves. Lastly, he was able to undertake words and simple phrases, leading up to sentences and quotations from old documents. One of the tablets found in the schoolhouse contains a proverb which shows how highly the Babylonians valued the art of writing. It reads: "He who shall excel in tablet-writing shall shine like the sun." Doubtless many a Babylonian lad was encouraged, in the long and wearisome task of learning to write, by copying this enthusiastic sentiment.

230. Of the higher life of Babylon in this age as expressed in great works of art and architecture very little has survived
Art and architec- on the spot. Indeed, the city of Hammurapi
ture in Hammu- has vanished. Not a single building erected
rapi's time by him now stands. Enough remains in other
Babylonian mounds to indicate that the arch had by this time assumed a prominent place on the fronts of buildings. The few pieces of sculpture found show little distinction. While the relief scene in which Hammurapi is represented as receiving the law from the Sun-god displays a certain fine dignity and impressiveness, it lacks the freedom and beauty of the Akkadian sculpture (Fig. 96). Even the work of the

lapidary in seal-cutting falls far short of the beauty which it had attained in the age of Sargon.

231. The decline in art was perhaps a prophecy of what was to come, for the Babylonian nation which Hammurapi had so splendidly organized and started on its way hardly survived his death. The Highland peoples, whom Hammurapi had driven out of the Sumerian cities, again descended upon the Babylonian Plain, as the Sumerians had probably done so long before. From the mountains of the east and northeast issued a rude Highland people called Kassites.[1] By gradual migration they filtered into the Fertile Crescent, especially after 1900 B.C., and settled in Babylonia. Hammurapi's successors seem to have been quite unable to keep them out. The Babylonians were now caught between two groups of invaders coming from opposite directions, for the Hittites advanced out of the northwest, and, moving down the Two Rivers, they captured Babylon itself and carried back the plunder of the city to their own country. This Hittite invasion was only a hurried raid, for the Hittites did not remain in Babylonia; but when they withdrew, they had completely overthrown the last of the great family of Hammurapi. Thus, about 1750 B.C., the rough and uncivilized Kassites, who were already settled in Babylonia, had no difficulty in making themselves masters of the country. Their triumph marked the end of old Babylonian progress in civilization. Until its revival under the Chaldeans, over a thousand years later, Babylonia relapsed into stagnation so complete that it was rarely interrupted.

Highlanders triumph over Hammurapi's line (about 1750 B.C.)

232. As we look back over this first chapter of early human progress along the Two Rivers we see that we have been able to follow it for about a thousand years, beginning probably 2900 B.C. The Sumerians laid the foundations of civilization in Shinar and began a thousand-year struggle with the Semites of the desert.

Summary and retrospect

---

[1] It was probably these Kassites who brought larger numbers of horses into Babylonia. although they did not appear in Egypt until some 200 years later (§ 125).

In spite of the mingling and union of the two races the Semites triumphed twice under two great leaders,— Sargon (Twenty-fifth Century B.C.) and Hammurapi (Twentieth Century B.C.). The Sumerians then disappeared, and the language of Babylonia became Semitic. The reign of Hammurapi, in spite of some deterioration in art, marks the highest point and the end of the thousand-year development,— the conclusion of the first great chapter of history along the Two Rivers. The scene of the second chapter will carry us up the river valley, just as it did in our study of the Nile.

QUESTIONS

Section 12. Describe the three geographic zones of the Great Northwest Quadrant and their population.

Section 13. Why was the Babylonian Plain long unsuited to settled life? Describe the Fertile Crescent. How can we summarize its history? Describe the life of the desert people. Into what lands did they shift at the west end of the Fertile Crescent? at the east end?

Section 14. Who were the early dwellers in the Plain of Shinar? Describe their writing materials and their writing. Were the Sumerians all united in one nation? List all the objects which an excavator might find in a Sumerian city mound.

Section 15. What outsiders defeated the Sumerians? Who was the first great Semitic king? What did the Akkadians accomplish in art?

Section 16. What nation resulted from the mingling of Sumerians and Akkadians? Discuss the development of trade and the rise of business methods. What became of the Sumerian language?

Section 17. Why may we call Hammurapi a great king? What city first became famous at this time?

BIBLIOGRAPHY FOR TOPICAL STUDIES

Industries and business: DELAPORTE, *Mesopotamia*, chap. iii; JOHNS, *Code*, §§ 4–126; WOOLLEY, *Sumerians*, pp. 112–119.

Royal tombs of Ur: GADD, *History and Monuments of Ur*, pp. 29–40; *Museum Journal of the University of Pennsylvania*, Vol. 19 (1928), pp. 5–34, Vol. 20 (1929), pp. 7–35, Vol. 22 (1931), pp. 248–260; WOOLLEY, *Sumerians*, pp. 35–40; *Ur of the Chaldees*, chap. ii.

Private houses: GADD, pp. 169–172; WOOLLEY, *Sumerians*, pp. 156–162: *Ur of the Chaldees*, pp. 164–171.

Chapter VI · Western Asia: The Assyrians and Chaldeans

Section 18. Early Assyria and her Western Rivals

233. The second chapter of history along the Two Rivers carries us up the river from Babylonia to the northeastern corner of the desert bay. Here was an easily defended elevation possessing a natural strength unknown to the towns in the flat Plain of Shinar. It overlooked the Tigris on the east and the desert on the west and south. The place was known as Assur

Situation of Assur, earliest capital of Assyria

Note. The headpiece shows an Assyrian King attacking a Fortified City (Ninth Century B.C.). A century before the Empire the Assyrians had already developed powerful appliances for destroying a city wall. The city at the right is protected by walls of sun-dried brick like those of Samal (Fig. 103). The defending archers on the wall are trying to drive away a huge Assyrian battering-ram, mounted on wheels, of which only the lower parts are visible, the upper parts being covered by the armor of the battering-ram, which is an ancient "tank" with its front protected by metal armor plate. It carries a fighting tower as high as the city wall, and Assyrians in the top of it direct arrows against the defenders of the wall. Within the tank unseen men work the heavy beam of the ram. It is capped with metal and is shown smashing a hole in the city wall, from which the bricks fall out. An observation tower, with a metal-covered dome and peep-holes, shields the officer in command as he directs operations. In the rear (at the left) is the Assyrian king shooting arrows into the hostile city. He uses a powerful bow, probably invented in Egypt, which will shoot an arrow with great force from 1000 to 1400 feet, and hence he can stand at a safe distance. A scene from the earliest Assyrian palace reliefs which have survived.

179

(see map, p. 146), which was likewise the name of its god; and it later gave its name also to the land of Assyria.

234. Being in a highland region, Assur enjoyed a climate much more invigorating than that of the hot Babylonian Climate, soil, and Plain. It had many fertile valleys winding products of Assyria up into the eastern and northern mountains, where rival cities were already in existence. It was a region where an occasional promontory of rock furnished quarries of limestone, alabaster, and harder stone. Herein Assyria differed greatly from Babylonia, which was without building stone and had therefore developed architecture in brick only. These eastern valleys were green with rolling pastures and billowing fields of barley and wheat. Herds of cattle and flocks of sheep and goats dotted the hillsides. Donkeys served as the chief draft animals, and the horse, while not unknown, was not common in the beginning. Here flourished an agricultural population, although the Assyrians finally built up also industries and trade.

235. This population of the region north of Babylonia was not purely Semitic but contained people of other tongues Founding of Assur and probably also of different races and blood. (2900 B.C.) under By 2900 B.C. there was already living at Assur Sumerian influence a small settlement of Sumerians, whose works of art have been excavated there. At the same time the men whom we call Assyrians were there. It is not wholly certain whence they came or whether they were of pure Semitic race; but they spoke a Semitic language closely related to that which was spoken at Akkad, where we have already seen the western Semites, led by Sargon, forming the first powerful Semitic kingdom in the Twenty-fifth Century B.C. The differences between the language of Akkad and that of Assur were hardly greater than we now find between the dialects of different parts of Germany. The men of Assur at first formed a tiny city-kingdom like those of their Sumerian neighbors in the south. They were in close contact with the Sumerians, whose sculpture and writing they adopted, along with many of the conveniences of Sumerian civilization.

236. While most of the *early* civilization of Assur thus came from the south, the little city-kingdom was equally exposed to influences from the north and west. In Asia Minor there were the hostile Hittite communities, some of which were venturing eastward to the Two Rivers. Assur was per-

Constant defensive warfare develops Assyrian military state

haps at times ruled by Hittite lords or other outsiders from the west, only to fall back again under the control of the south led by Sargon, the kings of Ur, Hammurapi, or some other ruler of Babylonia. Thus obliged, for over a thousand years after Sargon's reign, to defend their uncertain frontiers against their neighbors on both north and south, the Assyrians were toughened by the strain of unceasing war. The Assyrian state was therefore built up around the army, — at first militia and then a standing army, which became the chief strength of the government. This military state thus developed into a stable and powerful organization, unshaken by the rivalries of city-states such as those which so often weakened and finally overthrew Babylonia. Freed from such internal struggles, Assyria could muster her undivided strength and direct it against her foreign foes. The Assyrian kings early introduced the horse and added chariots to their army, which finally became the strongest military force the early world had yet seen.

237. At the same time commerce and traffic with surrounding nations brought wealth and power to the young nation. Attracted by the silver mines of southeastern Asia Minor (Cilicia, see map, p. 146), Assyrian merchants were drawn into commerce with the West. Assur thus became an

Assyrian merchants in Asia Minor (beginning in 23d Century B.C.)

important station on the trade route connecting the peoples in the mountains east of Assyria with those of the west. The Assyrian traders had learned the forms of business which were so highly developed in Ur under its kings of Sumer and Akkad, and settlements of these Assyrian merchants were established at various places in southeastern Asia Minor, in the region later known as Cappadocia. Here excavations have uncovered great quantities of the business records of these merchants in the form of cuneiform tablets like those of Assyria. They show us that these foreign merchants from the east continued to carry on business in Cappadocia for at least two hundred years, beginning while the kings of Sumer and Akkad were in power. We shall see later that these settlements from the east had an important part in carrying civilization farther west. Found, as they were, lying in the towns of southeastern Asia Minor, the clay tablets of these Assyrian merchants are for us today like milestones marking the march of civilization from the Two Rivers toward the southeastern part of Europe.

238. Access to the silver mines of Cilicia now greatly affected business and commerce, for silver rapidly displaced grain as a medium of exchange.

Plentiful silver introduces age of coined money

Fig. 102. *List of* Loans *of Silver made and* Securities *received by an Assyrian Merchant in Asia Minor named Enlil-bani*

Enlil-bani has carefully written out on this tablet a list of nine loans, all of silver, which various people are owing him. He did not make easy terms with these people, and the interest he charged ranged from 24 per cent to 30 per cent. Indeed, one unfortunate debtor was obliged to pay as interest 1½ shekels per month, or 18 shekels per year, on a loan of only 15 shekels, which shows that these Assyrian merchants had learned well the ways of the Babylonian business man

Small bars or rods of the metal, and likewise round pieces, were stamped with the weight of the piece and the name of the temple which had issued it. The caravans from the Two Rivers carried these forerunners of coin all over the Near East, and especially into central Asia Minor. Thus gradually began the age of metallic money. With it also arose the idea of credit. Among the tablets of the Assyrian merchants found in the ancient Hittite cities are some which state that each tablet represents so many shekels of silver. They are therefore practically checks or drafts sent in advance as payment for goods which the sender desires shall be forwarded to him. These tablets are the earliest known examples of credit transactions. It was from this region that the convenience of coined money and commercial operations of credit based on money finally passed into Greece and thence spread over Europe.

239. These connections with the west were of the greatest importance to Assyria. Not only did Assur need access to the metals produced by the west, but as an inland power it could not hope to rule Western Asia without access to the Mediterranean. *Western rivals of Assyria: Mitanni and the Phœnicians* Two serious obstacles lay between Assur and the western sea. In the bend of the Euphrates, right across the merchant roadways and caravan routes leading from Assyria to the west (see map, p. 146), was located the kingdom of Mitanni. The ruling class here were Indo-Europeans, descendants of those nomads of the northern grasslands who first learned to train horses (§ 316) and drill them for use in battle with the war chariot. Maintaining themselves on the Euphrates as the earliest known horse-breeding aristocracy, they made Mitanni a dangerous military state. The coming of the domestic horse was the beginning of a new age on the Fertile Crescent. When a squadron of chariots drawn by swift and heavy horses came thundering down upon infantry soldiers, they were scattered like autumn leaves. Driving their terrible chariots, the lords of Mitanni were able to carry their conquests northwestward across the Hittite frontiers. The Assyrians likewise were unable to stand against them. The Mitannians invaded Assyria, captured Nineveh, and for a time even held the Assyrians as a subject people. The second obstacle in the westward path of Assyria was her own kindred, the Semites, along the eastern coast of the Mediterranean. Here the harbor towns of the former Semitic nomads (§ 168)

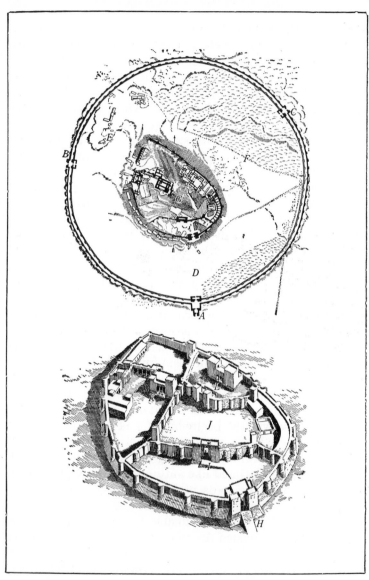

FIG. 103. The Aramean City of SAMAL, One of the Western Rivals of Assyria.
(Drawing after Von Luschan) *

had become a fringe of wealthy Phœnician city-kingdoms. These cities proved obstinate enemies of the Assyrian kings.

240. Besides the Mitannian horsemen and the Phœnician merchant princes of the west the Assyrians had to face also the dangerous hostility of a new Semitic migration which was both commercial and political. This new wave of Semitic nomads began to roll in upon the Fertile Crescent in the Sixteenth Century B.C. In the Fifteenth Century they were already trying to set up kingdoms on the western shores of the desert bay, that is, Palestine and Syria. These western nomads were the Hebrews in Palestine, and north of them the Arameans,[1] or Syrians, occupying Syria. We recall how the Hebrew nomads under Joshua began the conquest of Palestine, where they eventually gained possession of the whole country (see Chapter VII). They soon held the entire western end of the Fertile Crescent and aided in cutting off Assyria from the sea. After 1200 B.C. the Arameans established a group of flourishing kingdoms in the west. Here, under the influence of Hittite civilization on one side and Egyptian on the other, these Aramean kingdoms of Syria built royal cities and luxurious palaces filled with sumptuous furniture. Among the Aramean kingdoms of Syria the most powerful was Damascus.

New Semitic migration: Hebrews and Arameans

---

[1] The Arameans are often called Syrians, and the region north of Palestine (see map, p. 146) is commonly called Syria. These two names, Syria and Syrians, are not to be confused with Assyria and Assyrians.

---

* PLAN (on opposite page). The city was nearly half a mile across. It was defended by a double wall (*ABC*) of sun-dried brick on a heavy stone foundation. The wall was strengthened with towers every 50 feet, entirely around the city, making one hundred towers in all. The castle of the kings of Samal occupied a hill in the middle (*G*), and the houses of the townsmen filled the space between the city walls and the castle (*D, E, F*). These houses, built of sun-dried brick, have disappeared, but the castle can be restored.

RESTORATION OF THE CASTLE (*H, I, J, K, L*). This is the castle, or citadel, marked *G* in the city plan (on opposite page). The walls of sun-dried brick rest on heavy stone foundations widening at the base. Samal in north Syria, midway between the Mediterranean and the Euphrates, received influences both from the Hittites in Asia Minor and from Egypt. The columned porches (*K* and *L*) in front of the palaces were built on a Hittite plan, with columns suggested by Egyptian architecture. Hittite reliefs adorned this porch.

241. The energetic Aramean merchants extended their business far beyond their own kingdoms. They pushed

Peaceful penetration of Aramean commerce

their caravans all along the shores of the desert bay, even as far north as the sources of the Tigris, and they finally controlled the commerce of Western Asia. Their bronze weights, found in the ruins of Nineveh, show us how common were Aramean merchants in the Assyrian market places. Like their kinsmen the Jews in modern civilized states, although not organized as a single nation they were the great commercial leaders of the age.

242. The Arameans were a highly civilized race. By 1000 B.C., and probably several centuries earlier, they were

Aramean merchants spread first alphabet in Asia

using *alphabetic* writing, which they had borrowed from the Canaanites or the Phœnicians. It was the earliest system of writing known which employed *exclusively* alphabetic signs (Fig. 158). Along with the alphabet the Arameans received the Egyptian pen and ink also, conveniences indispensable in the use of the new alphabet. As the Babylonian caravans had in earlier times carried cuneiform tablets throughout Western Asia, so the Aramean caravans, with their bills and receipts, began to carry through the same region the alphabet which was to displace cuneiform signs. Thus the Phœnician-Aramean alphabet spread throughout Western Asia. It passed down the Euphrates to Persia, and, penetrating to the frontiers of India, even furnished the East Indian peoples with their (Sanskrit) alphabet.

243. The Aramean merchants of course carried their language (called Aramaic) with them, and Aramaic gradually

Assyrian and Aramaic side by side in business and government

became very common all around the desert bay. Indeed, in the old Assyrian communities the people who spoke Aramaic finally outnumbered the citizens of Assyrian speech. When an Aramean received a cuneiform tablet recording business matters in the Assyrian language, he sometimes took his pen and marked it with memoranda in Aramaic. Assyrian tablets bearing such notes in Aramaic have been found in the ruins of Assyrian buildings. Indeed, public business was finally carried on in both languages. Aramean clerks were appointed to government offices, and it was a very common thing for an Aramean official of the Assyrian Empire to keep his records on papyrus, writing with pen and ink on a roll, while his Assyrian associate in office wrote with a stylus on a tablet of clay.

Fig. 104. *An Aramean* King *of Samal and his* Secretary, *who holds an Egyptian Writing Outfit* (*Eighth Century* b.c.)

The king sits at the left on a richly carved throne of ebony, ivory, and gold, with a footstool of the same design. Before him stands his secretary, carrying under his left arm an object which is probably a papyrus roll, drawn in this manner so as to indicate that it is partially unrolled. In his left hand he holds an Egyptian writing case containing pen and ink. The flat relief in which the entire scene is carved had its origin on the Nile. From Syria, in such cities as Samal, it passed to Assyria, where it was immensely improved. (From a photograph by Von Luschan)

244. Aramaic finally became the language of the entire Fertile Crescent. It even displaced its very similar sister tongue, the Hebrew of Palestine, and thus the mercantile tongue of the Arameans, many centuries later, became the language spoken by Jesus and the other Hebrews of his time in Palestine. In the end this widespread commercial civilization of the Arameans left more lasting influences behind than even the powerful military state of the Assyrians. Unfortunately the Aramean city mounds of Syria, with one exception (Fig. 103), still remain unexcavated; hence we have recovered but few monuments to tell us of their builders. Damascus is still the largest city

Complete triumph of Aramaic along the Fertile Crescent

FIG. 105. *Assyrian and Aramean Scribes* RECORDING THE PLUNDER *taken from a Captured Asiatic City (Eighth Century* B.C.*)*

The captive women and children ride by in ox-carts on their way to slavery in Assyria, and a shepherd drives off the captured flocks. At the left an Assyrian officer reads from a tablet his notes of the spoil taken in the city. Two scribes write as he reads. The first (in front) holds in his left hand a thick *clay tablet*, from which he has just lifted the stylus, grasped in his right hand, as he pauses in his writing. The other scribe holds spread out on his left hand a *roll of papyrus*, on which he is busily writing with a pen held in his right hand. He is an Aramean, writing Aramaic with pen and ink. We see here, then, the two different methods of writing practiced at this time in Western Asia, — the outgoing Asiatic clay tablet and the incoming Egyptian paper, pen, and ink

of Syria, having nearly two hundred thousand inhabitants; but the ruins of all the ancient Aramean buildings must now lie under those of the modern city, and therefore it is unlikely that ancient Damascus will ever be unearthed.

245. We now understand that as the Assyrian armies faced the west they looked out upon an array of hostile nations which might have dismayed any people, however brave. In the foreground were the horsemen of Mitanni; behind them the powerful commercial cities of the Arameans, especially

Damascus; while farther in the rear, along the eastern end of the Mediterranean, was the line of flourishing harbor cities of the Phœnicians. In the far background rose the two mighty world-powers: Egypt on the southwest and the Hittites (Section 27) on the northwest. Undoubtedly the Assyrians remembered that the Hittites had once captured Babylon, and, as we shall later learn, the Hittites had now become a large and powerful empire. By the Fifteenth Century B.C. this Hittite Empire was a worthy rival of Egypt. The Assyrians watched the tremendous struggle between these two great powers for possession of the western end of the Fertile Crescent, which ended in a drawn battle in the Thirteenth Century B.C. They saw both of these powerful western rivals sorely weakened by the struggle until, toward 1200 B.C., as it was further weakened by invasion from behind, the Hittite Empire fell. Half a century later the empire of Egypt also collapsed. Mitanni had at first thrown in her lot with Egypt, but eventually the kingdom of the Mitannian horsemen was also crushed in the far-reaching international struggle. The leading contestants in the Near-Eastern arena had been three — Egypt, Assyria, and the Hittites — struggling in a three-cornered rivalry. By 1150 B.C. the two great western powers had fallen, leaving Assyria to inherit the empire of the East.

Fall of Assyria's greatest rivals: Hittites and Egyptians

246. Confronting Assyria in the west, after the fall of Mitanni, of Egypt, and of the Hittites, there still remained the powerful mercantile civilizations of the western Semites, — the line of harbor towns on the Phœnician coast and the Syrian cities of the Arameans farther inland, especially Damascus. As wealthy commercial rulers the Aramean kings of Damascus were long able to make their city so strong as to block any effort at permanent advance by Assyria toward the Mediterranean. One of the best illustrations of the effect of their power is the fact that for a considerable length of time Damascus sheltered the two little Hebrew kingdoms

Stubborn resistance of Assyria's smaller western rivals

from Assyrian attack (see map, p. 146). The Assyrian armies had marched westward and had crossed the Euphrates by 1300 B.C. They had looked out upon the Mediterranean by 1100 B.C., but for more than three and a half centuries after this the kings of Assur were unable to conquer and hold this western region against the strong group of Aramean, Phœnician, and Hebrew kingdoms. These western kingdoms thus held the Assyrian armies at bay until the Eighth Century B.C. It is important to remember, furthermore, that Assyria had dangerous enemies also in the Highland Zone on her north and east, while on the south was Babylon, likewise often a menace.

247. As Assyrian power after 1000 B.C. thus seemed to pause at the threshold of her coming empire, let us look back for a moment over the long two thousand years of development and see what progress Assur had made in civilization. Until nearly 2000 B.C. the Assyrians, like the Egyptians and Babylonians, used tools of copper. Then the discovery was made, probably by some northern people, that a small amount of tin mixed with copper would produce *bronze*, an alloy much harder and much more easily melted than pure copper. Tools of bronze were very much more effective, and weapons of bronze were far more dangerous, than any which could be made ot copper. The Age of Bronze lasted from about 2000 B.C. to about 1000 B.C. Thus the Assyrian armies which marched westward before 1000 B.C. bore weapons of bronze, but after this time iron weapons were obtainable. Iron was already known to man in prehistoric days, but it remained a rarity until the Hittites discovered it in northeastern Asia Minor. From the Thirteenth Century onward the Hittite kings distributed iron throughout the Near East. It was therefore in the first centuries of the Age of Iron [1] that the

Growth of Assyrian civilization before the Empire

---

[1] The three ages of metal are easily remembered :

The Copper Age, from the Fourth Millennium to about 2000 B.C.
The Bronze Age, from about 2000 to about 1000 B.C.
The Iron Age, from about 1000 B.C. to the modern Age of Steel.

Assyrians were preparing for western conquests, and their success was due, to a large extent, to the use of this metal in warfare.

248. Besides metal the west, particularly the Hittites, brought into Assyrian life other things important to civilization. Under influences from the Hittite art of north Syria the sculptors of Assur learned to tell the story of the king's valiant exploits in elaborate stone pictures cut in flat relief on great slabs of alabaster (Fig. 109 and headpiece, p. 179). These were set up in long rows along the palace walls. As in sculpture, so in architecture, the possession of stone enabled the Assyrians to do what had been impossible in almost stoneless Babylonia. The Assyrian builders could erect heavy foundations of stone under their buildings, as the Hittites and Syrians had long been doing. Above the foundation the Assyrian building itself, however, usually continued to be made of sun-dried brick, as in Babylonia.

Western contributions to Assyrian art and architecture

249. Many of the sacred stories and symbols of the gods which had grown up among the Babylonian communities were taken over by the men of Assur, who copied and studied and revered them; but the Assyrians clung to their old tribal god Assur, from whom came the name of their city and their tribe. In the earlier times, when the Assyrians were still chiefly tillers of the soil, they seem to have thought of Assur as a god of the dying and ever-reviving vegetation, like Osiris in Egypt. However that may be, Assur's oldest symbol was the tree of life, which the Assyrians set up and decorated every spring like a Maypole. Later, when Assyria became a nation of soldiers, they believed that Assur was a fierce god of war, whom they identified with the sun. Religion among the warlike Assyrians, as in Babylonia, had little effect upon the conduct of the worshiper. One reason for this was the fact that the Assyrians had much the same notions of the hereafter as the Babylonians, with no belief in a judgment to come.

Religion of Assur

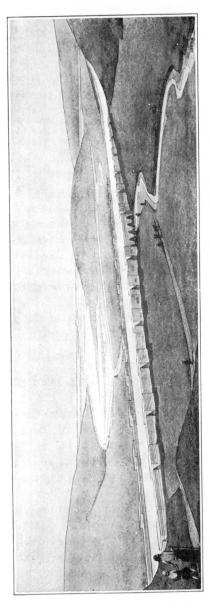

FIG. 106. THE OLDEST KNOWN AQUEDUCT: *Constructed by Sennacherib*

The remains of this remarkable feat of engineering skill were excavated in 1933 by the Oriental Institute of the University of Chicago. The aqueduct was a part of Sennacherib's great irrigation project for conveying water from the northern mountains thirty miles away to the fields around Nineveh. Finding that they must carry the water across a small river, the Assyrian engineers constructed a large stone-masonry channel over 900 feet long and almost 80 feet wide, along which the water flowed between parapets 9 feet wide. The water was thus carried not only across the little river, as if on a bridge, but also across the river valley, which was about 1000 feet wide. (Reconstruction and drawing by Seton Lloyd)

SECTION 19. THE ASSYRIAN EMPIRE (ABOUT 750 TO 612 B.C.)

250. While the great object of Assyrian expansion was the conquest of the west, in order to gain a foothold on the Mediterranean and to control the trade routes between the east and the west, hostile neighbors in the north, east, and south had often obliged the Assyrian kings to send their armies into these regions. They descended the Tigris with such power that they even captured and ruled for a time their old conqueror Babylon, while it was still under the rule of the half-barbaric Kassites.

Continued westward expansion of Assyria

After serious reverses Assyria was again pushing her plans of westward expansion by the middle of the Eighth Century B.C. Damascus, combined with the other western kingdoms, made a desperate resistance, only to be slowly crushed When at last Damascus fell (732 B.C.), the countries of the west were all subdued and made subject kingdoms. Thus the once obscure little city of Assur gained the lordship over Western Asia as head of an empire, a great group of conquered and vassal nations. The story of that empire forms the second great chapter of history along the Two Rivers.

251. In the midst of these great western campaigns of Assyria, while besieging the unhappy Hebrew city of Samaria, the Assyrian king died (722 B.C.,) and the throne then passed to his son. As king this prince took the name of Sargon, the first great Semite of Babylonia, who had reigned eighteen hundred years earlier. The new Sargon, whom we call Sargon II, raised Assyria to the height of her grandeur and power as a military empire. His descendants were the great emperors of Assyria.[1] On the northeast of Nineveh he built a new royal residence on a vaster scale and more magnificent than any Asia had ever seen before. He called it *Dur-Sharrukin* (Sar-

Sargon II of Assyria (722–705 B.C.)

---

[1] The leading kings of the dynasty of Sargon II are as follows:

Sargon II	722–705 B.C.
Sennacherib	705–681 B.C.
Esarhaddon	681–668 B.C.
Assurbanipal (called Sardanapalus by the Greeks)	668–626 B.C.

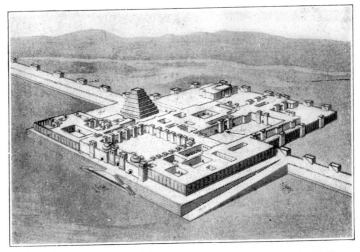

FIG. 107. *Restoration of the* PALACE *and a Portion of the* CITY *of Sargonburg,*
the Royal Residence of Sargon II

The palace stands partly inside and partly outside of the city wall, on a vast
elevated platform of brick masonry containing about 25 acres. Inclined roadways
and stairways rise on the *inside* of the city wall. The king could thus drive up in
his chariot from the streets of the city below to the palace pavement above. The
rooms and halls are clustered about a number of courts open to the sky. The
main entrance (with stairs before it leading down to the city) is adorned with
massive towers and arched doorways built of richly colored glazed brick and em-
bellished with huge human-headed bulls carved of alabaster. The streets and
houses of the city filled the space below the palace within the city walls, which
could accommodate some eighty thousand people. The Oriental Institute of The
University of Chicago is now engaged in completing the excavation of this city
and palace (see Fig. 108). (Drawing after Place)

gonburg). Babylonia in her greatest days had never possessed
a seat of power like this. In no uncertain terms it proclaimed
Assyria mistress of Western Asia.

252. The grandeur of Sargon II was even surpassed by his
son Sennacherib, one of the great statesmen of the early

Sennacherib   Orient. Far up in Asia Minor the name of
(705–681 B.C.)   Sennacherib was known and feared after he
plundered Tarsus and the easternmost Ionian Greek strongholds just after 700 B.C. Thence his campaigns swept southward, where he captured the Phœnician harbor towns along

FIG. 108. *A Colossal* WINGED BULL *from the Palace of Sargon*

The entrances to Assyrian palaces were usually guarded by a pair of these huge human-headed bulls. The one shown here is from the palace gateway at Sargon-burg (position indicated by arrow in Fig. 107). It now stands in the exhibition halls of the Oriental Institute at The University of Chicago. The figure, carved in calcareous stone similar to alabaster, is sixteen feet high and weighs forty tons. The excavation, transportation to the United States, and preparation for exhibition of this remarkable piece of sculpture therefore formed a very difficult task

the Mediterranean to the very borders of Egypt. To be sure, much of Sennacherib's army was destroyed by a pest from the Delta marshes, which the Hebrews regarded as the angel of the Lord (Yahveh); hence Sennacherib never crossed the Egyptian frontier. But against Babylon, his other ancient rival, he adopted the severest measures. Exasperated by one revolt after another, Sennacherib completely destroyed the venerable city of Hammurapi and even turned the waters of a canal over the desolate ruins.

253. Thus Babylon was annihilated, but the ancient power on the Nile remained a continual disturber of Assyrian con-

Egypt conquered by Assyria

trol. A crushing burden of Assyrian tribute had been laid on all subject states, and hence Egypt was constantly able to stir up revolt among the oppressed western peoples, who longed to be freed from the payment of this tribute. Assyria perceived that Egypt's interference must be stopped. Sennacherib's son therefore appeared before the gates of the eastern Delta forts by 674 B.C. Repulsed at first, he returned to the attack; and, although he died before entering the Delta, Egypt at last fell a prey to the Assyrian armies, and Sennacherib's grandson was for a time lord of the lower Nile.

254. By 700 B.C. the Assyrian Empire included all of the Fertile Crescent. It thus extended entirely around the great

Extent of the Assyrian Empire

desert bay, but it included furthermore much of the northern mountain country far behind. The conquest of Egypt gave it also the lower Nile valley in the west, though this last was too distant and too detached to be kept long. Built up by irresistible and far-reaching military campaigns which went on for two generations after Sargon II, the Assyrian conquests finally formed the most extensive empire the world had yet seen.

255. Sennacherib was not satisfied merely to enlarge the old royal residences of his fathers at Assur or at Sargonburg.

Nineveh becomes Assyrian capital

He devoted himself to the city of Nineveh, north of Assur, and it now became the farfamed capital of Assyria. To secure for the city a sufficient water supply Sennacherib connected it with the streams of the northern mountains by a canal with a magnificent aqueduct (Fig. 106), the oldest aqueduct known. Along the Tigris vast palaces and imposing tower-temples of the Assyrian emperors arose, reign after reign. The lofty and massive walls of Nineveh, which Sennacherib built, stretched two miles and a half along the banks of the Tigris, and it was about eight miles around the inner walls of the city. Here in his gorgeous palace he ruled the Western Asiatic

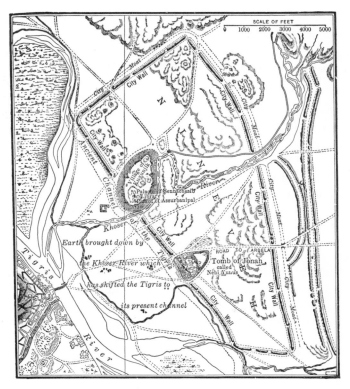

Sketch Map of NINEVEH

Notice the changes in the course of the Tigris, which formerly probably flowed along the west wall of the city. This change has been caused by the Khoser River, which has carried down soil and formed a plain between the wall of the city and the Tigris. In Fig. 199 we have a view from Nebi Yunis, the mound which covers the ruins of the palace of Esarhaddon; and we look along the city wall to the Mound of Kuyunjik. This mound covers the palaces of Sennacherib and Assurbanipal. The remainder of the city was filled with houses and shops of the citizens, and all these less important buildings have disappeared. A destructive overflow of the Khoser River, which flooded the city and broke down a section of the eastern wall, was one of the chief causes of the fall of Nineveh

world with an iron hand, and collected tribute from all the subject peoples, among whom the Hebrews were included.

256. The whole administration centered in the king's business office. He maintained a system of royal messengers.

The earliest known road-building in Asia now began, and the most ancient surviving road there was built by Sargon II to

Means of communication and organization of Assyrian Empire

connect Nineveh with his palace-town of Sargonburg. In each of the more important places on the main roads the king appointed an official to attend to the transmission of all royal business. In this manner all clay-tablet letters, produce, and merchandise belonging to the royal house were sure of being forwarded. This organization formed the beginnings of a postal system[1] which continued for many centuries in the Ancient Near East. The emperor received the letters and reports of over three score governors of districts and provinces, besides those of many subject kings who were sometimes allowed to continue their rule under Assyrian control. We even have a number of clay-tablet letters dispatched by Sennacherib himself while he was crown prince, and addressed to his royal father, Sargon. To maintain the army was the chief work of the state. The state was a vast military machine, more terrible than any mankind had ever yet seen. We shall understand this situation if we imagine the war department to be the central office in Washington or London, with the government devoting itself chiefly to supporting it.

257. We recall that the Assyrian forces were the *first large armies completely equipped with weapons of iron.* The bulk

The weapons of the Assyrians

of the Assyrian army was composed of archers, supported by heavy-armed spearmen and shield-bearers. Furthermore, Assyria had without doubt learned much from the skillful horsemen of Mitanni (§ 239). The famous horsemen and chariotry of Nineveh became the scourge of the East. For the first time, too, the Assyrians employed the battering-ram and formidable siege machinery. The sun-dried brick walls of the Asiatic cities could thus be battered down or pierced, and no fortified place could long repulse the assaults of the fierce Assyrian infantry.

---

[1] There are indications that it was already in existence in Asia, under Egyptian rule, as far back as 2000 B.C.

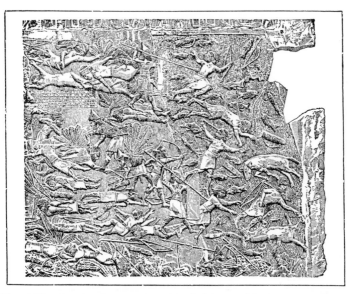

FIG. 109. *Assyrian* SOLDIERS *pursuing the* FLEEING ENEMY *across a Stream*

The stream occupies the right half of the scene. As drawn by the Assyrian artist, it may be recognized by the fish and the curling waves; also by the bows and quivers full of arrows floating downstream, along with the bodies of two dead horses, one on his back with feet up. Two dead men, with arrows sticking in their bodies, are drifting in midstream. Three of the living leap from the bank as their pursuers stab them with spears or shoot them with drawn bow. The Assyrian spearmen carry tall shields, but the archer needs both hands for his bow and carries no shield. The dead are strewn along the shore, occupying the left half of the scene. At the top the vultures are plucking out their eyes; in the middle an Assyrian is cutting off a head; beside him another plants his foot on a dead man's head and steals his weapons. The vegetation along the river is shown among the bodies, with abandoned weapons scattered between

258. Besides their iron weapons and their war machines the Assyrian soldiers displayed a certain inborn ferocity which held all Western Asia in abject terror before *The terrors of the* the thundering squadrons of the Ninevites.[1] *Assyrian army* Wherever the terrible Assyrian armies swept through the land they left a trail of ruin and desolation behind. Around smoking heaps which had once been towns stretched lines of tall stakes, on which were stuck the bodies of rebellious rulers

[1] See Nahum iii, 2–3.

impaled alive, while all around rose mounds and piles of the slaughtered, heaped up to celebrate the great king's triumph and serve as a warning to all revolters. Through clouds of dust rising along all the main roads of the Empire the men of the subject kingdoms beheld great herds of cattle, horses, and asses, flocks of goats and sheep, and long lines of camels loaded with gold and silver (the wealth of the conquered), converging upon the palace at Nineveh. Before them marched the chief men of the plundered kingdoms, with the severed heads of their former princes tied about their necks. As Assurbanipal sat at the banquet table and feasted with his queen in a garden bower, amid birds, fruit, flowers, and music, he looked up at the severed head of the King of Elam hanging on a tree before him.

259. While the wealth plundered from these defeated kings was necessary for the support of the army, it also served

Civilization of the Assyrian Empire: architecture

higher purposes. The Assyrian palaces were now imposing buildings, suggesting in architecture the far-reaching power of their builder. In the hands of the Assyrian architects the arch, inherited from Babylonia, for the first time became an imposing monumental feature of architecture. The impressive triple arches of the Assyrian palace entrance, faced with glazed brick in gorgeous colors, were the ancestors of the Roman triumphal arches (Fig. 243). On either side were gigantic human-headed bulls wrought in alabaster (Fig. 108), and above the whole towered lofty castellated walls of baked brick, visible far across the royal city.

260. Within the palace, as a dado running along the lower portion of the walls, were thousands of feet of relief pictures

Civilization of the Assyrian Empire: sculpture; music

cut in alabaster. At Nineveh, in a single mound, the excavators cleared seventy-one palace halls and laid bare nearly two miles of such relief scenes, many of which they carried away to the British Museum. These sculptures show much improvement over the work (headpiece, p. 179) of a century before the Empire. They display especially the great deeds of the

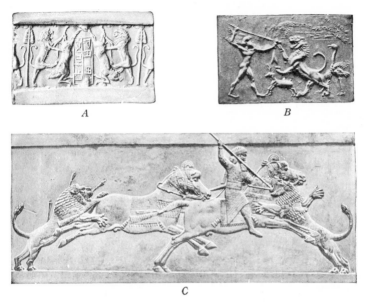

A   B

C

FIG. 110. ANIMAL SCULPTURE of the Babylonians and Assyrians

Seal *A* represents the wonderful work of a Babylonian seal-cutter in the time of Sargon of Akkad (§ 199). In balanced heraldic arrangement a lion is twice shown slaying a wild bull. A free and splendidly vigorous treatment of the old subject of combat between man and beast (Fig. 87) is found in Seal *B*. The ostrich adds a humorous touch which indicates that even the somber Assyrian could smile. In the lion hunt (*C*) we have one of the best examples of Assyrian relief sculpture of the reign of Assurbanipal. It clearly shows the influence of the early Babylonian seals on animal sculpture

emperor in campaign and hunting field. The human figures are monotonously alike, hard, cold, and unfeeling; nowhere is there a human form which shows any trace of feeling, either joy or sorrow, pleasure or pain. The Assyrian sculptor's wild beasts, however, are sometimes magnificent in the abandon of animal ferocity which they display. The tiger was in the blood of the Assyrian, and it came out in the work of his chisel. On the other hand, the pathetic expression of suffering exhibited by some of these wonderful animal forms was a triumph of art which the Assyrian sculptor owed to a study of the superb lions and bulls on the exquisite old Babylonian

Fig. 111. *The Egyptian* Well Sweep *introduced into Assyria*

With regard to his introduction into Assyria of the Egyptian well sweep (or *shadoof*; cf. Fig. 25) Sennacherib says, ''That daily there might be an abundant flow of water of the buckets, I had copper cables and pails made, and instead of pillars I set up great posts and cross-beams over the well-shafts.'' Then he had reliefs carved on his palace walls, picturing his people using the new device

seals of the age of Sargon of Akkad, nearly two thousand years earlier. Nevertheless the animal sculpture of Assyria was never surpassed, if ever equaled, by any other ancient people. The art of portraiture in statue form never got beyond very crude and unskillful efforts. A tablet recently (1924) discovered in the Berlin Museum contains a poem accompanied by a hitherto unknown system of musical notes intended for musical instruments. This oldest known musical notation shows a scale of five tones and a range of four of these scales. It was played upon a harp of twenty-two strings, an instrument common to the later Mediterranean world, and especially to Egypt. The Assyrians perhaps inherited this musical notation from Babylonia.

261. The emperors were obliged to depend much on foreign skill, both in art and in industries. The art of glazing colored brick had been borrowed from Egypt (§ 98). All the patterns of Assyrian decorative art likewise came from Egypt, and their furniture of ebony and ivory, made by Phœnician workmen, often betrays Egyptian origin. Phœnician craftsmen at Nineveh wrought splendidly engraved bronze platters. Sennacherib tells us that he had in his palace ''a portico patterned after a Hittite palace '' and

Assyrian borrow-
ing from abroad

his predecessors had long before built similar porticos like those they had seen in the Hittite west. It is in this ability to use foreign resources that we must recognize one of the greatest traits of the Assyrian emperors.

262. By means of his new canal and aqueduct Sennacherib was able to irrigate the fine gardens which he laid out along the river above and below Nineveh. Here he planted strange trees and plants from all quarters of his great empire. Among them were cotton trees, of which he says, "The trees that bore wool they clipped and they carded it for garments." These cotton trees came from India. We thus see appearing for the first time in the ancient world the cotton which now furnishes so large a part of our own national wealth.[1] These imports from distant regions show us how far-reaching were the foreign connections of the Assyrian Empire.

Introduction of foreign plants, including the earliest cotton

263. Higher interests were also cultivated among the Assyrians, and literature flourished. Sargon II had already begun collecting a tablet library of old writings, and his successors continued this interest in literature. Assurbanipal, the last great Assyrian emperor and the grandson of Sennacherib, boasts that his father instructed him not only in riding and shooting with bow and arrow but also in writing on clay tablets and in all the wisdom of his time. A great collection of twenty-two thousand clay tablets was discovered in Assurbanipal's fallen library rooms at Nineveh, where they had been lying on the floor for twenty-five hundred years. They are now in the British Museum. In this library the religious, scientific, and literary works of past ages had been systematically collected by the emperor's orders. These collections of tablets, begun under Sargon II, were the earliest libraries known in Asia. The Assyrians were far more advanced in these matters than the Babylonians, and Assyrian civilization was far from being a mere echo of Babylonian culture.

Assurbanipal's library

[1] This cotton tree was doubtless related to the lower-growing cotton plant of our Southern states.

Fig. 112. *Portion of Old Babylonian* Story of the Flood *from Assurbanipal's Library at Nineveh*

This large, flat tablet was part of an Assyrian cuneiform book consisting of a series of such tablets. This flood story tells how the hero, Ut-napishtim, built a great ship and thus survived a terrible flood, in which all his countrymen perished. Each of these clay-tablet books, collected in fresh copies by Assurbanipal for his library, bore a mark indicating the king's ownership, just like a bookplate in a modern library. To prevent anyone else from taking the book, or writing his name on it, the Assyrian king's bookplate contained the following warning: "Whosoever shall carry off this tablet, or shall inscribe his name upon it side by side with mine own, may Assur and Belit overthrow him in wrath and anger, and may they destroy his name and posterity in the land"

264. The social and business life of the Assyrians was regulated by a code of laws, which has unfortunately perished. In the ruins of the city of Assur, however, the German excavators found clay tablets forming part of a law book and containing the substance of nearly sixty laws. They reveal the strictest governmental control of marriage and of property rights. For transgressions of the law the punishments decreed are revoltingly cruel, quite commonly including, besides the death penalty, mutilations like the cutting off of fingers, ears, or nose, and even the tearing out of eyes. This over- *Internal decay; economic and agricultural decline* rigorous control of internal affairs by the Assyrian emperors included a serious mistake in policy. Their wars of conquest led to the destruction of the industrial and wealth-producing population, first within their own territory and then throughout the subject kingdoms. In spite of interest in introducing a new textile like cotton, the Assyrian rulers did not or could not build up industries or commerce like those of Babylonia. The people were chiefly agricultural, and in the old days it had sufficed to call them from their farming for short periods to defend the frontiers. With the expansion of the Empire, however, such temporary bodies of troops were insufficient, and the peasants were *permanently taken from the fields* to fill the ranks of an ever-growing standing army. It is not improbable that the ruling class was buying up the small farms to form great estates. We learn of disused canals and idle fields as we read of Sargon's efforts to restore the old farming communities. Nevertheless, so vast an expansion of the Empire exceeded the power of the standing army to defend it.

265. As reports of new revolts came in, the harassed ruler at Nineveh forced the subjects of his foreign vassal kingdoms to enter the army. With an army made up, *Foreign levies in the army; Arameans controlling trade* to a dangerous extent, of such foreigners, with industries declining, with fields lying idle, with the commerce of the country in the hands of the Aramean traders, and with Aramean speech more common in the cities of the Empire, even in Nineveh, than that of the Assyrians themselves, — under these conditions the Assyrian nation fast lost its inner strength.

266. In addition to such weakness within, there were the most threatening dangers from without. These came, as of old, from both sides of the Fertile Crescent. Drifting in from the desert, the Aramean hordes were constantly occupying the territory of the Empire. Sennacherib in one campaign took more than two hundred thousand captives out of Babylonia, mostly Arameans. At the same time another desert tribe called the Kaldi, whom we know as the Chaldeans, had been for centuries creeping slowly around the head of the Persian Gulf and settling along its shores at the foot of the eastern mountains. They were Semitic nomads, repeating what the Akkadians had done in Akkad and the Amorites in Babylon (§§ 195, 211).

Assaults from without: Chaldeans from the desert

267. On the other hand, in the northern mountains the advancing hordes of Indo-European peoples had been in full view since the incoming of the Mitannian horsemen. Mitanni had long ago disappeared, and the Indo-Europeans were now led by the tribes of the Medes and Persians. These migrations shook the Assyrian state to its foundations. By 616 B.C. the Chaldeans had mastered Babylonia. Nabopolassar, the new Chaldean king at Babylon, who called himself " King of Akkad," marched against the Assyrians and, having twice defeated them, conquered as far north as their earliest capital at Assur, which he failed to capture. The next year (614 B.C.), however, the Medes from the northeastern mountains marched down the Tigris and captured Assur. Nabopolassar arrived too late to share in the assault; but he established an alliance with Cyaxares, the Median king, and together they attacked Nineveh.

Assaults from without: Indo-Europeans from the mountains

268. Weakened by a generation of decline within, the once irresistible armies of Nineveh struggled for two years against this combined assault from without, and then the mighty city of the Assyrian emperors fell (612 B.C.). In the voice of the Hebrew prophet Nahum [1] we hear an echo of the exulting shout which resounded from the Caspian to the Nile as the nations discovered that the terrible scourge of the East had at last been

Fall of Assyria; destruction of Nineveh (612 B.C.)

[1] Nahum ii, 8, 13, and iii entire.

laid low. Its fall was forever; and when two centuries later Xenophon and his ten thousand Greeks marched past the place, the Assyrian nation was but a vague tradition, and Nineveh, its great city, was a vast heap of rubbish as it is today. Even Assyrian speech passed away, and Aramaic became the tongue of the region which had once been Assyria, just as it was also to become the language of Babylonia. The second great chapter of history on the Two Rivers was ended, having lasted but a scant century and a half (about 750 to 612 B.C.).

269. The fall of Assyria, while dramatically sudden and tragically complete, nevertheless left the nations of Western Asia in a very different situation from that in which the first Assyrian emperors had found them. The rule of a single sovereign had been *Progress effected by the Assyrian Empire* enforced upon the whole great group of nations around the eastern end of the Mediterranean, bringing these nations together in constant intercourse and thus for the first time creating a Near Eastern world having a common civilization. The methods of governing such an empire had been much improved. It was really in continuance of this organization that the great Persian Empire was built up, sixty years after the fall of Assyria. The Assyrian Empire, especially in its military organization, marked a long step forward in that gradual growth of the idea of all-including world power which culminated at last in the Roman Empire. In spite of its often ferocious harshness the Assyrian rule had furthered civilization. The building of the magnificent palaces in and near Nineveh formed the first chapter in great architecture in Asia. At the same time Nineveh possessed the first libraries as yet known there. Finally, the Assyrian dominion, as we shall see, created the international situation which enabled the Hebrews to gain the loftiest conceptions of their own God, as it obliged them to match him against the great war god of Assyria, — conceptions which have profoundly influenced the entire later history of mankind.

Section 20. The Chaldean Empire: the Last Semitic Empire

270. The Chaldeans, the new masters of Babylonia, now founded an empire whose brief career formed the third great **Rise of the Chaldean Empire** chapter of history on the Two Rivers.[1] They were the last Semitic lords of Babylonia. The Chaldeans made their capital at Babylon, rebuilt after its destruction by Sennacherib. They called the land Akkad, although we now know it as Chaldea. While they left the Medes in possession of the northern mountains, the empire of the Chaldeans included the entire Fertile Crescent.

271. At Babylon, Nebuchadnezzar, the greatest of the Chaldean emperors, now (604 B.C.) began a reign of over **Reign of Nebuchadnezzar (604–561 B. C.)** forty years, — a reign of such power and magnificence, especially as reflected to us in the Bible, that he has become one of the great figures of Oriental history. Exasperated by the obstinate revolts encouraged by Egypt in the west, Nebuchadnezzar punished the western nations, especially the little Hebrew kingdom of Judah. He finally carried away many Hebrews as captives to Babylonia and destroyed Jerusalem, their capital (586 B.C.).

272. In spite of long and serious wars the great king found time and wealth to devote to the enlargement and beautifi- **Magnificent buildings of Chaldean Babylon** cation of Babylon. Copying much from Assyria, Nebuchadnezzar was able to surpass his Assyrian predecessors in the splendor of the great buildings which he now erected. In the large temple quarter in the south of the city he rebuilt the temples of the

---

[1] The three great chapters of history on the Two Rivers are:

1. Early Babylonia, about 2900 to 1750 B.C. (Sargon I, about 2500 B.C.; Hammurapi, about 1948–1905 B.C.). See Sections 14–17.

2. The Assyrian Empire, about 750–612 B.C. See Section 19.

3. The Chaldean Empire, about 612–538 B.C. See Section 20.

With the exception of parts of the first, these three epochs were periods of *Semitic* power. To these we might in later times add a *fourth* period of Semitic supremacy, — the triumph of Islam in the Seventh Century A.D., after the death of Mohammed (§ 1191).

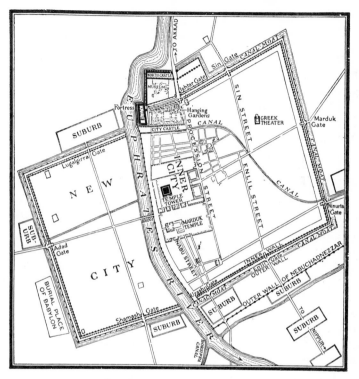

Plan of BABYLON *in the Chaldean Age*

This new plan of Nebuchadnezzar's city is based not only on the remains of buildings and streets as revealed by excavation, but also on ancient clay-tablet maps of Babylon found by the excavators. Such maps are evidence that Babylon, like certain other ancient cities (§ 131), was a "monumental city" built according to a city plan. (After Unger)

long-revered Babylonian divinities. Leading from these to the palace he laid out a festival avenue, or Procession Street, which passed through an imposing gateway called the Ishtar Gate, for it was dedicated to this goddess. Behind it lay the vast imperial palace and the offices of government, while high over all towered the temple-mount, which rose by the Marduk temple as a veritable Tower of Babel. Masses of rich tropical verdure, rising in terrace upon terrace and

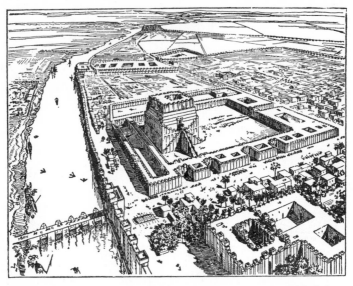

Fɪɢ. 113. *The* Rᴇꜱᴛᴏʀᴀᴛɪᴏɴ *of the City of* Bᴀʙʏʟᴏɴ *in the Age of* N*ebuchadnezzar*

The tower (cf. §182) in the foreground is the great temple of Marduk, surrounded by other buildings and temples of the sacred quarter in the southern section of the city. The group of buildings in the background, by the first bend in the river (see plan, p. 209), is the palace of Nebuchadnezzar, with its Hanging Gardens. On the east (right) side of the temple quarter the Procession Street runs northward to connect with the palace and the Ishtar Gate on the east (right) side of the palace (see Plate II). The Euphrates, flowing along the west (left) side of the city, is crossed by a bridge, the oldest passenger bridge known to us, dating from the Sixth Century ʙ.ᴄ. (cf. Fig. 106). Its ruinous piers still stand in the now dry bed of the Euphrates. The enormous fortified walls surrounding the city were the work of Nebuchadnezzar. A campaign of over eighteen years' excavation by the Germans under Koldewey has made this restoration possible. (Drawing after Koldewey)

forming a lofty garden, crowned the roof of the imperial palace. This garden, overlooking the Ishtar Gate, enhanced the brightness of its colored tiles. Here in the cool shade of palms and ferns, inviting to luxurious ease, the great king might enjoy an idle hour with the ladies of his court and look down upon the splendors of his city. These roof gardens of Nebuchadnezzar's palace were the mysterious Hanging Gardens of Babylon, whose fame spread far into the west until they were numbered by the Greeks among the Seven Won-

PLATE II. *Restoration of the* BABYLON *of* Nebuchadnezzar

Looking from the palace quarter, past the Ishtar Gate, and along Festival
Avenue to the temple quarter and the "Tower of Babel" (in right background).
Just at the right of the Ishtar Gate may be seen the palace roof gardens which
came to be known as the "Hanging Gardens." (After Unger)

ders of the World. Babylon thus became a monumental city like those of Assyria and Egypt.

273. For the first time Babylonia saw a very large city. It was immensely extended by Nebuchadnezzar, and enormous fortified walls were built to protect it, including one that extended entirely across the plain from the Tigris to the Euphrates above the city. It is this Babylon of Nebuchadnezzar whose marvels over a century later so impressed Herodotus, as is shown in the description of the city which he has left us. This, too, is the Babylon which has become familiar to all Christian peoples as the great city of the Hebrew captivity. Of all the glories which made it world-renowned in its time little now remains. The German excavations here, which continued from 1899 to 1917, revealed for the most part only broken fragments of dingy sun-baked brick walls. With the exception of the Ishtar Gate little is left to .suggest the brilliant life which once ebbed and flowed through these streets and public places. The Chaldeans seem to have absorbed the civilization of Babylonia in much the same way as other earlier Semitic invaders of this ancient plain. Commerce and business flourished, the arts and industries were highly developed, religion and literature were cultivated, and their records were put into wedge-writing on clay tablets as of old.

Chaldean Babylon and its civilization

274. Science made surprising progress in one important branch, — astronomy. The Babylonians had continued their ancient practice of trying to discover the future in the heavenly bodies (see § 227). The five planets then known (Mercury, Venus, Mars, Jupiter, and Saturn) were especially regarded as the powers controlling the fortunes of men, and as such the five leading Babylonian divinities were identified with these five heavenly bodies. The names of these Babylonian divinities have descended to us as the names of the planets, but on their way to us through Europe the ancient Babylonian divine names were translated into Roman forms. So the planet of Ishtar, the goddess of love, became Venus, while

Babylonian astrology and names of planets

that of the great god Marduk became Jupiter, and so on. The practice of astrology has survived to our own day; we still unconsciously recall it in such phrases as "his lucky star" or an "ill-starred undertaking."

275. Chaldean astrology has also left an indelible mark on our calendar in the names which we apply to the days of the week. The five planets just mentioned, together with the sun and the moon, make up a group of seven celestial bodies, each of which was an important divinity. As Chaldean temple worship spread into Syria it became customary finally to pronounce the ritual and sing the praise of each god on a certain particular day. Thus the worship of each one of these seven divinities came around every seventh day. The name of the god worshiped on that day was finally transferred to the day itself. In this way the day which was devoted to the Sun-god became Sun-day, the day sacred to the Moon became Mon-day, and so on through the week, until the last day, sacred to Saturn, was called Satur-day. As our language came to us along a northern route, and there are consequently Norse elements in it, the names of several of our week days have reached us in a northern form, like Wednesday (Woden's-day) or Thursday (Thor's-day). Nevertheless they all go back to the old Babylonian gods, who still live on among us in our names of the days of the week.

Celestial origin of names of our days of the week

276. Much more important than these surviving remains of Babylonian astrology were its services in gradually improving the observations of the skies till they became something more than mere fortune-telling. As far back as the Twenty-third Century B.C., in the days of the kings of Sumer and Akkad, the astrologers observed an eclipse of the moon which has now been calculated by a modern astronomer to have occurred in 2283 B.C. But at that remote date such observations were only occasional, and they were also very inaccurate and unsystematic. Gradually it became customary to make more frequent observations, until in 747 B.C., in

Beginning of continuous observations, 747 B.C.; astronomy

Fig. 114. *Both Sides of a Clay* Tablet *forming Part of a Chaldean* Astronomical Almanac *(Front at Left, Back at Right)*

The observations of the moon are in the left-hand column marked off by the vertical ruling. In the right-hand column are observations of the planets and fixed stars. The following four entries on the back are of great interest:

> On the first Mercury rises.
> On the third the Equinox.
> Night of the 15th, 40 minutes after sun-
> set, an eclipse of the moon begins.
> On the 28th occurs an eclipse of the sun.

Kugler has computed the dates of these two eclipses as October 9 and 23 in 425 B.C. This tablet therefore formed part of the great series of Babylonian observations which began in 747 B.C. (Courtesy of the University Museum of Philadelphia)

the reign of the Babylonian king Nabonassar, the series of observations became continuous, and a record of them was carefully kept on file. Unfortunately the complete file has not been preserved. So far as is now known, the oldest tablet from this list was made in the year 568 B.C. It is the oldest surviving carefully made astronomical observation. We now know that these records of the Chaldean astronomers continued for over three hundred and sixty years. They formed the first long series of astronomical observations and the first great body of astronomical knowledge. Indeed, modern astronomers have never yet made such a long-continued and uninterrupted series of observations.[1] It is especially remarkable that such scientific work continued to be carried on even after the Chaldean people had lost their independence and were ruled by Persian sovereigns.

277. More remarkable than this great body of observations, however, was the use to which the ablest Chaldean

Surveys of celestial motions; Nabu-rimannu; Kidinnu

astronomers put these records. Not long before 500 B.C., when the files of these continuous observations had been collecting for about two hundred and fifty years, a Chaldean astronomer named *Nabu-rimannu* used them to compile tables of the motions of the sun and moon, in which he recorded his calculations of the time required by these two heavenly bodies to make their revolutions, daily, monthly, yearly, and so forth, exactly dating the eclipses of the sun and the moon, and other important astronomical events. He calculated the length of the year as 365 days, 6 hours, 15 minutes, and 41 seconds. This measurement, made over two thousand years before the telescope was invented, is only 26 minutes, 55 seconds too long. It is the earliest known close approximation to the length of a year. This splendid time-table of the vast celestial clock, put together by Nabu-rimannu, was the earliest great constructive piece of astronomical work. There was a grandeur in it which the mind of man had never achieved before.

A little over a century later another Chaldean astronomer named *Kidinnu* made a similar group of tables of greatly increased accuracy. Indeed, one of his measurements of celestial motions even exceeds in accuracy the figures which have long been in practical use by modern astronomers. This was because he had before him the records of three hundred and sixty years of lunar observations, and no modern astronomer has any such records at his disposal. Kidinnu even proved that there was a difference between the length of the year as measured from equinox to equinox and as measured

---

[1] The only long-continued modern series of observations that can be compared with those of the Chaldeans are the meridian observations at Greenwich, England, which began in 1750, one hundred and eighty-five years ago.

between two successive arrivals of the earth at its nearest point to the sun.[1]

278. The century-long astronomical observations of the Chaldeans, together with the calculations of Nabu-rimannu and Kidinnu, passed over to the Greeks. They studied the calculations of these two great Chaldean astronomers, whom they called Naburianos and Kidenas; and when the Greek engineer Meton was trying to introduce a scientific calendar at Athens, he took the length of his year from the tables of Nabu-rimannu. Of these two Chaldeans a modern astronomer has said that they "are entitled to a place among the greatest of astronomers." These Chaldean pioneers in astronomy who first revealed to men a *system* of the celestial world, and thus became the founders of astronomical science, should be reverently remembered long after the kings and conquerors of the ancient world have been forgotten.

Chaldeans, the founders of astronomical science

279. While Chaldea thus surpassed in science anything accomplished by Assyria, we see in the new architecture of Chaldean Babylon the influence of Assyrian architecture. The Chaldeans themselves, however, fancied that they were restoring the civilization of the old Babylonia of Hammurapi. The scribes loved to employ an ancient style of writing and out-of-date forms of speech; the kings tunneled deep under the temple foundations and searched for years that they might find the old foundation records buried (like our corner-stone documents) by kings of ancient days.

Oriental revival of the past

280. This dependence upon the past meant decline. After the death of Nebuchadnezzar (561 B.C.), whose reign was the high-water mark of Chaldean civilization, the old civilized lands of the Orient seemed to have lost most of their former power to push forward and make fresh discoveries and new conquests in civilization,

Decline of the old Oriental lands

---

[1] Students who are taking courses in astronomy will understand that this is practically the discovery of the slow change in the obliquity of the earth's axis,— a change like the wabble of a spinning top, which is often called the precession of the equinoxes.

such as they had been making during three great ages on the Nile and three similar ages on the Two Rivers. Indeed, the leadership of the Semitic peoples in the early world was drawing near its close, and they were about to give way before the advance of the new peoples of the Indo-European race. But before we take up the movements of these new peoples, let us glance briefly at the little Hebrew kingdom, which was destined to influence the history of man more profoundly than any of the great empires of the early world.

QUESTIONS

Section 18. Where does the second chapter of history on the Two Rivers carry us? Describe the region around Assur. Whence did the people of Assur gain the beginnings of civilization? What were some of the results of Assyrian commercial expansion into Asia Minor? Who were the western rivals of Assur? Tell about the Arameans and what they accomplished. What did Assyrian civilization achieve before the Empire?

Section 19. Discuss Damascus and its capture by Assyria. Who was the founder of the leading line of Assyrian emperors? Describe his new city. What was the extent of the Assyrian Empire? How was its government carried on? What can you say about Assyrian warfare? about architecture and sculpture? What can you tell of Assurbanipal? What dangers within and without caused the fall of Assyria? What peoples destroyed Nineveh and when? What progress resulted from the rule of the Assyrian Empire?

Section 20. What empire formed the third chapter of history on the Two Rivers? Write a paragraph describing the achievements of Nebuchadnezzar. What astronomical names have descended to us from the Chaldeans? Explain how the names of our week days originated. Tell of the achievements of the Chaldean astronomers. What race followed the Semitic Chaldeans in Oriental leadership?

BIBLIOGRAPHY FOR TOPICAL STUDIES

Education and literature: DELAPORTE, *Mesopotamia*, pp. 198–223, 339–353; OLMSTEAD, *Sargon*, pp. 173–175; WOOLLEY, *Sumerians*, pp. 108–112.

Cities — Assyrian: BELL, *Architecture in Western Asia*, pp. 137–160; DELAPORTE, pp. 316–326; OLMSTEAD, *Sargon*, pp. 178–192; Babylonian: BELL, pp. 175–192; DELAPORTE, pp. 172–177; *History Teacher's Magazine*. Vol. 8 pp. 79–81

1900 BC

CHAPTER VII · Western Asia: The Hebrews

SECTION 21. PALESTINE AND THE PREDECESSORS OF THE HEBREWS THERE

281. The home of the Hebrews was on the western end of the Fertile Crescent, in a land now called Palestine.[1] It is the region lying along the southeastern corner of the Mediterranean, — a narrow strip between desert and sea; for, while the sea limits it on the west, the wastes of the desert bay *Situation and extent of Palestine, the home of the Hebrews* sweep northward, forming the eastern boundary of Palestine (see map, p. 146). It was about one hundred and fifty miles long, and less than ten thousand square miles are included within these limits; that is, Palestine was somewhat larger than the state of Vermont.

282. Much of this area is unproductive, for the desert intrudes upon southern Palestine and rolls northward in gaunt and arid limestone hills, even surrounding *Geographical character of Palestine* Jerusalem. The valleys of northern Palestine, however, are rich and productive. The entire land is without summer rains and is dependent upon the winter rainy season

NOTE. The above headpiece shows us a CARAVAN OF CANAANITES trading in Egypt about 1900 B.C. as they appeared on the estate of a feudal baron in Egypt. The Egyptian noble had this picture of them painted with others in his tomb, where it still is. Observe the shoes, sandals, and gay woolen clothing, the costume of the Palestinian towns, worn by these Canaanites; observe also the metal weapons which they carry. The manufacture of these things created industries which had begun to flourish among the towns in Syria and Palestine by this time. Notice also the type of face, with the prominent nose, which shows that Anatolian blood was already mixed with the Semitic blood of these early dwellers in Palestine.

[1] On the origin of the name see § 415.

FIG. 115. *Ancient Egyptian Painting of a* BRICKYARD *with Asiatic Captives engaged in Brickmaking* (*Fifteenth Century* B.C.)

The Hebrew slaves working in the Egyptian brickyards (see Exod. i, 14, and v, 6–19) must have looked like this when Moses led them forth into Asia. At the left below, the soft clay is being mixed in two piles; one laborer helps load a basket of clay on the shoulder of another, who carries it to the brick-molder, at the right above. Here a laborer empties the clay from his basket, while the molder before him fills with clay an oblong box, which is the mold. He has already finished three bricks. At the left above, a molder spreads out the soft bricks with spaces between for the circulation of air to make them dry quickly in the sun. The overseer, staff in hand, sits in the upper right-hand corner, and below him we see a workman carrying away the dried bricks, hanging from a yoke on his shoulders. Thus were made the bricks used for thousands of years for the buildings forming so large a part of the cities of the ancient world, from the Near East to Athens and Rome

for moisture. There is no opportunity for irrigation, and the harvest is therefore scantier than in lands enjoying summer rains. Only the northern end of the Palestinian coast has any harbors, but these were early seized by the Phœnicians (Sections 36–37). Palestine thus remained cut off from the sea. In natural resources it was too poor ever to develop prosperity or political power like its great civilized neighbors on the Nile and Euphrates or in Syria and Phœnicia.

283. Here at the western end of the Fertile Crescent, as at the eastern end, the Semitic nomads from the desert bay

Palestine, market place of Ancient Near East

(reread Section 13) mingled with the dwellers in the northern mountains of the Highland Zone. The northerners, chiefly Early Anatolians (later Hittites) from Asia Minor and Syria, left their mark on the Semites of Palestine. The prominent aquiline

FIG. 116. *Air View of* MOUND *covering* FORTRESS CITY *of Armageddon,
or Megiddo*

This city stands at the north end of the pass where the road from Egypt to Babylonia and Assyria crosses the Carmel Range. It is thus a natural fortress guarding
the ancient highway between Africa and Asia. For thousands of years, on the
Plain of Megiddo, the armies of Asia and Africa have met and fought, — from
Thutmose III to Lord Allenby and the Turks in the World War. This great
mound was formed by the accumulations of rubbish from fallen buildings (§ 186).
An expedition from the Oriental Institute of The University of Chicago is engaged
in peeling off stratum after stratum of this "layer cake" of ancient cities, the
one at present exposed being the city of Solomon's time (Tenth Century B.C.).
All that is preserved of the buildings are the stone foundations, the masonry of
which has been found to consist of no more than the "three rows of hewn stone"
mentioned in 1 Kings vii, 12. The headquarters of the archæological expedition
may be seen in the foreground. (Photograph by Mr. Charles Breasted)

nose, still considered to be the mark of the Semite, especially
of the Jew, was really a feature belonging to the non-Semitic
Anatolians, who intermarried with the people of Palestine
and gave them this Anatolian type of face (see Fig. 126 and
§ 320). Strange faces from many a foreign clime crowded
the market places of Palestine, amid a babel of various languages. Here the rich jewelry, bronze dishes, and ivory furniture of the Nile craftsmen mingled with the pottery of the
Ægean Islands and of the Highland civilization, and with the
gay woolens of Babylonia. The donkeys which lifted their
complaining voices above the hubbub of the market had

grazed along the shores of both Nile and Euphrates, and their masters had trafficked beneath the Babylonian tower-temples as well as under the shadow of the Theban obelisks. We recall how traffic with Babylonia had taught these western Semites to write the cuneiform hand. To the caravan coming out of Egypt Palestine was the entrance to the bridge between Africa and Asia, — a middle ground where the civilizations of Egypt and Babylonia, Phœnicia, the Ægean, and the Highland Zone, all represented by their wares, met and commingled as they did nowhere else in the Ancient Near East.

284. Just as the merchandise of the surrounding nations met in peaceful competition in the markets of Palestine, so the armies of these nations also met there in battle. The situation of Palestine, between its powerful neighbors on the Nile and on the Euphrates, made it the battleground where these great nations fought for many centuries. Over and over again unhappy Palestine went through the experience of little Belgium in the conflict between Germany and France in 1914. For many centuries Egypt held Palestine as a subject country. We recall how Assyria later conquered it and Chaldea enslaved it, and we shall yet find it in the power of Persia. When, therefore, the Hebrews originally took possession of the land, there was little prospect that they would ever long enjoy freedom from foreign oppression.

Palestine, battleground of Ancient Near East

SECTION 22. THE SETTLEMENT OF THE HEBREWS IN PALESTINE AND THE UNITED HEBREW KINGDOM

285. The Hebrews were all originally men of the Arabian Desert, wandering with their flocks and herds and slowly drifting over into their final home in Palestine. For two centuries (about 1400 to 1200 B.C.) their movement from the desert into Palestine continued. Another group of their tribes had been slaves in Egypt, where they had suffered much hardship

Hebrew invasion of Palestine (about 1400–1200 B.C.)

under a cruel Pharaoh. They were successfully led out of Egypt by their heroic leader Moses, a great national hero whose achievements his people never forgot. On entering Palestine the Hebrews found the Canaanites already dwelling there in flourishing towns protected by massive walls. The Hebrews were able to capture only the weaker Canaanite towns. As the rough Hebrew shepherds looked across the highlands of northern Palestine they beheld their kindred scattered over far-stretching hilltops, with the frowning walls of many a Canaanite stronghold rising between them. Even Jerusalem in the Judean

Fig. 117. *Mummy of* Ramses II, *commonly thought to be the Pharaoh who enslaved the Hebrews*

Ramses II died about 1225 B.C., that is, over thirty-one hundred years ago. He was about ninety years old

highlands for centuries defied the assaults of the Hebrew invaders, who had no siege machinery for attacking city walls.

286. Let us remember that by that time these unconquered Palestinian towns possessed a civilization fifteen hundred years old, with comfortable houses, government, industries, trade, writing, and religion, — a civilization which the rude Hebrew shepherds were soon adopting; for they could not avoid intercourse with the unsubdued Canaanite towns as trade and business threw them together. This mingling with the Canaanites produced the most profound changes in the life of the Hebrews. Most of them left their tents and began to build houses like those of the Canaanites; they put off the rough sheepskin they had

Hebrews adopt Canaanite civilization

worn in the desert, and they put on fine Canaanite raiment of gayly colored woven wool. After a time, in appearance, occupation, and manner of life the Hebrews were not to be distinguished from the Canaanites among whom they lived. In short, they had adopted Canaanite civilization, just as newly arrived immigrants among *us* soon adopt our clothing and our ways.

287. These changes did not proceed everywhere at the same rate. In the less fertile South the Hebrews were more at-
tached to the old desert life, so that many would not give up the tent and the old free-dom of the desert. The wandering life of the nomad shepherd on the Judean hills could still be seen from the walls of Jerusalem. Here, then, were two differing modes of life among the Hebrews: in the fertile North of Palestine we find the settled life of the town and its outlying fields; in the South, on the other hand, the wandering life of the nomad still went on. For centuries this difference formed an important cause of discord among the Hebrews.

Hebrews of South differ in mode of life from those of North

288. Fortunately for the Hebrews, Egypt was in a state of decline by 1100 B.C., and Assyria had not yet conquered the
west. But a Mediterranean people called Philistines had at this time migrated from the island of Crete to the sea plain at the southwest corner of Palestine (see map, p. 226). These Philistines formed a highly civilized and warlike nation, or group of city-kingdoms. Hard pressed by the Philistines, the Hebrew local leaders, or judges, as they were called, found it no easy task to unite their people into a nation. About a generation before the year 1000 B.C., however, a popular leader named Saul succeeded in gaining for himself the office of king. The new king was a southerner who still loved the old nomad customs; he was not fond of a fixed abode and preferred to dwell in a tent. In a fierce struggle to thrust back the Philistines, Saul was disastrously defeated, and, seeing the rout of his army, he fell upon his own sword and so died.

Foundation of He-brew nation; Saul, the first king

289. In a few years the ability of David, one of Saul's daring men-at-arms whom he had unjustly outlawed, won the support of the South. Seeing the David (about 1000–960 B.C.) importance of possessing a strong castle, the sagacious David selected the ancient fortress on the steep hill of Jerusalem, hitherto held by the Canaanites. The oldest occurrence of the name of the place has recently been found in Egyptian writings over a thousand years older than David's time. He took possession of the venerable city and made it his residence. Here he ruled for a time as king of the South, till his valor as a soldier and his victories on all sides won him also the support of the more prosperous North. The Philistines were now beaten off, and David ruled over an extensive Hebrew kingdom. He enjoyed a long and prosperous reign, and his people never forgot his heroic deeds as a warrior or his skill as a poet and singer.

FIG. 118. LETTER *of the Egyptian Governor of Jerusalem telling of the* INVASION OF PALESTINE *by the Hebrews (Fourteenth Century* B.C.)

The letter is a clay tablet written in Babylonian cuneiform by the terrified Egyptian governor, who begs the Pharaoh (Ikhnaton) for help, saying: "The Khabiru [Hebrews] are taking the cities of the king. No ruler remains to the king, my lord; all are lost." This letter is one of the group of three hundred such cuneiform letters found in a room of Ikhnaton's palace at Tell el-Amarna (or Amarna), and called the Amarna Letters

290. David's son, Solomon, became, like Hammurapi, one of the leading merchants of the East. He trafficked in horses Solomon and division of his kingdom (about 930 B.C.) and launched a trading fleet in partnership with Hiram, the Phœnician king of Tyre. His wealth enabled him to marry a daughter of the king of Egypt, and he delighted in Oriental luxury and display. He removed

FIG. 119. *Ruins of the* STABLES *of Solomon at Armageddon* (*Megiddo*)

Many of the square stone piers which supported the roof have disappeared, as has the roof itself, but a number of them remain to show the arrangement of the stables. The horses were tied to these piers, and the tie-holes in the corners of the piers are still preserved. In the middle between the piers we see two solid stone mangers and half of a third manger (*D, D, D*) looking like bathtubs. The horses, standing so that they could eat from these mangers, were ranged in a row of twelve stalls (row *A–A*), facing a second row of twelve (row *B–B*). The passage (*C–C*) between the two rows was intended to enable the grooms to reach and fill the mangers. With five such double rows of horses, these stables accommodated one hundred and twenty animals. (Excavated by the Oriental Institute of The University of Chicago)

the portable tent which the Hebrews had thus far used as a temple, and with the aid of his friend Hiram, who lent him skilled Phœnician workmen, he built a rich temple of stone in Jerusalem. Such splendor demanded a great income, and to secure it he weighed down the Hebrews with heavy taxes. The resulting discontent of his subjects was so great that, under Solomon's son, the Northern tribes withdrew from the nation and set up a king of their own. Thus the Hebrew nation was divided into two kingdoms before it was a century old.

SECTION 23. THE TWO HEBREW KINGDOMS

291. There was much hard feeling between the two Hebrew kingdoms, and sometimes fighting. Israel, as we call the Northern Kingdom, was rich and pros- Contrast between perous; its market places were filled with the two Hebrew industry and commerce; its fertile fields pro- kingdoms duced plentiful crops. Israel displayed the wealth and success of town life. On the other hand, Judah, the Southern Kingdom, was poor; its land was meager; besides Jerusalem it had no large towns; many of the people still wandered with their flocks.

292. These two methods of life came into conflict in many ways, but especially in religion. Every old Canaanite town for centuries had had its local town god, called Effect of this con- its *baal*, or "lord." The Hebrew townsmen trast upon religion therefore found it very natural to worship the gods of their neighbors, the Canaanite townsmen. They were thus unfaithful to their old Hebrew God Yahveh (or Jehovah).[1] To some devout Hebrews, therefore, and especially to those in the South, the Canaanite gods seemed to be the protectors of the wealthy class in the towns, with their luxury and injustice to the poor, while Yahveh appeared as the guardian of the simpler shepherd life of the desert, and therefore the protector of the poor and needy.

293. There was growing reason for such beliefs. Less than a century after the separation of the two kingdoms, Ahab, a king of the North, had had Naboth, one of his subjects, killed in order to seize a vineyard belonging to Naboth, and thus to enlarge his palace gardens. Reports of such wrongs

[1] The Hebrews pronounced the name of their God "Yahveh." The pronunciation "Jehovah" began less than six hundred years ago and was due to a misunderstanding of the pronunciation of the word *Yahveh*.

stirred the anger of Elijah, a Hebrew of old nomad habits, who lived in the desert east of the Jordan. Still wearing his desert sheepskin, he suddenly appeared before Ahab in the ill-gotten vineyard and denounced the king for his seizure of it. Thus this uncouth figure from the desert proclaimed war between Yahveh and the injustice of town life. Elijah's followers finally slew not only the entire Northern royal family but also the priests of the Canaanite gods (or baals). Such violent methods, however, could not accomplish lasting good. They were the methods of Hebrews who thought of Yahveh only as a war god.

Elijah and the violence of the older ideas of Yahveh

294. Besides such violent leaders as these there were also among the Hebrews more peaceable men who likewise chafed under the injustice of town life. These turned fondly back to the grand old days of their shepherd wanderings, out on the broad reaches of the desert, where no man "ground the faces of the poor." This point of view is picturesquely set forth in a simple narrative history of the Hebrew forefathers, — a glorified picture of their shepherd life, as we find it in the immortal tales of the Hebrew patriarchs, of Abraham and Isaac, of Jacob and Joseph. These tales belong among the noblest literature which has survived to us from the past.[1] We should notice also that they are the earliest example of *historical* writing in prose, of finished literary style, which we have inherited from any people.

Earliest historical writing among the Hebrews

295. It is now quite clear that such men were acquainted with the papyrus rolls written by Egyptian social reformers over a thousand years earlier, in defense of the poor and helpless (see § 117). We now know that such Egyptian documents were sometimes translated into Hebrew, for an Egyptian roll has been found containing a collection of wise proverbs, a section of which was included in the Book of Proverbs and later circulated under the name of Solomon. As they read such writings

Egyptian social writings and the Hebrew reformers

---

[1] See Gen. xxiv, xxvii, xxviii, xxxvii, xxxix–xlvii, 12.

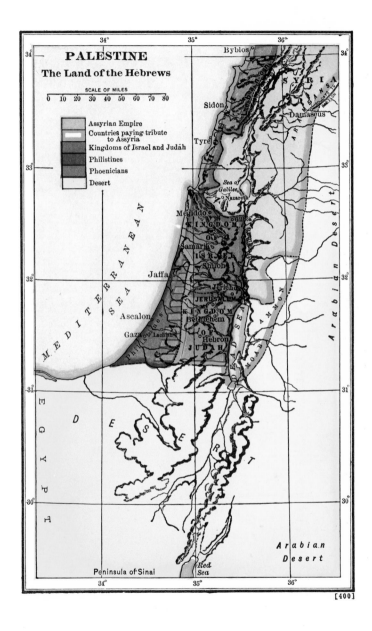

PALESTINE
The Land of the Hebrews

SCALE OF MILES
0 10 20 30 40 50 60 70 80

Assyrian Empire
Countries paying tribute
   to Assyria
Kingdoms of Israel and Judáh
Philistines
Phoenicians
Desert

Byblos

SYRIA

Sidón

Damascus

Tyre

Sea of
Galilee
Nazareth

Megiddo
KINGDOM
OF
Samaria
ISRAEL
Shiloh

Jaffa

Jericho
JERUSALEM
KINGDOM
Bethlehem
OF
Hebron
JUDAH

Ascalon

Gaza
Lachish
Philistines

MEDITERRANEAN SEA

DEAD SEA

MOAB

AMMON

Arabian Desert

EGYPT

DESERT

Peninsula of Sinai

Red
Sea

Arabian
Desert

[400]

of the old Egyptian champions of the poor the Hebrew prophets and reformers took courage and gained new ideas.

296. Another century passed, and about 750 B.C. another dingy figure in sheepskin appeared in the streets of Bethel, where the Northern Kingdom had an important temple. It was Amos, a shepherd from the hills of Judah in the South. In the solitudes of his shepherd life Amos had learned to see in Yahveh far more than a war god of the desert. To him Yahveh seemed to be a God of fatherly kindness, not demanding bloody butchery like that practiced by Elijah's followers, but nevertheless a God who rebuked the selfish and oppressive wealthy class of the towns. The simple shepherd could not resist the inner impulse to journey to the Northern Kingdom and proclaim to the luxurious townsmen there the evils of their manner of life.

Amos: peaceful methods of the reformer and prophet

297. We can imagine the surprise of the prosperous Northern Hebrews as they suddenly met this rude shepherd figure, clad in sheepskin, standing at a street corner addressing a crowd of townsmen. He was denouncing their showy clothes, fine houses, beautiful furniture, and, above all, their corrupt lives and hard-heartedness toward the poor among their fellow Hebrews, whose lands they seized for debt and whose labor they gained by enslaving them. These things had been unknown in the desert. By such addresses as these Amos, of course, endangered his life, but he thus became the first social reformer in Asia. We apply the term "prophet" to the great Hebrew leaders who pointed out the way toward unselfish living, brotherly kindness, and a higher type of religion. Thus began in Western Asia the same kind of effort to lead men to show justice and kindness toward all, especially toward the poor, which had long been known in Egypt, and it is probable that Amos had heard of such Egyptian teachings. Fearing that his teachings might be lost if they remained merely spoken words, Amos finally sat down and put his sermons into writing, and thus they have survived to us.

Amos denounces corrupt living of Northern Kingdom

298. While all this had been going on, the Hebrews had been learning to write, as so many of their nomad predeces-

Hebrews learn to write

sors on the Fertile Crescent had done before them. They were now abandoning the clay tablet, and wrote on papyrus with the Egyptian pen and ink. They borrowed their alphabet from the Phœnician and Aramean merchants. It is certain that our earliest Hebrew historian's admiration for the *nomad* life did not prevent him from making use of this new and great convenience of *town* life, that is, writing. The rolls containing the beautiful tales of the patriarchs, or bearing the teachings of such men as Amos, were the first books which the Hebrews produced, — their first literature. Such rolls of papyrus were exactly like those which had been in use in Egypt for over two thousand years. The discovery of the household papers of a Hebrew community in Egypt has shown us just how such a page of Hebrew or Aramaic writing looked (Fig. 122). But literature remained the only art the Hebrews possessed. They had no painting, sculpture, or architecture, and if they needed these things they borrowed from their great neighbors, — Egypt, Phœnicia, Damascus, and Assyria.

SECTION 24. THE DESTRUCTION OF THE HEBREW KINGDOMS BY ASSYRIA AND CHALDEA

299. While the Hebrews had been deeply stirred by their own conflicts *at home*, such men as Amos had also perceived

Destruction of the Northern Kingdom by Assyria (722 B.C.)

and proclaimed the dangers coming from *abroad*, from beyond the borders of Palestine, especially Assyria. Amos, indeed, announced the coming destruction of the Northern King-

dom by Assyria because of the evil lives of the people. As Amos had foreseen, Assyria first swept away Damascus (§§ 240 and 250). The kingdom of Israel, left thus exposed, was the next victim, and Samaria, its capital, was captured by the Assyrians in 722 B.C. (§ 251). Of the unhappy Northern Hebrews 27,290 well-to-do people were carried away as

FIG. 120. *Hebrews* PAYING TRIBUTE *to the King of Assyria*

The Assyrian king, Shalmaneser III, stands at the left, followed by two attendants. Before him hovers the winged sun-disk. His appearance in the middle of the Ninth Century B.C., campaigning in the west against Damascus, so frightened the Hebrews of the Northern Kingdom that their king (Jehu) sent gifts to the Assyrian king by an envoy, whom we see here bowing down at the king's feet. Behind the Hebrew envoy are two Assyrian officers who are leading up a line of thirteen Hebrews (not included here) bearing gifts of silver, gold, etc. The scene is carved on a black stone shaft set up by the Assyrian king in his palace on the Tigris, where the modern excavators found it. It is now in the British Museum

captives, and the Northern nation, called Israel, was destroyed after having existed for a little over two centuries.

300. The national hopes of the Hebrews were now centered in the helpless little kingdom of Judah, which struggled on for over a century and a quarter more, in the midst of a great world conflict in which Assyria was the unchallenged champion. Thus far thoughtful Hebrews had been accustomed *Yahveh, God of Palestine, rival of Assur, god of Assyria* to think of their God as ruling in Palestine only. But now they were learning that Palestine was part of a great political world. Did he have power also over the vast world arena where all the mighty nations were fighting? But if so, was not Assur, the great god of victorious Assyria, stronger than Yahveh, God of.the Hebrews? And many a despairing Hebrew, as he looked out over the hills of Palestine, wasted by the armies of Assyria, felt in his heart that Assur, the god of the victorious Assyrians, who ruled nearly all Western Asia, must indeed be stronger than Yahveh, God of the Hebrews.

3(1. It was in the midst of somber doubts like these, in the years before 700 B.C., that the princely prophet Isaiah, in one

Isaiah and siege of Jerusalem by Sennacherib great oration after another, addressed the multitudes which filled the streets of Jerusalem. The hosts of Sennacherib were at the gates, and the terrified throngs in the city were expecting at any moment to hear the thunder of the great Assyrian war engines battering down the crumbling walls of their city, as they had crushed the walls of Damascus and Samaria. Then the bold words of the dauntless Isaiah lifted them from despair like the triumphant call of a trumpet. He told them that Yahveh ruled a kingdom far larger than Palestine, — that He controlled the great world arena, where *He*, and not Assur, was the triumphant champion. If the Assyrians had wasted and plundered Palestine, it was because they were but the lash in the

Fig. 121. Sennacherib, *King of Assyria, receiving* Captive Hebrews

The artist, endeavoring to sketch the stony hills of southern Palestine, has made the surface of the ground look like scales. We see the Assyrian king seated on a throne, while advancing up the hill is a group of Assyrian soldiers headed by the grand vizier, who stands before the king, announcing the coming of the Hebrew captives. At the left, behind the soldiers, appear three of the captives kneeling on the ground and lifting up their hands to appeal for mercy. The inscription over the vizier's head reads, "Sennacherib, king of the world, king of Assyria, seated himself upon a throne, while the captives of Lachish passed before him." Lachish was a small town of southern Palestine. Sennacherib captured many such Hebrew towns and carried off over two hundred thousand captives, but even his own records make no claim that he captured Jerusalem. The scene is engraved on a large slab of alabaster, which with many others adorned the palace of Sennacherib at Nineveh as evidence of his power and glory

hands of Yahveh, who was using them as a scourge in his own hands to punish Judah for its wrongdoing.

302. Thus while the people were momentarily expecting the destruction of Jerusalem, Isaiah undauntedly proclaimed a great and glorious future for the Hebrews and speedy disaster for the Assyrians. When at length a pestilence from the marshes of the eastern Nile Delta swept away the army of Sennacherib and saved Jerusalem, it seemed to the Hebrews the destroying angel of Yahveh who had smitten the Assyrian host.[1] Some of the Hebrews then began to see that Yahveh ruled a larger world than Palestine. Their own ideas were stimulated by the great Sun-hymn of Ikhnaton which had long been circulating in Western Asia, as one of the Hebrew Psalms shows. Compare these two passages:

Sennacherib's army destroyed; justification of Isaiah's words

From Ikhnaton's Sun-hymn	*From the 104th Psalm*
How manifold are thy works! They are hidden before men O sole God, beside whom there is no other. Thou didst create the earth according to thy will.	O Lord, how manifold are thy works! In wisdom hast thou made them all: The earth is full of thy riches.

303. Nearly a century after the deliverance from Sennacherib they beheld and rejoiced over the destruction of Nineveh (612 B.C.), and they fondly hoped that the fall of Assyria meant final deliverance from foreign oppression. But they had only exchanged one foreign lord for another, and Chaldea followed Assyria in control of Palestine. Then the unsubmissive Hebrews of Judah met the same fate which their kindred of Israel had suffered. In 586 B.C. Nebuchadnezzar, the Chaldean king, destroyed Jerusalem and carried away the people to exile in Babylonia. The Hebrew nation, both North and South was thus wiped out after having existed about four and a half centuries.

Destruction of the Southern Kingdom by Chaldea (586 B.C.)

[1] See 2 Kings xix, 32–37.

Section 25. The Hebrews in Exile and their Deliverance by the Persians

304. Some of the fugitives fled to Egypt. Among them was the melancholy prophet Jeremiah, who had foreseen the com-

Jeremiah and a temple of the Hebrews in Egypt

ing destruction of Jerusalem with its temple of Yahveh. He strove to teach his people that each must regard his own heart as a temple of Yahveh, which would endure long after His temple in Jerusalem had crashed into ruin. Recent excavation has restored to us the actual papers of a colony of Hebrews in Egypt at Elephantine (see map, p. 66). These papers (Fig. 122) show that the exiled Hebrews in Egypt had not yet reached Jeremiah's ideal of a temple of Yahveh in every human heart; for they had built a temple of their own, in which they carried on the worship of Yahveh.

305. Similarly, the Hebrew exiles in Babylonia were not yet convinced of the truth of the teaching they had heard

Doubts of exiled Hebrews; great prophet of the exile

from their great leaders the prophets. There were at first only grief and unanswered questionings, of which the echo still reaches us:

> By the rivers of Babylon,
> There we sat down, yea, we wept,
> When we remembered Zion [Jerusalem].
> Upon the willows in the midst thereof
> We hanged up our harps.
>
> .   .   .   .
>
> How shall we sing Yahveh's song
> In a strange land? (Psalms cxxxvii, 1–4)

Had they not left Yahveh behind in Palestine? And then arose a wonderful teacher [1] among the Hebrew exiles, and out of centuries of affliction gave them the answer. In a series of triumphant speeches this greatest of the earlier Hebrews declared Yahveh to be the creator and sole God of the universe.

---

[1] A great poet-preacher, a prophet of the exile, whose addresses to his fellow exiles are preserved in sixteen chapters embedded in the Old Testament book of Isaiah (chaps. xl–lv, inclusive).

He explained to his fellow exiles that suffering and affliction were the best possible training and discipline to prepare a people for service. He announced, therefore, that by afflicting them Yahveh was only preparing His suffering people for service to the world, and that He would yet restore them and enable them to fulfill a great mission to all men. He greeted the sudden rise of Cyrus the Persian with joy. All kings, he taught, were but instruments in the hands of Yahveh, who through the Persians would overthrow the Chaldeans and return the Hebrews to their land.

306. Thus had the Hebrew vision of Yahveh slowly grown, from the days of their nomad life, when they had seen him only as a fierce tribal war god, having no power beyond the corner of the desert where they lived, until now, when they had come to Monotheism reached by Hebrews in exile see that He was a kindly father and a righteous ruler of all the earth. This was monotheism, a belief which made Yahveh the sole God. They had reached it only through a long development, which brought them suffering and disaster, — a discipline lasting many centuries. Just as the individual today, especially a young person, learns from his mistakes, and develops character as he suffers for his own errors, so the suffering Hebrews had outgrown many imperfect ideas. They thus illustrated the words of the greatest of Hebrew teachers, "First the blade, then the ear, then the full grain in the ear." [1] By this rich and wonderful experience of the Hebrews in religious progress the whole world was yet to profit.

307. When the victorious Persian king Cyrus entered Babylon (§ 344), the Hebrew exiles there greeted him as their deliverer. His triumph gave the Hebrews a Persian ruler. With great humanity the Persian kings allowed the exiles to return Restoration of exiled Hebrews by Persian kings to their native land. Some had prospered in Babylonia and did not care to return, but at different times enough of them went back to Jerusalem to rebuild the city on a very modest scale and to restore the temple.

[1] The words of Jesus; see Mark iv, 28.

FIG. 122. *Aramaic* LETTER *written by a* HEBREW COMMUNITY IN EGYPT
to the Persian Governor of Palestine in the Fifth Century B.C.

This remarkable letter was discovered in 1907, with many other similar papers, lying in the ruins of the town of Elephantine in Upper Egypt. Here lived a community of some six or seven hundred Hebrews, some of whom had probably migrated to Egypt before Nebuchadnezzar destroyed Jerusalem. They had built a temple to Yahveh (Jehovah) on the banks of the Nile. This letter tells how the jealous Egyptian priests formed a mob, burned the Hebrew temple, and plundered it of its gold and silver vessels. Thereupon the whole Hebrew community sat down in mourning, and for three years they tried in vain to secure permission to rebuild. Then, in 407 B.C., their leaders wrote this letter to Bagoas, the Persian governor of Palestine, begging him to use his influence with the Persian governor of Egypt to induce him to permit them to rebuild their ruined temple. They refer by name to persons in Palestine who are also mentioned in the Old Testament. The letter is written with pen and ink on papyrus, in the Aramaic language, which was now rapidly displacing Hebrew. This writing used the Phœnician letters long before they were adopted throughout Western Asia. This beautifully written sheet of papyrus, about 10 by 13 inches, bearing the same letters which the Hebrews used (§ 298), shows us exactly how a page of their ancient writings in the Old Testament looked. They read the stories of Abraham, Isaac, Jacob, and Joseph from pages like this

308. The authority given by the Persian government to the returned Hebrew leaders enabled them to establish and publish the religious laws which have ever since been revered by the Jews. The religion thus organized by the returned Hebrew leaders we now call Judaism, the religion of the *Jewish law and Judaism; restored Jewish state a church* Jews. Under it the old Hebrew kingship was not revived. In its place a high priest at Jerusalem became the ruler of the Jews. The Jewish state was thus a *religious* organization, a church with a priest at its head.

309. The leaders of this church devoted themselves to the study of the ancient writings of their race still surviving in their hands. A number of the old writings, some of them mentioned in the Old Testament, had been lost. They arranged and *Editing of Hebrew writings: Prophets and Psalms* copied the orations and addresses of the prophets, and all the old Hebrew writings they possessed. As time went on, and the service of the restored temple developed, they arranged a remarkable book of a hundred and fifty religious songs, — the hymn book of the second temple, known to us as the Book of Psalms. For a long time — indeed, for centuries — these various Hebrew books, such as the Law, the Prophets, and the Psalms, circulated in separate rolls, and it did not occur to anyone to put them together to form one book.

310. It was not until Christian times that the Jewish leaders put all these old writings of their fathers together to form one book. Printed in Hebrew, as they were originally written, they form the Bible of the Jews at the present day. These *Old Testament and our legacy in Hebrew religion* Hebrew writings have also become a sacred book of the Christian nations. In the form of an English translation it is called the Old Testament, and is today the most precious legacy which we have inherited from the Ancient Near East before the coming of Christ. It tells the story of how a rude shepherd folk issued from the wilds of the Arabian Desert to live in Palestine, where they were prepared to understand the religious writings of the earlier great nations of the East, especially Egypt, and thus to pass through experiences which made them the religious teachers of the civilized world. And we should further remember that, crowning all their history, there came forth from them in due time the Founder of the Christian religion. One of the most important things that we owe to the Persians, therefore, was their restoration of the Hebrews to Palestine. The Persians thus saved and aided in transmitting to us the great legacy from Hebrew life which we have in the Old Testament and in the life of the Founder of Christianity.

QUESTIONS

Section 21. Describe the situation and character of the land of the Hebrews. Was it likely to offer a tranquil home?

Section 22. Where was the *original* home of the Hebrews? What was the result of their living among the Canaanites? When did they gain their first king and who was he? Who was their leading enemy? Describe the reign of David; of Solomon. What happened to the kingdom after Solomon?

Section 23. Contrast the two kingdoms. How did this contrast affect religion? Compare the methods of Elijah and Amos. What was the work of a prophet? From what people did the Hebrews learn to write and what were the first books of the Hebrews?

Section 24. What danger threatened the Hebrews from abroad? What happened to the Northern Kingdom? What can you say of the work of Isaiah? Tell about Sennacherib's campaign against Jerusalem.

Section 25. What became of the Hebrews of Judah? Discuss the Hebrew conception of Yahveh at the time of the Babylonian exile. What did the returned Hebrews accomplish and by what authority?

BIBLIOGRAPHY FOR TOPICAL STUDIES

Jeremiah and the destruction of Judah: BAILEY and KENT, *Hebrew Commonwealth*, pp. 239–251; CHAMBERLIN, *Hebrew Prophets*, pp. 132–168; KITTEL, *Great Men and Movements*, pp. 334–366; KNOTT, *Student's History of the Hebrews*, pp. 258–264.

Nehemiah: KENT, *History of the Jewish People*, §§ 155–170; KNOTT, *Student's History*, pp. 293–298.

Chapter VIII · Western Asia: The Coming of the Indo-Europeans

Section 26. The Indo-European Peoples and their Dispersion[1]

311. We have seen that the Arabian Desert was once a great reservoir of unsettled population, which was continually leaving the grasslands on the margin of the desert and shifting over into the towns to begin a settled life. Corresponding to these grasslands of the *south* there are similar grasslands in the *north*. These northern grasslands stretch from the lower Danube eastward along the north side of the Black Sea through southern Russia

Northern Grass-lands

Note. The headpiece above shows Ancient Fire Altars used by the great Persian kings and located not far from their tombs (Fig. 136).

[1] Section 26 should be carefully worked over by the teacher with the class before the class is permitted to study it alone. The diagram (Fig. 123) should be put on the blackboard and explained in detail by the teacher, and the class should then be prepared to put the diagram on the board from memory. This should be done again when the study of the Greeks is begun (§ 405), and a third time when Italy and the Romans are taken up.

and far into Asia north and east of the Caspian (see map, p. 754). In ancient times they always had a wandering shepherd population, and time after time, for thousands of years, these northern nomads have poured forth over Europe and Western Asia, just as the desert Semites of the south have done over the Fertile Crescent.

312. Among these nomads of the north there was in very early times an important branch of the Great White Race

Two lines,—Indo-European and Semitic

which we call *Indo-European*. The early Indo-Europeans were the ancestors of the leading peoples of Europe today. As our forefathers came from Europe, the Indo-European nomads were also our own ancestors. These nomads of the *northern* grasslands began to migrate in very ancient times, moving out along diverging routes. The earliest group of them known to us is the Hittites, who appeared in Asia Minor not later than 2500 B.C., and perhaps earlier. The recent decipherment of Hittite writing has disclosed such words as *vadar*, meaning "water," showing the relation between our own language and that of these ancient Indo-Europeans. The Indo-Europeans as a whole at last extended in an imposing line from the frontiers of India on the east, westward across all Europe to the Atlantic, as they do today; and hence their name, Indo-Europeans. This great northern line was confronted on the south by a similar line of Semitic peoples, extending from Babylonia on the east, through Phœnicia and the Hebrew kingdoms, westward to Carthage and similar Semitic settlements of Phœnicia in the Western Mediterranean (§ 162 and map, p. 346).

313. The history of the ancient world, as we are now to follow it, was largely made up of the struggle between this

Struggle between Indo-European and Semitic lines

southern Semitic line, which issued from the southern grasslands, and the *northern Indo-European* line, which came forth from the northern grasslands to confront the older civilizations represented in the southern line. Thus as we look at the diagram we see the two great races facing each other across the Medi-

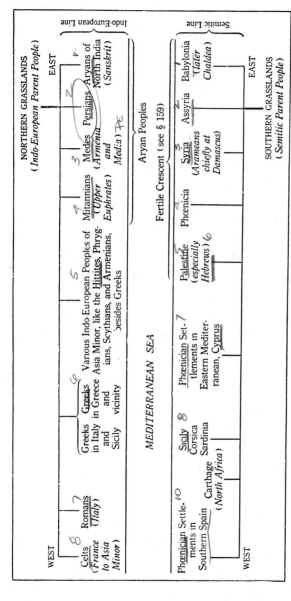

FIG. 123. DIAGRAM *suggesting the* TWO LINES *of Semitic and Indo-European* DISPERSION

In this explanation and in § 312 the word "line" means much the same as "row." The geographic lines along which these peoples lie are of course not straight. The racial lines sometimes overlie each other, as in Sicily, and are mentioned in both lines. The Egyptians, who physically belong in the southern line, have been omitted because they are not purely Semitic, although physically and in language closely related to the Semites. Notice also that in the West the two races face each other for the most part across the Mediterranean; in the East they confront each other along the Fertile Crescent

terranean like two vast armies stretching from Western Asia westward to the Atlantic. The later wars between Rome and Carthage represent some of the operations on the Semitic left wing, while the triumph of Persia over Chaldea is a similar outcome on the Semitic right wing.

314. The result of the long conflict was the complete triumph of our ancestors (the Indo-European line), who

Triumph of European end of Indo-European line

conquered along the center and both wings and finally, as represented by the Greeks and Romans, gained unchallenged supremacy throughout the Mediterranean world. This triumph was accompanied by a long struggle for the mastery between the members of the northern line themselves. Among them the victory moved from the east end to the west end of the northern line, as first the Persians, then the Greeks, and finally the Romans gained control of the Mediterranean and Oriental world.

315. Let us now turn back to a time before the Indo-European people had left their original home on the grass-

Indo-European parent people and their original home

lands. Modern study has not yet determined with certainty the region where the parent people of the Indo-European nomads had their home. The indications now are that this original home was on the great grassy steppe in the region east and north-east of the Caspian Sea. Here, then, probably lived the parent people of all the later Indo-Europeans. At the time when they were still one people they were speaking one and the same tongue. From this tongue have descended all the languages later spoken by the civilized peoples of modern Europe, including, of course, our own English, as we shall see.

316. Before they dispersed, the parent people were still in the Stone Age for the most part, though copper was beginning

Civilization of Indo-European parent people

to come in, and the time was not later than 3000 B.C. Divided into numerous tribes, they wandered at will, seeking pasture for their flocks, for they already possessed domestic animals, including cattle and sheep. But chief among their domesticated beasts was the *horse*, which, as we recall, was at first entirely unknown to the civilized Oriental nations. The animal must have been known on the Fertile Crescent not much later than 3000 B.C. The Indo-Europeans employed the horse not only for riding but also for drawing their wheeled carts. The ox already bore the yoke and drew the plow, for some of the tribes had adopted a settled mode of life, and cultivated grain, especially barley. Being without writing, they possessed but little government and organization, but they were the most gifted and the most highly imaginative people of the ancient world.

317. As their tribes wandered farther and farther apart they lost contact with each other. Local peculiarities in speech and customs became more and more marked, finally producing great differences such as always result when peoples speaking the same language are widely separated. We are familiar, for example, with the noticeable differences between the spoken English of England and that of America. While at first the Indo-European groups could doubtless understand one another when they met, these differences in speech gradually became so great that the widely scattered tribes, even if they happened to meet, could no longer make themselves understood, and finally they lost all knowledge of their original kinship. This kinship has been rediscovered in very recent times. The final outcome, in so far as speech was concerned, was the languages of modern civilized Europe; so that, beginning with England in the west and going eastward, we can trace more than one common word from people to people entirely across Europe into northern India. Note the following:

Dispersion of Indo-European parent people

WEST			EAST		
English	German	Latin	Greek	Old Persian and Avestan	East Indian (Sanskrit)
brother	*bruder*	*fräter*	*phrātēr*	*brātar*	*bhrātar*
mother	*mutter*	*māter*	*mētēr*	*mātar*	*mātar*
father	*vater*	*pater*	*patēr*	*pitar*	*pitar*

In the west the earliest known group of these wanderers
from the northern grasslands had entered Asia Minor by
2500 B.C. These were the invaders who founded the Hittite
Empire (Section 27). Another Indo-European group pushed
southward and westward and easily subdued the population
in the great western bend of the Euphrates, where they became the ruling class of a new nation called Mitanni (§ 239).
Mitanni, we remember, threatened to block the westward
advance of Assyria, but was eventually crushed in the conflict between the Egyptians and the Hittites (§ 245). Farther
west the most advanced tribes of the Indo-Europeans had
already crossed the Danube and were far down in the Balkan
Peninsula by 2000 B.C. Some of them had doubtless entered
Italy by this time. These western tribes were, of course, a
part of the mixed ancestry of the Greeks and Romans; at
least they brought the earliest dialects of Greek and Roman
(Latin) speech into Greece and Italy. We shall join them
and follow them in their conquest of the Mediterranean.
Before doing so, however, we have to watch the advance of
the Indo-Europeans in Western Asia and at the eastern end
of the Fertile Crescent.

SECTION 27. EARLIEST KNOWN INDO-EUROPEANS AND THE HITTITE EMPIRE

318. As we look at the Highland Zone in Western Asia
we are aware that, hidden within and behind its screen of
Highland civili-   mountains, important movements of mankind
zation   had been going on for a long time in a region
we have not yet discussed. Before we do so let us look backward for a moment. In this book we have thus far found
that the Stone Age peoples of the Near East rose to a high
civilization in two regions: the Nile valley and the Fertile
Crescent (especially the valley of the Two Rivers). Recent
discoveries are showing us more and more of what was hap-
pening in Western Asia farther north. The Highland Zone here
includes a broad band of country extending from the Ægean

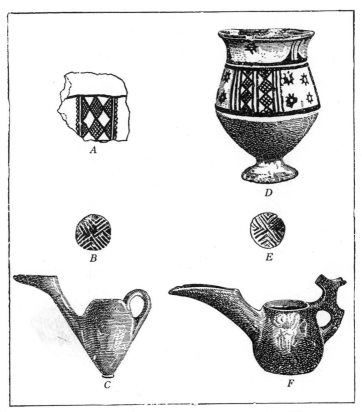

FIG. 124. *Early* POTTERY *and* SEALS *of the Highland Zone*

The left-hand column (*A*, *B*, and *C*) is a group from Anatolia and represents the craft of the Hittites, who occupied a large western section of the Highland Zone. In the right-hand column we have a similar group (*D*, *E*, and *F*) from Persia. The resemblance between these pairs (*A* and *D*, *B* and *E*, *C* and *F*) suggests the great uniformity of the Highland civilization stretching along the Highland Zone from Persia to Anatolia. It must be remembered that this Highland civilization was older than the Iranian migration which brought the Medes and Persians into the Highland Zone and into its sphere of influence

Sea on the west, eastward along the north side of the Fertile Crescent, and then farther eastward, between the Caspian Sea and the Persian Gulf, to the Iranian Plateau. A glance at the map (p. 146) will show that this region comprises, from west to east, Anatolia (Hittite Asia Minor), Armenia, Media, and Persia. Throughout all this extensive region the Late Stone Age peoples advanced to a Bronze Age civilization, which in many important respects was uniform for this whole Asiatic section of the Highland Zone. Beautiful painted pottery recently found in Persia can sometimes hardly be distinguished from the pottery found in the Hittite country at the other end of the Highland Zone civilization. We cannot yet give this far-reaching early civilization a name; but, naming it geographically, it is convenient to call it the Highland civilization. It is thought to have originated on the Iranian Pla-

FIG. 125. *Remains of a* ROOF SUPPORT *(X) from a Wooden House of the Late Stone Age, excavated beneath an Ancient Hittite City of Central Asia Minor*

This support was a tree trunk used to prop the roof timbers of the house. Thousands of years ago the house was covered by the fallen remains of an ancient Hittite city which was built over the spot. When excavated by the Oriental Institute of The University of Chicago the blackened stump of the tree trunk was found, as seen here, still standing on its stone base (*Y*). Very little of the house itself remained, but the stone tools and weapons found in it showed that it was erected by men of the Late Stone Age. The sides of the excavation pit, against which the archæologist is leaning as he makes his notes, are not the walls of the ancient house, but are the accumulated rubbish of later houses which were built on this spot and then fell to ruins. Down through this rubbish, now packed hard, the excavators have dug a pit over 90 feet deep, with vertical walls, which show the marks of the modern pickaxes and shovels

teau, and great quantities of its pottery and bronzes have recently been found in western Persia and Media. Connected with it was the earliest civilization in Elam (map, p. 146), which seems to have been very old, — as old, indeed, as the Sumerian civilization. Regarding the race of the Highland peoples who developed this civilization we can say very little. Without doubt they were not all of one race, and they seem not to have been Indo-Europeans in the beginning. A very important part in the development of the Highland civilization was played by the peoples who occupied Anatolia, or Hittite Asia Minor, especially because of the metals which they found in their mountains.

319. Asia Minor, or Anatolia,[1] the greater part of which was for so long occupied by the Hittites, is a vast peninsula from six hundred and fifty to seven hundred ⟨Asia Minor (Anatolia), the land of the Hittites⟩ miles long and from three to four hundred miles wide, being about as large as the state of Texas. The interior is a lofty table-land, little better than a desert in its central region. Around most of this table-land rise mountain ridges, fringing both the table-land and the sea. On both sides of the mountain fringe are fertile valleys and plains, producing plentiful crops. The seaward slopes of the mountains, especially along the Black Sea, are clad with flourishing forests. The northern shores of Asia Minor, east of the Halys River, rise into ridges containing rich deposits of metal ores, especially iron. The Hittites thus became the earliest distributors of iron when it began to displace bronze in the Mediterranean world and the Near East (§ 247).

320. In the earliest period before the Indo-European invasions it is convenient to call the inhabitants of the western end of the Highland Zone in Asia *Early Ana-* ⟨Race and prehistoric movements of Early Anatolians⟩ *tolians.* The climate is not favorable to the preservation of ancient bodies, and as yet excavation has recovered the skeletons of very few Early Anatolians. They were without doubt inhabiting this region already in the Late Stone Age, and, like the oldest inhabitants of the Highland Zone elsewhere (Fig. 80), they were a round-

---

[1] "Anatolia" is a Greek word equivalent to the Latin "Orient"; but usage has given it a much more limited meaning; for it is used to designate only Asia Minor as far east as the upper Euphrates. It has now been discovered that the earliest peoples of this region were not identical with the historic Hittites. Before the incoming of the Hittites we may therefore call the peoples of Asia Minor Anatolians, a term which implies nothing regarding their race or nationality.

headed people. Neither in type of body nor in language were
they Indo-Europeans.[1] The Early Anatolians overflowed
at both ends of
Asia Minor. At
the western end
some of them mi-
grated to Crete
and to the main-
land of Greece as
early as the Late
Stone Age. At
the eastern end
they poured into
Palestine in such
multitudes that
their unmistak-
able type of fea-
tures, with promi-
nent aquiline nose,
became the pre-
vailing (Jewish)
type in the whole

FIG. 126. *An Ancient* HITTITE *and his Modern*
Armenian DESCENDANT

At the left is the head of an ancient Hittite as carved
by an Egyptian sculptor on the wall of a temple at
Thebes, Egypt, over three thousand years ago. It strik-
ingly resembles the profile of the Armenians still living
in the Hittite country, as shown in the modern portrait on the right. The shape of both these heads is
that of the typical "round heads" of the Highland
Zone. Such a skull is flat behind; its back does not
project or overhang (cf. Fig. 80)

region of Palestine (§ 283). This marked example of the influence of the Early Anatolians in neighboring regions is a
striking illustration of their importance in the ancient world.

321. We know very little of these Early Anatolians, and
it will require decades of persistent excavation among their
Early Anatolians   earliest settlements before we shall be able
and Indo-Euro-   to piece together any considerable account of
pean invasion   their life and history (Fig. 125). Probably as
early as 2500 B.C. the Indo-Europeans of the north and east

[1] Scientifically speaking, there is no Indo-European type of body. It is important to bear in mind that while the vast majority of the Indo-European
peoples today are long-heads, there are nevertheless round-headed peoples, like
the Swiss and the Armenians, who now speak Indo-European languages. In the
same way, there is in the United States a large colored population speaking
English, but speaking English — an Indo-European language — does not make
Indo-Europeans out of Negroes. Nevertheless, in ancient times the prevailing
Indo-European type was long-headed.

began to push in, perhaps through the Caucasus Mountains. Forming the vanguard of Indo-European migration, they were the earliest Indo-Europeans to appear in the arena of history. The latest discoveries have shown that it is these Indo-European invaders of Anatolia whom we should call Hittites. Their invasion was the first of those vast movements of Indo-European migration in Western Asia which, as we shall see later, resulted finally in the conquest of the Fertile Crescent and the whole Near East by the Indo-European Medes and Persians. The Hittites first brought in the horse among the Early Anatolians, as the other Indo-Europeans did also along the Fertile Crescent. The Early Anatolians were not exterminated, but, just as in Mitanni, these horse-breeding invaders seem to have formed the ruling class. In language the result was a mixture of speech. The new, mixed language of course contained some Early Anatolian words, appearing side by side with Indo-European words and grammatical forms. For over a thousand years this mixed speech was an important language of Western Asia, and we shall call it Hittite.

322. When they entered Anatolia the Hittites were barbarians. The rise of the civilization which we may call Hittite was at first due to influence from the Fertile Crescent. In times past, as we re- **Rise of Hittite civilization** member, Babylonian caravans had traded in Asia Minor, and later Assyrian merchants had settled there. These business communities from the Fertile Crescent made the Hittites acquainted with commercial transactions. In transacting their business the Hittites themselves gradually learned to read clay-tablet bills and invoices written in cuneiform. Excavations have even uncovered fragments of their clay-tablet dictionaries with three columns, the first Sumerian, the second Babylonian or Akkadian, and the third Hittite. Thus they learned to write their own Hittite words in cuneiform. At first they used cuneiform writing only to write Babylonian or Akkadian, the language of Akkad. When they wrote letters to foreigners abroad, they

continued to do so in the speech of Babylonia. Eventually, however, they learned to use the cuneiform signs for writing their own mixed speech, which we have called Hittite.[1] Thus the clay tablet became common in the Hittite world, and it was probably through the Hittites that the use of clay tablets passed over into Crete. After the introduction of writing the Hittites made noticeable progress, and by 2000 B.C. they were a highly civilized people. Fully able to compete with the greatest nations of the Ancient Near East, they twice rose, as the rival of Egypt and Assyria. These two great periods we shall call the First Hittite Empire (about 1900 to 1650 B.C.) and the Second Hittite Empire (about 1400 to 1200 B.C.).

323. The earliest Hittite king of whom we have any knowledge is Anitta, who arose in the city of Kussar, in eastern

First Hittite Empire — Asia Minor, perhaps about 2000 B.C. The exact location of Kussar is not known. It is quite clear that the Hittites did not then form a single nation, but lived in a number of kingdoms which, like the later Greek kingdoms, were often at war with one another. The leadership was finally gained by the kingdom of Hatti,[2] which lay inside the great bend of the river Halys in central Asia Minor. Its capital was called Hattusas. The kings of Hatti were able to conquer neighboring kingdoms and build up a small empire. Early in the Eighteenth Century B.C. the great king Mursil, the first of that name, arose in Hattusas. In the days when the power of Hammurapi's successors at Babylon was tottering, it was Mursil I who marched down the Euphrates, captured Babylon, and overthrew the last of Hammurapi's line, the First Dynasty of Babylon, about 1750 B.C. (§ 231). Eventually the successors of Mursil I weakened, and before 1600 B.C. the First Hittite Empire fell.

[1] The Hittite tablets contained so many Babylonian word signs that during the World War the Czechoslovakian scholar Bedřich Hrozný succeeded in deciphering the Hittite cuneiform. Since the war our knowledge of Hittite has increased greatly, and the German scholar Emil Forrer has shown that the tablets found at Hattusas contain examples of seven languages besides Hittite.

[2] The name *Khatti* or *Hatti* is of course the origin of our modern name "Hittite." The closeness of the resemblance will be evident when the modern ending *ite* is removed, leaving *Hitt*.

324. The Second Hittite Empire, which arose after 1400 B.C., remained for two centuries the greatest power in Western Asia. Its founder bore the long name Suppilulyuma.[1] He was the ablest soldier Western Asia had seen since the campaigns of Thutmose III, which had begun almost exactly a century before those of the great Hittite king. But now there was no Thutmose III to turn back the powerful Hittite soldier. Weakened by the religious revolution of Ikhnaton, the Egyptians could only helplessly watch the advance of the Hittites as they conquered all Syria and made it Hittite territory. Thereupon Suppilulyuma crossed the Euphrates and crushed the power of Mitanni. Feeble Assyria was at that time the vassal of Mitanni, and the Hittite conqueror of Mitanni was therefore lord over the greater part of Western Asia.

Rise of Second Hittite Empire

325. Among the clay tablets which have been dug up in the Hittite capital of Hattusas there is a remarkable cuneiform letter, written at this time to the great Hittite emperor by a queen of Egypt, possibly the widow of Ikhnaton. She is the queen whose graceful figure we have seen sitting at dinner with her husband and their little daughters, but with no son, in the palace at Amarna (Fig. 72). This letter is striking evidence of the Hittite conqueror's greatness and power, for the Egyptian queen tells him that she has no son to occupy her dead husband's throne, and she begs the Hittite ruler to send one of his sons to become her husband and thus to be the king of Egypt. This marriage, if it had taken place, would have made the Hittite royal family the lords of both the Egyptian and the Hittite Empire. The two together would have formed the greatest empire the world had ever seen. But the Hittite emperor was suspicious of the Egyptian queen's extraordinary proposal, and before sending his son he made an investigation. When, after this delay, he did finally send one of his sons, it was too late. Arriving in Egypt after the

Second Hittite Empire, leader of Western Asia

---

[1] We do not know much about the pronunciation of Hittite proper names, but this name was probably pronounced "Soop-pee-lool'yu-ma."

powerful enemies of Ikhnaton's family had pushed aside the
widowed queen, the young Hittite prince was seized and slain.
Thus Suppilulyuma lost the opportunity of gaining control
of Egypt without striking a blow. But he had other sons, and
these he crowned as the leading kings of Syria, and thus made
the northern end of the Egyptian Empire his own. On the
south his empire extended down to Palestine, which Egypt
continued to hold; on the east beyond the Euphrates his
territory included much of Mitanni; and his eastern boundary for a time lay far over toward Assyria. On the north and
the west the Second Hittite Empire included the larger part
of Asia Minor, and the commercial city of Troy must have
felt the pressure of Hittite power, if it was not, indeed, a
vassal of the Hittite conqueror. By 1350 B.C. the Hittite
Empire was the most powerful state that had ever arisen
in Western Asia.

326. The two empires, Egyptian and Hittite, were now
rivals for the leadership of the world. It was a rivalry which
was fought out for over a quarter of a century

Egypto-Hittite ri-
valry and treaty
of peace
between the grandsons of Suppilulyuma and
the great Pharaohs Seti I and Ramses II. As
the war went on, especially after 1300 B.C., the rise of Assyria
gave the Hittite emperors increasing uneasiness. They made
treaties with their vassal kings in Syria which pledged them
to act as enemies of Assyria. Among the clay tablets dug up
at Hattusas is a very interesting letter written by the Hittite
emperor, urging the young king of Babylon to attack Assyria
from behind. Then, as dissensions arose among the Hittites
themselves, Suppilulyuma's grandson, Hattusil, arranged a
treaty of peace with Ramses II, who received it from the
Hittite king engraved upon a silver tablet. Thus the struggle
between these powerful rivals ended. Intimate relations between the two royal families were established. Even the two
queens, of Egypt and Hatti, exchanged friendly greetings
and letters of congratulation on the new peace pact. These
clay-tablet letters, written some time in the 1270's B.C.,
were found by the modern excavators lying among the royal

files and records dug up at the Hittite capital. Later on the Hittite emperor sent his daughter to Egypt to become the wife of Ramses II. On the walls of the Egyptian temples, almost as far south as the Second Cataract in Nubia, the Pharaoh's sculptors carved the scene depicting the arrival of his Hittite bride.

327. The civilization of the Second Hittite Empire attained a high level and had a far-reaching influence. It is important to notice some of its leading achievements. The Hittite state was built up out of a large group of weaker kingdoms *Hittite civilization: the state and its laws* conquered by the original kingdom of Hatti. Every year the subject states were obliged to contribute infantry and chariotry to the emperor's army. The emperor's power consisted of this composite army, combined with the soldiers drawn from his own kingdom of Hatti. The government operated under a system of wise laws which even the king himself was bound to obey. The advance of Hittite civilization is disclosed to us in the fact that after the peace with Egypt the Hittite king, perhaps Hattusil, issued a revised code of these laws which was much more humane than formerly. Nearly two hundred paragraphs, forming a large part of this code, have survived on the clay tablets. In this code the king often refers to former, more severe punishments which he is making less severe. For stealing a head of cattle the penalty had formerly been a fine of thirty head, but in the new code this fine was reduced to fifteen. Even for murder capital punishment was not inflicted, and mutilation of the culprit by cutting off ears or nose was not practiced. This Hittite code is therefore far more humane than the savage laws of Assyria, and more so indeed than the codes of Babylonia or Egypt. The respect for law which the Hittite kings display is very remarkable. Indeed, Suppilulyuma admits that his invasion of the Egyptian Empire in Syria was unlawful, and regards an epidemic of plague among his people as a punishment for his offense.

328. The enlightened attitude of the Hittite kings was doubtless responsible in some degree for the remarkable de-
Hittite architec-
ture; sculpture
velopment among the Hittites along lines other than statecraft. The earliest impressive stone architecture in Asia was the work of the Hittite architects. The powerful walled city of Hattusas which they erected was the first really large city ever built in Asia. It far surpassed the Babylon of that day in size, and the Nineveh of the Assyrian emperors was still some six centuries in the future. The most notable form which the Hittite architects introduced into building was the front of the king's palace, which consisted of a porch in the middle, with its roof supported on two columns, while on either side of the porch was a square tower. The building was called "a house of two towers." It was such a porch which was adopted by the Assyrian emperors in their palaces (§ 261), and it finally reached the Persians.

The Hittite architects understood the value of sculpture as an adornment of architecture. Set up on either side of the central doorway of the king's palace were two splendid sentinel lions carved in stone. This idea of protective animal images was drawn from the similar use of the Egyptian sphinxes, which were likewise taken over by the Hittites. (See also Fig. 108.) Sculpture was further employed in the embellishment of the wall by a dado, consisting of large, flat slabs of stone carved with relief pictures. These were transmitted by the Hittites to Assyria. The Hittites likewise adopted the Egyptian winged sun-disk, which then seems to have passed from them to the Assyrians. At the same time the Hittite sculptors received the early Babylonian symbol of the eagle with outspread wings and a lion's head or sometimes a double head. They passed it on across the Ægean to later Europe, from which it finally came to us in the United States as the American eagle.

329. The clay-tablet cuneiform records of the Hittite emperors are the earliest historical narratives which display a literary prose style. The Hittite scribes were interested in

Fig. 127. A *Hittite Prince* HUNTING DEER

The prince, accompanied by his driver, stands in the moving chariot, shooting
with bow and arrow at the fleeing stag. A hound runs beside the horses. Over the
scene is an inscription in Hittite hieroglyphs (§ 329). The whole is sculptured
in stone and forms a good example of the rather crude Hittite art

literature, and this interest led them to make copies of the
old Babylonian writings with evident pleasure. The story
of the Babylonian hero Gilgamesh was known
throughout the whole of Asia Minor, and   Hittite literature
he passed from there to Greece under the new name of
"Heracles," later "Hercules." Besides historical composi-
tions there were even special treatises, such as an essay on
horse-breeding which the Hittites borrowed from Mitanni.

Unlike the scribes of other great civilizations the Hittite
writers were interested in being known as authors, and attached their names to their writings. They were the earliest
known self-conscious authors, and they thus show a very
modern spirit. As the Hittite emperors began to erect stone
buildings they felt the need of a larger monumental style of
writing which would make it possible to decorate a building
with historical records as the Egyptians did. They therefore
devised a system of writing made up of picture signs. With
these new hieroglyphic signs they engraved great stone records like those of Egypt. Carved in the face of rocky cliffs

or masonry walls, these records still look down upon the traveler throughout a large part of Asia Minor from the Ægean to the Euphrates. Unfortunately this *hieroglyphic* writing of the Hittites has not yet been fully deciphered,[1] and we are still unable to read more than parts of it.

330. In religion likewise the Hittites were greatly influenced by Babylonian and Egyptian beliefs. This is especially evident in the symbols like the Babylonian eagle and the Egyptian winged sun-disk. The Hittites worshiped two great groups of gods: those of the earth and those of the sky. Side by side with the Earth-Mother, to whom the Hittites were devoted, was their Sun-god, who was evidently taken over from Egypt. He was so prominent that the Hittite emperor even called himself "the Sun."

Hittite religion

331. Lying between southeastern Europe and the great civilizations of the Near East, Hittite civilization served as a link connecting the two, and the influences which it passed on to the early Ægean world were of permanent importance. From the Hittite world the Greeks received coinage (§ 495), besides important items in art, architecture, and religion. However, the Hittites are not to be considered as merely carriers of civilization. As we have seen (§§ 328–329), the Hittite Empire made significant original contributions to the cultures of the Ancient Near East. These influences were passed on by Assyria to the Persians, that other great Indo-European people of Western Asia, whom we shall now study.

Permanent influence of Hittite civilization

SECTION 28. THE ARYAN PEOPLES AND THE IRANIAN PROPHET ZOROASTER

332. It is now an established fact that the easternmost tribes of the Indo-European line, having left the parent people, were pasturing their herds in the great steppe on the east of the Caspian by about 2000 B.C. Here they formed

---

[1] The decipherment, while not yet completed, has made great progress.

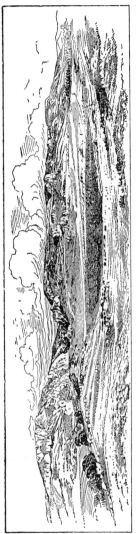

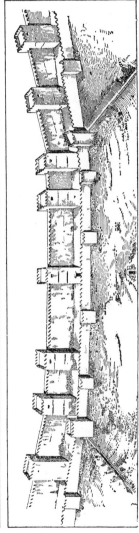

Fig. 128. *The Ancient* Capital *of the Hittites in Central Asia Minor*

The view at the top shows the ruins of the great walled city which covered a group of hills like those of Rome. A modern village close by, called Boghaz-Köi, has given the place its modern name: but the Hittites called the city Hattusas. The view below shows a portion of the masonry walls of the city as they once were, when the Hittite kings lived here in the Thirteenth Century B.C. Excavation by German archæologists at Hattusas revealed also the clay tablets which once filled the state record chambers in the Hittite palace. These records have given us an entirely new conception of the international situation during the Second Hittite Empire. (After Puchstein)

a people properly called the Aryans [1] (see Fig. 123), and here they made their home for some time. The Aryan people

Aryans; advance of the eastern wing of the Indo-European line

had no writing, and they have left no monuments. Nevertheless, the beliefs of their descendants show that the Aryan tribes already possessed a high form of religion, which summed up conduct as "good thoughts, good deeds." Fire occupied an important place in this worship, and they had a group of priests whom they called "fire-kindlers."

333. When the Aryans broke up, perhaps about 1800 B.C., they separated into two groups. The eastern tribes wandered

Sanskrit-speaking tribes in India

southeastward and eventually arrived in India. In their sacred books, which we call the *Vedas*, written in Sanskrit, there are echoes of the days of Aryan unity, and they furnish many a hint of the ancient Aryan home on the east of the Caspian.

334. The tribes of the other group kept the name "Aryan" in the form "Iran," [2] so that we call them Iranians. They

Mitannians, Medes, and Persians on the Fertile Crescent

also left the Aryan home and pushed westward and southwestward into the mountains bordering the Fertile Crescent. The Mitannians were a horse-breeding tribe of this Iranian group. Farther east were two powerful groups of the Iranians called the Medes and the Persians, who were yet to conquer the Fertile Crescent and establish the last great Oriental empire in Western Asia.

---

[1] The Indo-European parent people seemingly had no common name for all their tribes as a great group. The term "Aryan" is often popularly applied to the parent people, but this custom is incorrect. "Aryan" (from which "Iran" and "Iranian" are later derivatives) designated a group of tribes, a fragment of the parent people, which detached itself and found a home for some centuries just east of the Caspian Sea. When we hear the term "Aryan" applied to the Indo-European peoples of Europe, or when it is said that we ourselves are descended from the Aryans, we must remember that this use of the word is historically incorrect, though very common. The Aryans, then, were *Eastern* descendants of the Indo-European parent people, as we are *Western* descendants of the parent people. The Aryans are our distant cousins but not our ancestors.

[2] They have given their name to the great Iranian Plateau, which stretches from the Zagros Mountains eastward to the Indus River. This whole region was known in Greek and Roman days as Ariana, which (like "Iran") is of course derived from "Aryan" (see map, p 198).

FIG. 129. HOUSES of a STONE AGE VILLAGE in Persia, probably about
Six Thousand Years Old

In the background we see the palace terrace of Persepolis (compare Fig. 200), built
some 3500 years after this village was forsaken. The walls of the houses throughout the village are still standing up to a height of six or seven feet, with doors and
the earliest known windows still preserved. Stone knives and other implements,
together with beautifully painted pottery — sometimes containing remnants of
food — were found on the floors of these houses in front of the hearths over which
the food was cooked. The art displayed in the painted decorations on the pottery
is surprisingly advanced. These people lived just at the dawn of the age of metal,
as shown by one or two pieces of copper found in the village. At the present day
the entire village is about 600 feet long and half as wide. When discovered by
Dr. Herzfeld it was covered by a mound rising only ten or twelve feet above the
surrounding plain. The village is being excavated by the Oriental Institute of The
University of Chicago, and the clearance is still incomplete

335. By the time of the coming of the Iranians the fringe
of peoples along the north and east of the Fertile Crescent
had adopted much of the more advanced civi-   Medes receive civ-
lization of the Two Rivers. Especially in   ilization of Fertile
Elam on the east and in Urartu (Hebrew   Crescent
Ararat), in the later Armenian country on the north, the
civilization of the Fertile Crescent had been very influential.
The Assyrian emperors, especially after 700 B.C., had completely defeated these frontier peoples and broken their

power. This was particularly true of the Elamites, whose country was taken over by the Persians. The Indo-European invaders were therefore able to settle in these border states on the east and north of the Fertile Crescent, and there they found cuneiform writing, which had been adopted by the Elamites many centuries earlier and was common in Urartu also. The Medes, who were the leaders of the Indo-European invasion, soon learned cuneiform writing, and the Persians seem to have taken it over from the Medes.

336. After they invaded the Highland Zone, therefore, but before they conquered the Fertile Crescent, the once rude

The Indo-European Medes threaten Semitic Chaldeans

Indo-European shepherds and herdsmen acquired at least a veneer of civilization, although their life and government long remained simple and crude, and in some ways almost barbarous. By 700 B.C. the Medes had established a powerful Iranian empire in the mountains east of the Tigris. It extended finally from the Persian Gulf, where it included the Persians, northwestward in the general line of the mountains, to the Black Sea region. The front of the Indo-European eastern wing was thus roughly parallel with the Tigris at this point, but its advance was not to stop here. As their capital the Medes founded the city of Ecbatana (see map, p. 146) about 700 B.C. It lay directly opposite the pass that led through the Zagros Mountains to the Fertile Crescent and to the city of Babylon itself. A century later Nebuchadnezzar and his successors at Babylon looked, therefore, with anxious eyes at this dangerous Median power, recalling no doubt how in 612 B.C. these same people had so willingly united in the assault against Nineveh.

The Chaldeans on the Euphrates represented the leadership of men of Semitic blood from the southern pastures. Their leadership was now to be followed by that of men of Indo-European blood from the northern pastures. As we see the Chaldeans giving way before the Medes and Persians, let us bear in mind that we are watching a great racial change, and remember that these new Iranian masters of the East were our kindred; for both we and they have descended from the same wandering shepherd ancestors, the Indo-European parent people, who once dwelt in the far-off pastures of inner Asia, probably five thousand years ago.

337. All of these Iranians possessed a beautiful religion inherited from old Aryan days before their migration. A generation after the fall of Nineveh, perhaps Religion of Iranians about 570 B.C.,[1] there was born a Median prophet named Zoroaster. He began to look out upon the life of men in an effort to find a new religion which would supply the needs of man's life. He watched the ceaseless struggle between good and evil which seemed to meet him wherever he turned, and which he found already expressed in the beliefs of his people about the old gods. To him there seemed to be a struggle between a group of good beings, on the one hand, and a group of evil powers, on the other. The Good became to him a divine person, whom he called Mazda, after one of the old gods, or Ahuramazda, which means "Lord of Wisdom," and whom he regarded as God. Ahuramazda was surrounded by a group of helpers much like angels, of whom one of the greatest was the Light, called Mithras. Opposed to Ahuramazda and his helpers, it was finally believed, there was an evil group led by a great Spirit of Evil named Ahriman. It was he who was later inherited by Jews and Christians as Satan.

338. Thus the faith of Zoroaster grew up out of the struggle of life itself and became a great power in life. It was one of the noblest religions ever founded. It Judgment hereafter called upon every man to stand on one side or the other,— to fill his soul with the Good and the Light or to dwell in the Evil and the Darkness. Whatever course a man pursued, he must expect a judgment hereafter. This was the earliest appearance in Asia of belief in a last judgment. Zoroaster's new faith was an idealization of the old

---

[1] There has been much difference of opinion about the date of Zoroaster. Several earlier dates formerly seemed possible, but the evidence now seems to favor the Sixth Century B.C.

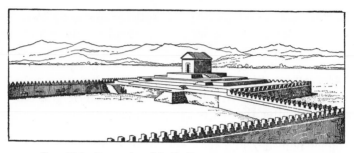

FIG. 130. *Restoration of the Earliest Known Persian* TEMPLE

This temple was recently discovered at Pasargadæ by Herzfeld, who concludes that it was erected by Cyrus himself, near whose palace and tomb it stands. (After Herzfeld)

beliefs and the old gods of his people. Therefore he retained the old Aryan veneration of fire as a visible symbol of the Good and the Light, and he preserved the ancient fire-kindling priests.

339. Unable to influence his own people, Zoroaster left the Medes and finally went south to the Persians, preaching

Zoroaster establishes his new religion

his new religion, and perhaps for many years he found but little response to his efforts. We can discern his hopes and fears alike in the little group of hymns he has left, probably the only words of the great prophet which have survived. It is characteristic of the horse-loving Iranians that Zoroaster is said finally to have converted one of their great kings by miraculously healing the king's crippled horse. The new faith had gained a firm footing before the prophet's death, however, and before 500 B.C. it was the leading religion of the Iranians and accepted by the Persian emperors. It is even possible that Darius erected the prophet's tomb. Besides the hymns mentioned above, fragments of his teaching have descended to us in writings put together in the early Christian Era, many centuries after the prophet's death. All together these sacred writings form a book known as the *Avesta*. This we may call the Bible of the Persians.

WERE ELIMITES

SECTION 29. THE RISE OF THE PERSIAN EMPIRE

340. No people became more zealous followers of Zoroaster than the group of Iranian tribes known as the Persians. Through them a knowledge of him has de- *Emergence of the* scended to us. As we have seen (§ 335), the *Persians; their* Persians had settled in Elam at the south- *land and traditions* eastern end of the Zagros Mountains, just north of the Persian Gulf. Its shores are here little better than desert, but the valleys of the mountainous hinterland are rich and fertile. In these valleys the Persians occupied a district some four hundred miles long. They were still a plain peasant folk, feeding their flocks and herds on the hills and leading a settled agricultural life, with simple institutions, no art, no writing or literature, but with stirring memories of their past.

341. They acknowledged themselves vassals of their kinsmen the Medes, who ruled far to the north and northwest of them. One of the Persian tribes, dwelling in *Cyrus unites Per-* the mountains of Elam, was organized as a *sian tribes and* little kingdom called Anshan. About sixty *conquers Medes* years after the fall of Nineveh Anshan was ruled over by a Persian named Cyrus, who succeeded in uniting the other tribes of his kindred Persians and forming a nation. Thereupon Cyrus rebelled against the rule of the Medes. He gathered his peasant soldiery, and within three years he defeated the Median king and made himself master of the Median territory (549 B.C.). The extraordinary career of Cyrus was now a spectacle upon which all eyes in the lands of the west were fastened with wonder and alarm.

342. The overflowing energies of the new conqueror and his peasant soldiery proved irresistible. The Persian peasants seem to have been remarkable archers. *Persian army* The mass of the Persian army was made up of bowmen whose storm of arrows at long range overwhelmed the enemy long before the hand-to-hand fighting began. Bodies of the skillful Persian horsemen, hovering on either wing, then rode in and completed the destruction of the foe

These arrangements were taken by the Persians from the Assyrians, the greatest soldiers whom the East had ever seen.

343. The great states of Chaldea (Babylonia) **Cyrus conquers the west** and Egypt, Lydia under Crœsus in western Asia Minor, and even Sparta in Greece formed a powerful combination against this sudden menace, which had risen like the flash of a meteor in the eastern sky. Without an instant's delay Cyrus struck at Crœsus of Lydia, the chief author of the hostile combination. One Persian victory followed another. By 546 B.C. Sardes, the Lydian capital, had fallen, and Crœsus, the Lydian king, was a prisoner in the hands of Cyrus. Cyrus at once gained also the southern coasts of Asia Minor. Within five years the power of the little Persian kingdom in the mountains of Elam

FIG. 131. *Persian* SOLDIERS

Although carrying spears when doing duty as palace guards, these men were chiefly archers, as is shown by the size of the large quivers on their backs. The bow hangs on the left shoulder. The royal bodyguard may also be seen wielding their spears around the Persian king at the battle of Issus (Fig. 198). Notice the splendid robes worn by these palace guards. The figures are done in brightly colored glazed brick,— an art borrowed by the Persians and employed to beautify the palace walls

had swept across Asia Minor to the Mediterranean, as the genius of Cyrus made it the leading nation of the world.

344. Turning eastward again, Cyrus had no trouble in defeating the Chaldean army led by the young crown prince Belshazzar, whose name in the Book of Daniel (see Dan. v) is a household word throughout the Christian world. In spite of the vast walls erected by Nebuchadnezzar to protect Babylon, the Persians entered the great city in 538 B.C., seemingly without resistance. Thus, only seventy-four years after the fall of Nineveh had opened the conflict between the former dwellers in the northern and the southern grasslands, the Semitic East completely collapsed before the advance of the Indo-European power.

Cyrus conquers Chaldea; collapse of Semitic East

345. Cyrus established his capital and royal residence at Pasargadæ, where the palace of the heroic conqueror has recently been excavated. Very little of it has survived; but on one of the reliefs the lower portion of a royal figure is preserved, and on a fold of the garment, in cuneiform signs, we may still read the words "Cyrus, the great king." Here, also, he built a temple for the faith of Zoroaster, who was probably still living. It is the oldest known Persian temple. Nine years after his capture of Babylon, Cyrus, the first great conqueror of Indo-European blood, fell in battle (529 B.C.) as he was fighting with the nomads in northeastern Iran. His body was reverently laid away in a massive tomb of impressive simplicity at Pasargadæ, and there it was found two hundred years later by Alexander the Great.

Capital and tomb of Cyrus; his death, 529 B.C.

346. All Western Asia was now subject to the Persian king.[1] In 525 B.C., only four years after the death of Cyrus, his son Cambyses conquered Egypt. This conquest of the only remaining ancient Oriental power rounded out the Persian Empire to include the whole civilized East from the Nile Delta, around the entire eastern end of the Mediterranean, to the Ægean, and from this western boundary

Cambyses conquers Egypt; Persia rules the whole civilized East

---

[1] It will aid the memory to note the three great invasions of the Indo-Europeans in Western Asia. There were, of course, others less important. It will be helpful also to notice that two intervals, of roughly 1000 years each, separate I and II, and II and III.

   I. Conquest of Early Anatolian country, about 2500 B.C.
   II. Conquest of Mitanni, about 1500 B.C.
   III. Conquest of the Fertile Crescent and entire Near East, completed and organized 500 B.C. by the capture of Nineveh (612 B.C.), Sardes (546 B.C.), and Babylon (538 B.C.) and the conquest of Egypt (525 B.C.).

FIG. 132. *The* TOMB *of* CYRUS *at Pasargadæ*

Perhaps built by Cyrus himself alongside his temple and his palace. The columns are a later addition, not belonging to the original monument. The body of Cyrus had lain in this tomb for nearly two hundred years when Alexander the Great (§ 733) found it plundered of its royal ornaments and lying on the floor. He ordered the body restored to its place, and had the tomb chamber closed up. It is now empty. (Photograph by the Oriental Institute of The University of Chicago)

eastward almost to India (see map IV, p. 266). The great task had consumed just twenty-five years (550 to 525 B.C.) since the overthrow of the Medes by Cyrus. It was an achievement for which the Assyrian Empire had prepared the way, and the Persians were now to learn much from the great civilizations which had preceded them.

SECTION 30. THE CIVILIZATION OF THE PERSIAN EMPIRE
(530–330 B.C.)

347. The Persians found Babylon a great and splendid city, with the vast fortifications of Nebuchadnezzar stretching from river to river, and his sumptuous buildings visible far across the Babylonian Plain. The city was the center of the commerce of Western Asia, and the greatest market in the early Oriental world. Along the Nile the Persian emperors now ruled the splendid cities whose colossal monuments we have visited. These things and the civilized life which the Persians found along the Nile and the Euphrates soon influenced them greatly, as we shall see.

Persian kings absorb civilization of the East they rule

348. Aramaic, the speech of the Aramean merchants who filled the busy market places of Babylon, had by that time become the language of the whole Fertile Crescent. Business documents were now written in Aramaic, with pen and ink, on papyrus; and clay tablets, bearing cuneiform writing, were slowly disappearing. The Persian officials were therefore obliged to carry on their government business, such as the collection of taxes, in the Aramaic tongue throughout the western half of the Persian Empire, and probably also in much of the eastern half. Even as far as the Nile and western Asia Minor they sent out their government documents in Aramaic, this universal language of business.

Aramaic becomes language of Persian administration in the west

349. The government of the Persian kings, like that of the Assyrian Empire, was thus bilingual, by which we mean that it employed two languages,— Aramaic and the old Persian tongue. Even in writing Persian the Persians often employed Aramaic letters, as we write English with Roman letters. But they already possessed a cuneiform *alphabet*, having probably gained the idea of an alphabet from Aramaic writing. Recent discoveries at Ecbatana, the Median capital, indicate that the Medes devised this new alphabet of thirty-nine *cuneiform* signs, which was now employed for writing Persian on clay tablets. They also used it when they wished to make records on large monuments of stone (Fig. 133).

Persians devise a cuneiform alphabet

350. These cuneiform records of the Persians are very important in that they first enabled us to read the cuneiform inscriptions of Western Asia. When Aramaic had displaced the Babylonian and Assyrian languages, there came a time when no one wrote any more clay tablets or other records in the ancient wedge writing. The latest cuneiform tablet known

Importance of Persian cuneiform documents

belongs among the astronomical records of the Chaldeans and was written in the year 7 B.C.[1] Nearly two thousand years ago, therefore, the last man who could read a cuneiform tablet had passed away. The history of Babylonia and Assyria was consequently lost under the city mounds along the Tigris and Euphrates.

351. Now the Persian cuneiform, consisting of only thirtynine alphabetical signs, was not difficult. In the early Nine-

Value of Persian cuneiform in deciphering Babylonian cuneiform

teenth Century A.D. Grotefend, a German schoolmaster, identified and read the names of Darius and Xerxes (Fig. 134) and some other Persian words. Various interested European scholars were later able to discover the sounds of nearly all the signs in the Persian cuneiform alphabet. By 1847 Sir Henry Rawlinson, a British army officer, had completed the decipherment of Persian cuneiform, and scholars were then able to read the old Persian inscriptions. But the number of these inscriptions then known was very small. Indeed, the chief value of the ability to read ancient Persian cuneiform records lay in the fact that this Persian writing might form a bridge leading over to an understanding of ancient *Babylonian* cuneiform.

352. Scholars had early discovered that the inscription C on the great Behistun monument of King Darius (see

History of Babylonia and Assyria recovered

Fig. 133) was written with the same cuneiform signs which were also observable on many of the older clay tablets and stone monuments found in Babylonia. It was understood, therefore, that if inscription C at Behistun could be deciphered, it would be possible then to read all the ancient documents of Babylonia and Assyria. Within three years Rawlinson, working from the Behistun inscriptions, had deciphered

---

[1] The tablet is dated in the year 305 of the Seleucid Era. This era began in 312 B.C. The date of this latest cuneiform document is therefore 7 B.C.

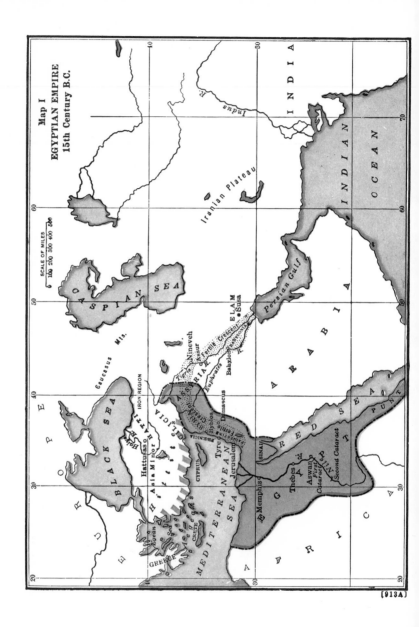

Map I
EGYPTIAN EMPIRE
15th Century B.C.

SCALE OF MILES
0 100 200 300 400 500

INDIA

Indus

Iranian Plateau

CASPIAN SEA

Persian Gulf

Caucasus Mts.

Tigris R.

Nineveh
Assur
ASSYRIA

Fertile Crescent

Euphrates R.

Babylon
Akkad

ELAM

Susa

ARABIA

INDIAN OCEAN

BLACK SEA

IRON REGION

HATTI

Hattusas

Asia Minor

CILICIA

CYPRUS

MEDITERRANEAN SEA

Damascus

SYRIA

Byblos
PHOENICIA
Tyre

PALESTINE
Jerusalem

Fertile Crescent

(SINAI)

RED SEA

PUNT

GREECE

CRETE

Aegean Sea

E U R O P E

Memphis

E G Y P T

Thebes

Aswan
First Cataract

NUBIA

Second Cataract

A F R I C A

[913A]

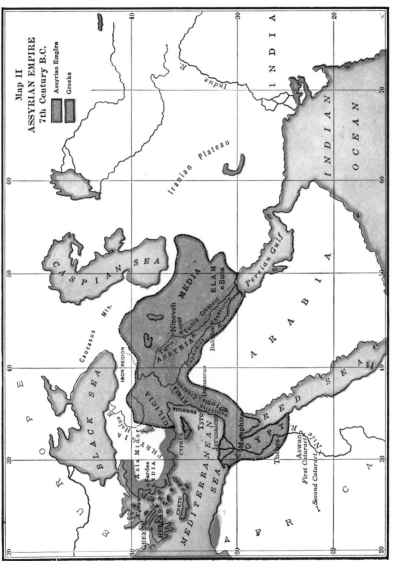

Map II
ASSYRIAN EMPIRE
7th Century B.C.
Assyrian Empire
Greeks

SEQUENCE MAP SHOWING EXPANSION OF THE ORIENTAL EMPIRES FOR A THOUSAND YEARS (FROM ABOUT 1500 TO 500 B.C.). IN FOUR PARTS. (See Map III and Map IV following)

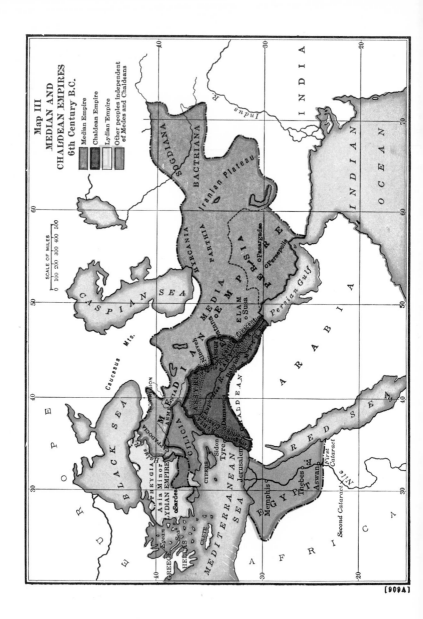

Map III
MEDIAN AND
CHALDEAN EMPIRES
6th Century B.C.

Median Empire
Chaldean Empire
Lydian Empire
Other peoples independent
of Medes and Chaldeans

SCALE OF MILES
0 100 200 300 400 500

INDIA

Indus R.

Iranian Plateau

SOGDIANA

BACTRIANA

HYRCANIA

PARTHIA

CASPIAN SEA

MEDIA

PERSIA EMPIRE

ELAM
Susa

Pasargadae
Persepolis

Persian Gulf

Caucasus Mts.

ARMENIA

ASSYRIA
Nineveh

CHALDEAN

Babylon

ARABIA

BLACK SEA

CAPPADOCIA

PHRYGIA

Asia Minor
LYDIAN EMPIRE
Sardes

CILICIA

Sidon
Tyre
Damascus
Jerusalem

CYPRUS

MEDITERRANEAN SEA

CRETE

GREECE
Aegean Sea

EUROPE

Memphis

Thebes
Aswan
First Cataract

EGYPT

RED SEA

Second Cataract

Nile

AFRICA

INDIAN OCEAN

INDIA

[909A]

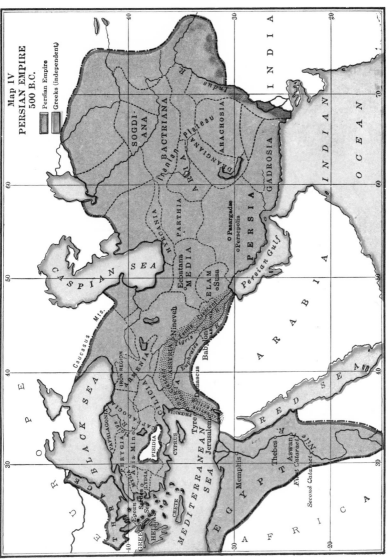

Map IV
PERSIAN EMPIRE
500 B.C.

Persian Empire
Greeks (independent)

SEQUENCE MAP SHOWING EXPANSION OF THE ORIENTAL EMPIRES FOR A THOUSAND YEARS (FROM ABOUT 1500 TO 500 B.C.) IN FOUR PARTS. (See Map I and Map II preceding)

Fig. 133. *Triumphal Monument of* Darius the Great, *the* Rosetta Stone of Asia, *on the Cliff of Behistun*

This impressive monument is the most important historical document surviving in Asia. It is made up of four important parts: the relief sculptures (*A*) and the three inscriptions (*B, C, D*). *B* is a great inscription in columns some 12 feet high, recording the triumph of Darius over all his enemies in the extensive revolts which followed his coronation. It is in the Persian language, written with the new cuneiform alphabet of thirty-nine letters which the Medes probably devised (§ 349). The other two inscriptions (*C* and *D*) are translations of the Persian (*B*). *C* therefore contains the same record as the Persian (*B*), but it is in the Babylonian language and is written in Babylonian cuneiform, with its several hundred wedge-signs (§ 178). *D*, the third inscription, is also cuneiform, in the language of the region of Elam, and hence is called Elamite. Thus the Great King published his triumph in the three most important languages of this eastern region and placed the record overlooking a main road at Behistun (see map, p. 498), where the men of the caravans passing between Babylon and the Iranian Plateau would look up 300 feet and see the splendid monument 25 feet high and 50 feet wide. To reach it requires a dangerous climb, and it was on this lofty cliff, at the risk of his life, that Sir Henry Rawlinson copied all three of these cuneiform inscriptions (1835–1847). By the use of these copies Rawlinson succeeded in deciphering the ancient Babylonian cuneiform, and this great monument of Darius therefore enabled modern historians to recover the lost language and history of Babylonia and Assyria. It did for Western Asia what the Rosetta Stone did for Egypt. (Drawn from photographs of the British Museum Expedition)

FIG. 134. The Two Old Persian Inscriptions which were first
Deciphered and Read

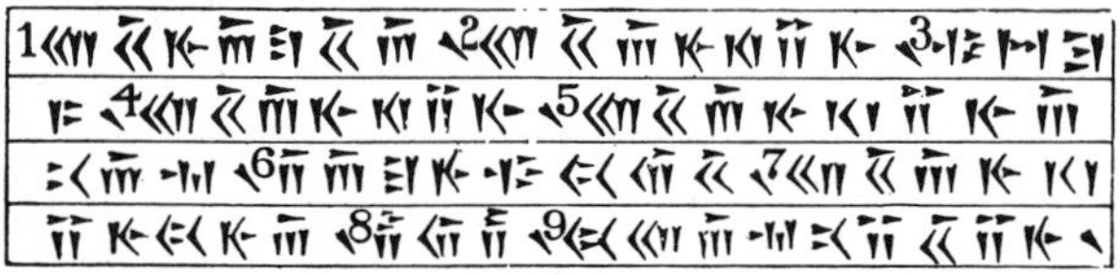

The Persian scribes separated the words in their inscriptions by inserting an oblique wedge between the words. The above Arabic numbers are here added that we may be able to refer to the different words. It will be seen that these numbers (except 1) always stand where the oblique wedge shows a new word begins. Grotefend noticed that the same word is repeated a number of times in each of these inscriptions. In *A* compare Nos. 2, 4, 5, and 6, and they will be recognized as the same word. In *B* it occurs also four times (Nos. 2, 4, 5, and 7). As these inscriptions were found above the figures of Persian kings, Grotefend therefore suspected that this frequent word must be the Persian word for "king." Moreover, as it occurs in both inscriptions as No. 2, the preceding word (No. 1) would probably be the *name* of the king, the two words being arranged thus: "Darius [the] king." Grotefend then found that the words for the titles of the kings of Persia were known in later Persian documents. Guided by the known titles, he attempted the following guess as to the arrangement and meaning of the words:

1	2	3	4
unknown name of a Persian king	[the] king	[the] great	king

5	6	7	8
of kings,	of king	unknown name of a Persian king	the son

etc. (6, 7, and 8 meaning "the son of King So-and-so"). He next experimented with the known names of the kings of Persia, and, judging from their length, he found that the probable name for No. 1 in *A* was "Darius," and for No. 1 in *B* was "Xerxes." The result may be seen in Fig. 135

Babylonian cuneiform also. At once the city mounds of Babylonia and Assyria began to speak and tell us, piece by piece, the three great chapters of history along the Two Rivers, — something over twenty-five hundred years of the story of man in Western Asia, of which the world before had been entirely ignorant. The ability to read the cuneiform records and thus gain this knowledge we owe to the documents left us by the Persian kings.

Kh - sha - y - a - r - sha - a

FIG. 135. *The Name of* XERXES *in Old Persian* CUNEIFORM

This is the first word in Fig. 134 (*B*), supposed by Grotefend to be "Xerxes." Now, just as our "Charles" is an imperfect form of the ancient name "Carolus," so the name we call "Xerxes" was pronounced by the old Persians *Khshayarsha*. The above seven signs, therefore, should be read Kh-sha-y-a-r-sha-a. Grotefend in this way learned the sounds for which these signs stood. Now some of these signs appear in the word Grotefend thought was "king" in Persian. Hence it was now possible for Grotefend to see if he could find out how to pronounce the ancient Persian word for "king." And the reader can do the same. Let him copy on a slip of paper the first three signs in the word supposedly meaning "king"; for example, use word 2 in Fig. 134. Now take these three signs and compare them with the signs in "Xerxes." The student will find that the three signs he has copied are the same as the first, second, and seventh signs in the word "Xerxes." Let us write down in a row the sounds of these three signs (first, second, and seventh), and we find we have *Kh-sha-a*. The ancient Persian word for "king" must have begun with the sounds *Kh-sha-a*. When we compare this with *shah*, the title of the present king of Persia, it is evident that Grotefend was on the right road to decipher Old Persian cuneiform

353. The organization of the great Persian Empire, stretching from the river Indus to the Ægean Sea (almost as long as the United States from east to west) and from the Indian Ocean to the deserts of the Caspian, was a colossal task. It demanded an effort of organization on a greater scale than any ruler had ever attempted before. It was much too great an undertaking to be completed by Cyrus. Begun by him, it was carried through by Darius the Great (521–485 B.C.), whose organization remains one of the most remarkable achievements in the history of the ancient Orient, if not of the world. The rule of Darius was just, humane, and intelligent, but the subject peoples had of course no voice in government. The Persian sov-

Organization of Persian Empire by Darius

ereign had already come to be called the Great King in the time of Cyrus. All that the Great King decreed was law, and all the peoples bowed to his word. Darius says in the Behistun inscription, "By the grace of Ahuramazda these lands have conformed to my decree; even as it was commanded unto them by me, so was it done." Let us therefore notice an important fact here revealed: this system was not only attempting government on a larger scale than the world had ever seen before, but it was government controlled by *one man*. The ancient world never forgot the example of the vast Persian Empire controlled by one-man power.

354. In developing his colossal organization Darius caused himself to be made actual king in Egypt and in Babylonia, Persian provincial but the rest of the Empire he divided into system twenty provinces. Each of these provinces was called a satrapy, because it was under a governor called a satrap, who was appointed by the Great King. These arrangements, while similar to those of the Chaldean, Assyrian, and Egyptian empires, were a further development of provincial rule under governors. Indeed, the Persian Empire was the first example of a fully organized group of subject peoples and nations ruled as provinces, — an arrangement which we may call a provincial system. The subject nations, or provinces under Persian rule, enjoyed a good deal of independence in the local matters of their own government as long as they paid regular tribute and furnished recruits for the Great King's army. To discover and prevent local rebellion, such as the revolt of a governor or people against the Persian government, the Great King kept officials residing in each subject state, who were called, after an old Egyptian custom, the King's Ears or the King's Eyes, and whose duty it was to report any evidence of disobedience. All this was an advance upon the rule of the Assyrian Empire.

355. Farm lands were divided into vast domains held by powerful nobles and other great landowners. There were few small land-owning farmers. All paid dues to help make up the tribute collected from every division of the Empire. In the eastern part of the Empire it was paid, as of old, in produce (see Fig. 138). In the western part of the Empire, chiefly Lydia and the Greek settlements in   Lands, tribute, and western Asia Minor, the coinage of metal was   coinage common by 600 B.C., and there this tribute was paid in coined money. The eastern countries — Egypt, Babylonia, and Persia herself — were not quick to adopt this new convenience. Darius, however, began the coinage of gold and permitted his satraps to coin silver. The rate was about thirteen to one; that is to say, gold was worth about thirteen times as much as silver. Thus the great commercial convenience of coined money issued by the state began to be more common in the Near East during the Persian period.

356. In general, Darius, like the modern Japanese, showed surprising discernment in selecting the most valuable things in the great civilizations about him for adop-   Darius introduces tion in his own government. He speed-   Egyptian calendar ily perceived the practical convenience of   and encourages the Egyptian calendar of twelve thirty-day   science months, and he introduced it as the calendar of the Persian government. He was likewise impressed with the value of Egyptian medical knowledge. He therefore sent back to Egypt a learned Egyptian high priest, who was a captive in Persia, and gave him instructions to go to Sais, a city of the western Delta, and to restore there an Egyptian medical school which had fallen into decay. Upon a statue of this high priest, now in the Vatican collections at Rome, there is engraved an interesting account of how he carried out the orders of Darius and restored the two buildings of the school. One of these was the school building itself and the other was probably the library. Students from the best families were placed in the school, and it was equipped with all needed "instruments," probably for the practice of surgery. The inscription further states: "His majesty [that is, Darius] did this because he knew the value of this art [the practice of medicine], in order to save the life of every one having sickness." Thus the great Persian established the earliest known medical school as a royal foundation. It was also under Darius that the astronomical studies of the great Chaldean astronomer Nabu-rimannu were carried on at Babylon; and similar researches, continued by Kidinnu, likewise took place under Persian rule (see §§ 276–278).

357. Nothing shows the wise statesmanship of Darius the Great more clearly than his remarkable efforts to make Persia

Darius turns to the sea

a great sea power. It was no easy task for an inland nation of shepherds and peasants like the Persians, separated from the water by desert shores, to gain control of the sea. Darius was obliged to employ foreign navigators. He dispatched a skillful Mediterranean sailor named Scylax to explore the course of the great Indus River in India. Then Darius ordered him to sail along the coast of Asia from the mouth of the Indus westward to the Isthmus of Suez. Scylax was the first Western sailor known to have sailed along this south coast of Asia, so little known to Western peoples at that time (about 500 B.C.).

358. At Suez, Darius restored the ancient but long filled-up canal of the Egyptians connecting the Nile with the Red Sea.

Darius links East and West by a Suez canal

Along the ancient route of this canal have been found fragments of great stone tablets erected by Darius (see map, p. 66). They bear an account of the restoration of the canal, in which we find the words of Darius: "I commanded to dig this canal, from the stream flowing in Egypt, called the Nile, to the sea [Red Sea] which stretches from Persia. Then this canal was dug as I commanded, and ships sailed from Egypt through this canal to Persia, according to my will." Darius evidently cherished what proved to be a vain hope, that the south coast of Persia might come to share in the now growing commerce between India and the Mediterranean world. As Persia was now lacking in small landowners, so also was she lacking in small and enterprising merchants, who might have become great promoters of commerce.

359. Unlike the Assyrians, Darius treated the Phœnician cities with kindness, and succeeded in organizing a great

FIG. 136. TOMBS OF DARIUS THE GREAT (*Right*) and ARTAXERXES I (*Left*)
near Persepolis

The tomb of Darius the Great is inscribed with his name, besides a long inscription on the front (still unpublished) describing the beautiful Zoroastrian religion.
Out of range on the left is the tomb of Darius II, and on the right, also out of
range, is the tomb of Xerxes. The remaining three royal tombs belonging to the
last three kings of the Achæmenian line (the line of Darius) — Artaxerxes II,
Artaxerxes III, and Darius III — are cut in the cliff behind the palaces of Persepolis (Fig. 200). Including the tomb of Cyrus (Fig. 132), we thus have the tombs
of all nine of the great kings of Persia, except that of Cambyses, the conqueror of
Egypt, which has never been found. The door of the burial chamber in each tomb
is in the middle of the colonnade front. Above this colonnade is a square containing a sculptured picture of the king worshiping Ahuramazda before a fire altar.
All these tombs were broken open and robbed in ancient times, like the tomb of
Cyrus, and all are now empty except that inside, in niches, still rest the massive
stone coffins in which Darius, Xerxes, and the other kings and their families were
buried. (Air view by the Oriental Institute)

Phœnician war fleet. We shall find that Darius's son Xerxes
could depend upon many hundreds of ships for warfare and
transportation in the Eastern Mediterranean   Persia becomes
when such shipping was needed for the in-   earliest great sea
vasion of Europe. Thus the more enlightened   power in Asia
Persian kings accomplished what the Assyrian emperors never
achieved, and Persia became the first great sea power in Asia.

360. For the first time the ancient world began to develop
a wide-spread system of good roads, by which the Persian

emperors maintained communication from end to end of the vast Empire. On a smaller scale these roads must have done System of roads for the Persian Empire what railroads do for and communication us. Royal messengers maintained a much more complete postal system than that which had already been introduced under the Assyrian Empire. These messengers were surprisingly swift, although merchandise required about as much time to go from Susa or Persepolis to the Ægean Sea as we now need for going around the world. A good example of the effect of these roads was the incoming of the domestic fowl, which we commonly call the chicken. It was originally a wild jungle hen of India which the East Indians tamed, and it was unknown in the Mediterranean until Persian communications brought it from India to the Ægean Sea.

361. The ancient Elamite city of Susa, in the Zagros Mountains, was the chief residence and capital. The mild win-
Capital and royal ter air of the Babylonian Plain, however, residences attracted the sovereign during the colder months, when he went to dwell in the palaces of the vanished Chaldean Empire at Babylon. In spite of its remoteness the earlier kings had made an effort to live in their old Persian home. We have seen that Cyrus built a splendid palace at Pasargadæ, near the battlefield where he had defeated the Medes (see map, p. 498), and Darius also established a magnificent residence at Persepolis, some forty miles south of the palace of Cyrus. It is near the ruins of Persepolis that the tombs of Darius, Xerxes, and the later Persian emperors still stand in their native Persia.

362. The Persian architects had to learn architecture from the old Oriental peoples now subject to Persia. The enor-
Architecture mous terraces on which the Persian palaces stood were imitated from Babylonia. The winged bulls at the palace gates, like the magnificent stairways leading up to them, were copied from those of Assyria and the west. The vast colonnades stretching along the front and filling the enormous halls — the earliest colonnades of Asia — had grown up over two thousand years earlier on the

FIG. 137. *Excavation of* GRAND STAIRWAY *Leading to* AUDIENCE HALL
of Darius the Great at Persepolis

Only the nearer half of the stairway is visible from this point, for it is nearly three hundred feet long. It enabled visitors coming from the court below to ascend to the elevated floor of a vast royal audience hall, some of the columns of which are visible on the right (see also Fig. 201). The man at the extreme left is standing on the rubbish which was higher toward the right and had completely covered the stairway from view. At this point the rubbish is made up of the crumbled bricks of a lofty sun-dried brick wall which stood on the right of the stairway and fell down over it, completely concealing it. Most of the workmen engaged in clearing it away are hidden behind the high wall of rubbish at the left. The tripod in the rear is a strong derrick for raising the heavy stones of the sculptures and of the stepped balustrade which were knocked off by the fall of the great sun-dried brick wall and had likewise fallen down into the court. The entire face of the stairway is covered with beautiful relief sculptures, revealing the remarkable art of the Persians in the days of Darius, whose gold and silver tablets bearing his building inscriptions were discovered in the summer of 1933 by the Oriental Institute of The University of Chicago, which is carrying on the Persepolis excavations

Nile. Likewise the gorgeously colored palace walls of enameled brick reached Persia from the Nile by way of Assyria and the west.[1] Thus the great civilizations over which the Persian emperors ruled were merged together in the life of their Empire.

[1] It is very noticeable that the Persian architects did not adopt the arch from Babylonia. On the contrary, each door in the palace of Darius is topped with a *horizontal* block of stone, called a lintel, copied from Egyptian doors.

Fig. 138. *Relief from the* Sculptures *on the Face of the* Grand
Stairway *at Persepolis*

The reliefs on the face of the grand stairway shown in the preceding illustration
picture the reception of the envoys of twenty-eight Oriental nations, who have
come to Persepolis to present their tribute to the Persian emperor. The frieze
shown above represents the natives of Cilicia with two magnificent rams forming
part of their tribute

363. Such a consolidation of all the civilizations of the
Ancient Near East into one vast organization produced **a**
Europe and the   new situation, and one of tremendous impor-
Persian Empire   tance for the history of Europe. We have
seen that Cyrus had carried his victories westward to the
shores of the Ægean Sea, and the Greek cities of western Asia
Minor fell under Persian sway. Thus the Oriental colossus
arose directly alongside southeastern Europe. If we look at
the map (map IV, p. 266) and observe how the western advance of the great Empire finally extended, under Darius, to
include European territory as far as the Danube, we shall
understand that a hostile collision with Greece was unavoid-
able. This situation was yet to bring about a more complete
commingling of the civilizations of the Near East with the life

of neighboring Europe than had ever been possible before.
These wars between Persia and Europe were not of any great
importance to Persia, but they were epoch-making for little
European nations like the Greeks, and we must therefore
take them up later as a part of the history of Greece.

364. For the Oriental world as a whole, Persian rule meant
about two hundred years of peaceful prosperity (ending about
330 B.C.). The Persian kings, however, as   Decline of Persia
time went on, were no longer as strong and
skillful as Cyrus and Darius. They loved luxury and ease,
and left much of the task of ruling to their governors and
officials. This meant corrupt and ineffective government;
the result was weakness and decline.

365. The later world, especially the Greeks, often represented the Persian rulers as cruel and barbarous Oriental
tyrants. This unfavorable opinion is cer-   Character of Per-
tainly not justified as far as it refers to the sian kings and
earlier Persian rulers. Most of the Persian their rule
emperors felt a deep sense of obligation to give just government to the nations of the earth. Darius the Great in the
Behistun inscription says: "On this account Ahuramazda
brought me help, . . . because I was not wicked, nor was I a
liar, nor was I a tyrant, neither I nor any of my line. I have
ruled according to righteousness." There can be no doubt
that the Persian Empire, the largest the ancient world had
thus far seen, enjoyed a government far more just and humane than any that had preceded it in the East.

366. Many such statements as that of Darius just quoted
show that the Persian rulers were devoted followers of Zoroaster's teaching. Their power carried this   Spread of Persian
noble faith throughout Western Asia and   religion; competi-
especially into Asia Minor. Here Mithras,   tion among Orien-
regarded by Zoroaster as a helper of Ahura-   tal religions
mazda, appeared as a hero of light, and finally as a Sun-god,
who gradually outshone Ahuramazda himself. From Asia
Minor, Mithras passed into Europe, and, as we shall see, the
faith in the mighty Persian god spread far and wide through

Fig. 139. *Discovery of the* Foundation Records *of Darius the Great's* Vast Audience Hall *at Persepolis*

We are looking into an excavation under the northeast corner of the great audience hall of Darius. At the bottom of the excavation we see a shallow square box of stone, from which the lid has been removed. The archæologist at the left holds in his hand a large tablet of solid silver, over thirteen inches square, on which is engraved in cuneiform characters a record of Darius the Great. When the archæologist lifted this silver plate out of the box he saw below it another of the same size, but of solid *gold*, bearing the same record as that on the silver plate. After the architects of Darius had deposited the records here they closed the box containing the gold and silver plates with a stone lid and then placed over it the rough stone which is seen here under the left arm of the workman at the right. Since this discovery, excavation at the southeast corner of the same building disclosed another deposit of the same kind containing two more plates of gold and silver bearing records identical with those on the first two plates. These discoveries were made by the Persian Expedition of the Oriental Institute of The University of Chicago, which is excavating at Persepolis

the Roman Empire, to become a dangerous competitor of Christianity; for in matters of religion, as in many other things, the Persian Empire completed the breakdown of national boundaries and marked the beginning of a long period when the leading religions of the East were called upon to compete in a great contest for the mastery among all the nations (§ 1106).

Section 31. Decline of Oriental Leadership · Estimate of Oriental Civilization

367. Persia was the last of the great Oriental powers. Before we turn to the rise of civilized Europe let us look back over Oriental civilization for a moment **End of leadership** and review what it accomplished in over **of Ancient Near** thirty-five hundred years. **East (after 400 B.C.)**

368. First the Ancient Near East domesticated the wild animals, especially cattle, sheep, and goats, which served as food or produced food in the form of dairy **Achievements of** products. It domesticated likewise the wild **Ancient Near East:** grasses, the seeds of which became our wheat, **first food-produc-** barley, and other cereal grains, which could **tion** be cultivated in large quantities. By these achievements it transformed early men from merely food-gatherers to food-producers. It invented the plow, and by substituting animal power for man power in agriculture it greatly increased the cultivated area, thus putting into the hands of government and society for the first time a large amount of portable wealth. It was these great contributions which made possible the rise of civilized society.

369. While Europe still lay in Stone Age barbarism the peoples of the Ancient Near East gave the world for the first time a whole group of further inventions **Achievements of** surpassed in importance only by those of the **Ancient Near East:** modern world. Among these were the first **inventions** highly developed practical arts, such as the use of the potter's wheel, the potter's furnace, the loom and highly elaborate weaving, the earliest metal work (including the difficult art of hollow casting), glass-making, paper-making, and many other similar industries. To distribute the products of these industries among other peoples and carry on commerce the Ancient Near East built the earliest seagoing ships propelled by sails. Its engineers were the first to move great weights and undertake large building enterprises,— large even for us of today.

370. The Ancient Near East also gave us the earliest architecture in stone masonry, the clerestory, the colonnade,
Achievements of Ancient Near East: art, writing, etc.
the arch, and the tower or spire. It produced the earliest refined sculpture, from the wonderful portrait figures and colossal statues of Egypt to the exquisite seals of early Babylonia. It gave us writing and the earliest alphabet. In literature it brought forth the earliest known tales in narrative prose, poems, historical works, social discussions, and even drama. It gave us the calendar we still use. It made a beginning in mathematics and laid the foundations of scientific astronomy. In this work and in the development of surgery it began the practice of a scientific attitude of mind. It first produced government on a large scale, whether of a single great nation or of an empire made up of a group of nations.

371. Finally, in religion the East developed the earliest belief in a sole God and his fatherly care for all men, and it
Achievements of Ancient Near East: religion
laid the foundations of a religious life from which came forth the Founder of the leading religion of the civilized world today. For these things — accomplished, most of them, while Europe was still without civilization — our debt to the Ancient Near East is enormous.

372. Let us see, however, if there are not some important things which the East had not yet gained. The East had
Lack of citizenship in Ancient Near East
always accepted as a matter of course the rule of a king, and believed that his rule should be kindly and just. It had never occurred to anyone there that the *people* should have anything to say about how they should be governed. No one had ever gained the idea of a free citizen, a man feeling what we call patriotism, and under obligations to vote and to share in the government. Liberty as we understand it was unknown, and the rule of the people, which we call democracy, was hardly dreamed of in the Ancient Near East. Hence the life of the individual man lacked the stimulating responsibilities which come with citizenship. Such responsibilities, like that

of thinking about public questions and then voting, or of serving as a soldier to defend the nation, quicken the mind and force men to action, and they were among the strongest influences in producing great men in Greece and Rome.

373. Just as the Orientals accepted the rule of *kings* without question, so they believed in the rule of the *gods*. It was a tradition which they and their fathers had always accepted. This limited their ideas of the world about them. They thought that every storm was due to the interference of some god, and that every eclipse must be the act of an angry god or demon. Hence the Orientals made little inquiry into the *natural* causes of such things. In general, then, they suffered from a lack of freedom of the mind, — a kind of intellectual bondage to religion and to old ideas.[1] Under these circumstances natural science could not go very far, and religion was much darkened by superstition, while art and literature lacked some of their greatest sources of stimulus and inspiration.

Lack of freedom of mind in Ancient Near East

374. There were still, therefore, boundless things for mankind to do, — in government, in thought about the natural world, in gaining deeper views of the wonders and beauties of nature, as well as in art, in literature, and in many other lines. This future progress was to be made in Europe, — that Europe which we left at the end of the second chapter in the Late Stone Age. To Europe, therefore, we must now turn, to follow across the Eastern Mediterranean the course of rising civilization as it passed from the Ancient Near East to our European forefathers from four to five thousand years ago.

Future progress to be made in Europe

[1] Some degree of intellectual freedom from tradition was earliest shown by the great unknown surgeon of Egypt (§ 119), and especially by the Egyptian king Ikhnaton, by the Hebrew prophets, and by the Chaldean astronomers; perhaps we could also include Zoroaster. But complete intellectual freedom was first attained by the Greeks.

QUESTIONS

Section 26. Explain in detail what is meant by the term "Indo-Europeans." List the various conflicts between Indo-Europeans and Semites.

Section 27. What is meant by "Highland civilization"? Discuss the first Indo-European invasion of Western Asia. Describe the civilization of the Second Hittite Empire. What influences reached the Hittites from the Fertile Crescent and from Egypt? Why did the Hittites not use their hieroglyphic writing on the clay tablets? What part did the Hittite Empire play in the progress of civilization?

Section 28. What became of the Aryan people when they left their first home? What is the chief difference between the Zoroastrian religion and the other religions which we have previously studied? When did Zoroaster live?

Sections 29–30. What race did Cyrus subdue in the Fertile Crescent? How were the Persian documents used in the decipherment of Babylonian cuneiform? Describe the organization of the Empire by Darius. Discuss his plans for commercial expansion. How did Persian architecture arise?

Section 31. What were the most important things which the Ancient Near East contributed to human life? What other important things had the Ancient Near East not yet produced?

BIBLIOGRAPHY FOR TOPICAL STUDIES

Clay tablets from Hattusas: *Classical Weekly*, Vol. XVIII, No. 22 (April 20, 1925), pp. 171–175.

The spread of Hittite civilization southward: GARSTANG, *Hittite Empire*, pp. 236–278; HOGARTH, *Ancient East*, pp. 50–52; WOOLLEY, *Dead Towns*, pp. 74–95.

The conquests of Cyrus: HOGARTH, pp. 159–167; ROGERS, *History of Ancient Persia*, pp. 35–64.

BIBLIOGRAPHY

It has not been possible in this bibliography to mention all of even the important books which might be listed. It is important to include such books as the teacher has some chance of procuring. It not infrequently happens that the best account of a particular period or topic is in a foreign language or in a rare publication, such as a doctor's dissertation, which could be found only in one of our largest libraries. All such titles, however valuable, are omitted from this list.

CHAPTERS I–II

Antiquity, 1927– (Assistant Editor, 24 Parkend Road, Gloucester, England). AVEBURY, Sir J. L., *Prehistoric Times* (7th ed., N.Y., 1913). BRITISH MUSEUM, *Flints* (London, 1928). BURKITT, M. C., *Old Stone Age* (Cambridge University Press, 1933) ; *Our Early Ancestors* (Cambridge University Press, 1929) ; *Our Forerunners* (London, 1924). BUXTON, L. H. D., *Primitive Labour* (London, 1924). CHILDE, V. G., *The Most Ancient East* (N.Y., 1929). CLELAND, H. F., *Our Prehistoric Ancestors* (N.Y., 1928). COLE, F. C., *The Long Road from Savagery to Civilization* (N.Y., 1933). DAVISON, D., *Our Prehistoric Ancestors* (London, 1926). DAWSON, C. H., *Age of the Gods* (London, 1933). GARDNER, H., *Art through the Ages* (N.Y., 1926), chap. i. HIBBEN, T., *The Carpenter's Tool Chest* (Philadelphia, 1933). KROEBER, A. L., *Anthropology* (N.Y., 1923). KUMMER, F., *First Days of Knowledge* (N.Y., 1923). MACALISTER, R. A., *A Text-book of European Archæology* (Cambridge, 1921). MACCURDY, G. G., *Human Origins* (2 vols.; N.Y., 1924). MAGOFFIN, R. V. D., and DUNCALF, F., *Ancient and Medieval History* (N.Y., 1934) MARETT, R. R., *Anthropology* (N.Y., 1912). MORGAN, J. M. DE, *Prehistoric Man* (N.Y., 1925). MORGAN, L. H., *Ancient Society* (N.Y., 1878). OBERMAIER, H., *Fossil Man in Spain* (Yale University Press, 1924). OSBORN, H. F., *Man Rises to Parnassus* (Princeton University Press, 1928) ; *Men of the Old Stone Age* (3d ed., N.Y., 1919). PARSONS, G., *The Stream of History* (N. Y., 1928). PEAKE, H. J. E., and FLEURE, H. J., *Hunters and Artists* (Yale University Press, 1927). QUENNELL, M. and C. H. B., *Everyday Life in Prehistoric Times* (2d ed., London, 1931). RENARD, G. F., *Life and Work in Prehistoric Times* (N.Y., 1929). SOLLAS, W. J., *Ancient Hunters and their Modern Representatives* (3d ed., N.Y., 1924). TYLER, J. M., *The New Stone Age in Northern Europe* (London, 1921). WILDER, H. H., *Man's Prehistoric Past* (rev. ed., N.Y., 1923).

CHAPTERS III–IV

A. Histories. BREASTED, J. H., *History of the Ancient Egyptians* (N.Y., 1913) ; *History of Egypt* (2d ed., N.Y., 1924). *Cambridge Ancient History* (Cambridge University Press), Vols. I and II, *passim* (Vol. I, 2d ed., 1928; Vol. II, 1926). HALL, H. R. H., *The Ancient History of the Near East* (7th ed., London, 1927). QUIBELL, A. A., *Egyptian History and Art* (N.Y., 1923). ROSTOVTZEFF, M. I., *A History of the Ancient World* (Oxford, 1926), Vol. I.

B. Art and archæology. BELL, E., *The Architecture of Ancient Egypt* (London, 1915). BOSTON MUSEUM OF FINE ARTS, *Bulletin,* 1903– . BRITISH MUSEUM,

A General Introductory Guide to the Egyptian Collections (London, 1930). *Cambridge Ancient History*, Vol. I, chap. xvi; Vol. II, chap. xv. CAPART, J., *Egyptian Art* (London, 1923); *Lectures on Egyptian Art* (University of North Carolina Press, 1928). CLARKE, S., and ENGELBACH, R., *Ancient Egyptian Masonry* (Oxford University Press, 1930). CROSS, L. (Ed.), *Pre-Greek Art* (Student Series M of The University Prints, Cambridge, Mass., 1925). FECHHEIMER, H., *Die Plastik der Ägypter* (Berlin, 1920). GARDNER, H., *Art through the Ages*, chaps. ii–iii. MASPERO, SIR G., *Art in Egypt* (Ars Una: Species Mille. General History of Art series, N.Y., 1930). METROPOLITAN MUSEUM OF ART (New York), *Bulletin*, 1905– . MURRAY, M. A., *Egyptian Sculpture* (London, 1930). NELSON, H. H., and HÖLSCHER, U., *Medinet Habu Reports* (University of Chicago Press, 1931). PETRIE, SIR W. M. F., *The Arts and Crafts of Ancient Egypt* (Edinburgh and London, 1923). ROSS, SIR E. D., *The Art of Egypt through the Ages* (London, 1931). WEIGALL, A., *Ancient Egyptian Works of Art* (London, 1924).

C. **Mythology and religion.** BREASTED, J. H., *The Dawn of Conscience* (N.Y., 1933); *Development of Religion and Thought in Ancient Egypt* (N.Y., 1912). *Cambridge Ancient History*, Vol. I, chap. ix; Vol. II, chap. ix. GARDINER, A., article "Egypt: Ancient Religion" in *Encyclopædia Britannica* (11th ed.). PETRIE, SIR W. M. F., *Religious Life in Ancient Egypt* (London, 1924). SHORTER, A. W., *An Introduction to Egyptian Religion* (London, 1931).

D. **Social life.** BLACKMAN, A. M., *Luxor and its Temples* (London, 1923). ERMAN, A., *Life in Ancient Egypt* (N.Y., 1894) (new edition in German by Ranke, Tübingen, 1923). GLANVILLE, S. R. K., *Daily Life in Ancient Egypt* (London, 1930); *The Egyptians* (London, 1933). SHORTER, A. W., *Everyday Life in Ancient Egypt* (London, 1932).

E. **Excavation and discovery.** BAIKIE, J., *A Century of Excavation in the Land of the Pharaohs* (N.Y., 1924); *Egyptian Papyri and Papyrus-Hunting* (N.Y., 1925). CARTER, H., and MACE, A. C., *The Tomb of Tut-ankh-amen* (3 vols.; N.Y., 1923–1933). *Journal of Egyptian Archæology* (Egypt Exploration Society; Secretary, American Branch, Riverbank Lodge, Antrim, New Hampshire), 1914– PETRIE, SIR W. M. F., *Seventy Years in Archæology* (London, 1931).

F. **Original sources in English.** BREASTED, J. H., *Ancient Records of Egypt* (5 vols.; University of Chicago Press, 1906–1907); *The Edwin Smith Surgical Papyrus* (Oxford University Press, 1930). ERMAN, A., *The Literature of the Ancient Egyptians* (London, 1927). MASPERO, SIR G., *Popular Stories of Ancient Egypt* (N.Y., 1915). PEET, T. E., *A Comparative Study of the Literatures of Egypt, Palestine, and Mesopotamia* (Oxford University Press, 1931). PETRIE, SIR W. M. F., *Egyptian Tales, Translated from the Papyri* (London, 1913).

G. **The monuments as they are today.** BAIKIE, J., *Egyptian Antiquities in the Nile Valley* (London, 1932). BORCHARDT, L., and RICKE, H., *Egypt: Architecture, Landscape, Life of the People* (London, 1930). BREASTED, J. H., *Egypt through the Stereoscope; a Journey through the Land of the Pharaohs* (Keystone View Co., Meadville, Pa., 1908; 100 views, with guidebook and maps). MURRAY, M. A., *Egyptian Temples* (London, 1931).

CHAPTERS V–VI

A. **Histories.** *Cambridge Ancient History*, Vols. I, II, and III (1929), *passim.* DELAPORTE, L. J., *Mesopotamia* (N.Y., 1925). DOUGHERTY, R. P., *Nabonidus and Belshazzar* (Yale University Press, 1929). GADD, C. J., *History and Monuments of Ur* (N.Y., 1929). GOODSPEED, G. S., *History of the Babylonians and Assyrians* (N.Y., 1917). HALL, H. R. H., *Ancient History of the Near East.* JOHNS, C. H. W., *Ancient Babylonia* (N.Y., 1913); *Ancient Assyria* (Cambridge University Press, 1912). KING, L. W., *History of Babylon from Foundation of Monarchy to Persian Conquest* (N.Y., 1915); *History of Sumer and Akkad* (London, 1916). OLMSTEAD,

A. T. E., *History of Assyria* (N.Y., 1923); *Western Asia in the Days of Sargon of Assyria* (N.Y., 1908). ROGERS, R. W., *History of Babylonia and Assyria* (6th ed., N.Y., 1915). ROSTOVTZEFF, M., *History of the Ancient World*, Vol. I. WOOLLEY, C. L., *The Sumerians* (Oxford, 1928).

B. Art and archæology. BELL, E., *Early Architecture in Western Asia* (London, 1924), chaps. i–iv, vii–x. *Cambridge Ancient History*, Vols. I–II, *passim*. CROSS, L. (Ed.), *Pre-Greek Art*. FRANKFORT, H., *Archeology and the Sumerian Problem* (University of Chicago Press, 1932). GARDNER, H., *Art through the Ages*, chap. iv. HARCOURT-SMITH, S., *Babylonian Art* (N.Y., 1928). MEISSNER, B., *Babylonien und Assyrien* (2 vols.; Heidelberg, 1920–1925) (invaluable to teachers who read German). OLMSTEAD, A. T. E., "A Visit to Babylon," in *History Teacher's Magazine*, Vol. VIII (1917), pp. 79–81. PATERSON, A., *Assyrische Skulpturen* (Haarlem, Holland, 1901–1907; Kleinmann, London; plates, with descriptions in German, French, and English).

C. Mythology and religion. *Cambridge Ancient History*, Vol. III, chap. xi JASTROW, M., *Aspects of Religious Belief and Practice in Babylonia and Assyria* (N.Y., 1911).

D. Social life. JASTROW, M., *The Civilization of Babylonia and Assyria* (Philadelphia, 1915). MEISSNER, B., *Babylonien und Assyrien*. SAYCE, A. H., *Babylonians and Assyrians: Life and Customs* (N.Y., 1899).

E. Excavation and discovery. *American Journal of Archæology* (Baltimore), 1885– . KOLDEWEY, R., *The Excavations at Babylon* (London, 1914). *Museum Journal of the University of Pennsylvania*, 1910– . ROGERS, R. W., *History of Babylonia and Assyria*, Vol. I. THOMPSON, R. C., and HUTCHINSON, R.W., *A Century of Exploration at Nineveh* (London, 1929). WOOLLEY, C. L., *Ur of the Chaldees; a Record of Seven Years of Excavation* (London, 1929).

F. Original sources in English. BOTSFORD, G. W. and L. S., *Source Book of Ancient History* (N.Y., 1913), chap. iii. JOHNS, C. H. W. (Tr.), *The Oldest Code of Laws in the World* (Edinburgh, 1911). KING, L. W. (Tr.), *Letters and Inscriptions of Hammurabi* (London, 1900), Vol. III. LUCKENBILL, D. D., *Ancient Records of Assyria and Babylonia* (2 vols.; University of Chicago Press, 1926–1927). SAYCE, A. H., *Records of the Past* (6 vols.; London, 1889–1893). SMITH, S., *Babylonian Historical Texts relating to the Capture and Downfall of Babylon* (London, 1924).

G. The monuments as they are today. The buildings surviving in Babylonia and Assyria are in a ruinous state. Photographs of sites in Mesopotamia may be obtained from the Keystone View Co., Meadville, Pa.

CHAPTER VII

A. Histories. BAILEY, A. E., and KENT, C. F., *History of the Hebrew Commonwealth* (N.Y., 1920). BAYNES, N. H., *Israel amongst the Nations* (Student Christian Movement, London, 1927). BLUNT, A. W. F., *Israel in World History* (Oxford University Press, 1927). GOLUB, J. S., *In the Days of the First Temple* (Cincinnati, 1931). GOODSPEED, E. J., *The Story of the Old Testament* (University of Chicago Press, 1934). KENT, C. F., *History of the Hebrew People* (N.Y., 1906; Vol. I, 10th ed.; Vol. II, 9th ed.): *A History of the Jewish People during the Babylonian, Persian, and Greek Periods* (N.Y., 1927); *The Kings and Prophets of Israel and Judah* (N.Y., 1909). KITTEL, R., *Great Men and Movements in Israel* (N.Y., 1929). KNOPF, C. S., *The Old Testament Speaks* (N.Y., 1933). KNOTT, L. A., *Student's History of the Hebrews* (N.Y., 1927). LODS, A., *Israel, from its Beginnings to the Middle of the Eighth Century* (London, 1932). MACALISTER, R. A. S., *History of Civilization in Palestine* (N.Y., 1921). NOYES, C. E., *The Genius of Israel* (Boston, 1924). OLMSTEAD, A. T., *History of Palestine and Syria to the Macedonian Conquest* (N.Y., 1931). PERITZ, I. J., *Old Testament History* (N.Y., 1923). PRICE, I. M., *The Dramatic Story of Old Testament History* (N.Y., 1929); *The Monuments and the Old Testament* (Philadelphia, 1925). SMITH, SIR G. A., *The Historical Geography of the Holy Land* (25th ed., 1932).

B. Mythology and religion. BARTON, G. A., *Religion of Israel* (2d ed., University of Pennsylvania Press, 1928). BUDDE, K. F. R., *Religion of Israel to the Exile* (N.Y., 1899). CADMAN, S. P., *The Prophets of Israel* (N.Y., 1933). CHAMBERLIN, T. K., *Jewish Religious Life after the Exile* (N.Y., 1915). COOK, S. A., *Religion of Ancient Palestine in the Light of Archæology* (Oxford University Press, 1930). GRAHAM, W. C., *The Prophets and Israel's Culture* (University of Chicago Press, 1934). OXTOBY, F. B., *Israel's Religious Development* (Philadelphia, 1927). PEAKE, A. S., *Religion of Israel* (London, 1908). PEDERSEN, J., *Israel; its Life and Culture* (London, 1926). SMITH, H. P., *Religion of Israel* (N.Y., 1928). SMITH, J. M. P., *The Prophet and his Problems* (N.Y., 1923). WOOD, W. C., *Religion of Canaan from Earliest Times to Hebrew Conquest* (Newmarket, Ontario, 1916; offprint of *Journal of Biblical Literature*).

C. Excavation and discovery. ALBRIGHT, W. F., *The Archæology of Palestine and the Bible* (N.Y., 1932). BARTON, G. A., *Archæology and the Bible* (5th ed., American Sunday-School Union, Philadelphia, 1927). GARSTANG, J., *Foundations of Bible History: Joshua, Judges* (N.Y., 1931). JACK, J. W., *Samaria in Ahab's Time* (N.Y., 1929). MACALISTER, R. A. S., *A Century of Excavation in Palestine* (N.Y., 1926). PEET, T. E., *Egypt and the Old Testament* (London, 1924). WOOLLEY, C. L., *Excavations at Ur and the Hebrew Records* (London, 1929).

D. Social life. BUDDEN. C. W., and HASTINGS, E., *Local Colour of the Bible* (3 vols.; Edinburgh, 1922–1925). HENRY, L. I., *Paul, Son of Kish* (University of Chicago Press, 1923). HUNTING, H. B., *Hebrew Life and Times* (N.Y., 1921). SMITH, J. M. P., *The Prophets and their Times* (University of Chicago Press, 1925).

E. Literature. *Abingdon Bible Commentary* (N.Y., 1929). BOTSFORD, G. W. and L. S., *A Source Book of Ancient History*, chap. iv. CORNILL, C. H., *Introduction to the Canonical Books of the Old Testament* (N.Y., 1907). FOWLER, H. T., *History of the Literature of Ancient Israel* (N.Y., 1922). GENUNG, J. F., *Guidebook to the Biblical Literature* (Boston, 1919). LEWIS, F. G., *How the Bible Grew* (University of Chicago Press, 1919). *Old Testament* in the Revised Version. PEAKE, A. S., *Commentary on the Bible* (N.Y., 1920). PENNIMAN, J. H., *Book about the English Bible* (University of Pennsylvania Press, 1931). ROGERS, R. W., *Cuneiform Parallels to the Old Testament* (2d ed., N.Y., 1926). SANDS, P. C., *Literary Genius of the Old Testament* (Oxford University Press, 1932). WILD, L. H., *Literary Guide to the Bible* (rev. ed., N.Y., 1925).

F. Palestine, its people and monuments as they are today. BAIKIE, J., *Ancient Jerusalem* (N.Y., 1930). CROSBY, R. L., *Geography of Bible Lands* (N.Y., 1921). ELMENDORF, D. L., *A Camera Crusade through the Holy Land* (N.Y., 1912). HURLBUT, J. L., *Traveling in the Holy Land through the Stereoscope* (the Keystone View Co., Meadville, Pa., 1900; 100 views, with guidebook and maps). PREISS, L., and ROHRBACH, P., *Palestine and Transjordania* (N.Y., 1926).

CHAPTER VIII

A. Histories. AHL, A. W., *Outline of Persian History* (N.Y., 1922). *Cambridge Ancient History*, Vols. II, III, IV (1926), and VI (1927), *passim*. COWLEY, A. E., *The Hittites* (Oxford University Press, 1920). GROUSSET, R., *Civilizations of the East* (N.Y., 1931), pp. 112–133. HALL, H. R. H., *Ancient History of the Near East.* HOGARTH, D. G., *The Ancient East* (N. Y., 1915). HUART, C. I., *Ancient Persia and Iranian Civilization* (N. Y., 1927). MEYER, E., *Reich und Kultur der Chetiter* (Berlin, 1914). ROGERS, R. W., *History of Ancient Persia* (N. Y., 1929). ROSS, SIR E. D., *The Persians* (Oxford University Press, 1931). SAYCE, A. H., *The Hit-*

tites; the Story of a Forgotten Empire (rev. ed., London, 1925). SYKES, SIR P. M. *A History of Persia* (2d ed., London, 1921), Vol. I.

B. Art and archæology. BELL, E., *Early Architecture in Western Asia*, chaps. v–vi, xi. BRITISH MUSEUM (Department of British and Mediæval Antiquities), *Treasure of the Oxus* (2d ed., London, 1926). PERROT, G., and CHIPIEZ, C., *History of Art in Persia* (N.Y., 1892). SARRE, F. P. T., *Kunst des alten Persien* (Berlin, 1922) (valuable for plates). WEBER, O., *Die Kunst der Hethiter* (Berlin, 1922) (valuable for plates). WOOLLEY, C. L., *Dead Towns and Living Men* (Toronto, 1932).

C. Mythology and religion. CARNOY, A., *Iranian Mythology* (Boston, 1917). EAKIN, F., *Revaluing Scripture* (N.Y., 1928), chap. iv. MOULTON, J. H., *Early Religious Poetry of Persia* (N.Y., 1911).

D. Social life. GLOVER, T. R., *From Pericles to Philip* (4th ed., London, 1926), chap. vii. JACKSON, A. V. W., *Zoroaster, the Prophet of Ancient Iran* (N.Y., 1899). RAWLINSON, G., *Seven Great Monarchies*: "The Fifth Monarchy: Persia" (N.Y., 1885).

E. Exploration and discovery. BREASTED, CHARLES, "Exploring the Secrets of Persepolis," in the *National Geographic Magazine*, Vol. 64 (1933), pp. 381–420. GARSTANG, J., *The Hittite Empire* (London, 1929) ; *The Land of the Hittites* (N.Y., 1910). GELB, I., *Hittite Hieroglyphs* (University of Chicago Press, 1931). HERZFELD, E. E., *Archäologische Mitteilungen aus Iran* (Berlin, 1929–1930), Vol. I, pp. 4–40 and Pls. 1–30 ; *A New Inscription of Xerxes from Persepolis* (University of Chicago Press, 1932). HOGARTH, D. G., *Kings of the Hittites* (Oxford University Press, 1926). JACKSON, A .V. W., *Persia, Past and Present* (N.Y., 1909). OSTEN, H. H. VON DER, *Discoveries in Anatolia, 1930–31* (University of Chicago Press, 1933). SCHMIDT, E. F., *Anatolia through the Ages* (University of Chicago Press, 1931). STURTEVANT, E. H., "The Hittite Tablets from Boghaz Kevi," in *Classical Weekly*, Vol. XVIII, No. 22 (April 20, 1925).

F. Original sources in English. BOTSFORD, G. W. and L. S., *Source-Book of Ancient History*, chap. v. DARMESTETER, J. (Tr.), *Zend-Avesta* (Christian Literature Co., N.Y., 1898). TOLMAN, H. C., *The Behistan Inscription of King Darius* (Vanderbuilt University Studies, Nashville, Tenn., 1908).

CHAPTERS IX–XVIII

A. Ægean civilization. BAIKIE, J., *Sea-Kings of Crete* (4th ed., London, 1926). BELL, E., *Prehellenic Architecture in the Ægean* (London, 1926). BOSSERT, H. T., *Alt Kreta* (2d ed., Berlin, 1923) (valuable for illustrations). BURN, A. R., *Minoans, Philistines, and Greeks, B.C. 1400–900* (N.Y., 1930). BURROWS, R. M., *Discoveries in Crete* (London, 1907). EVANS, SIR A. J., *Palace of Minos* (3 vols.; London, 1921–1928). GARDNER, H., *Art through the Ages*, chap. v. GLASGOW, G., *The Minoans* (London, 1923). GLOTZ, G., *The Ægean Civilization* (N.Y., 1925). HALL, H. R. H., *The Civilization of Greece in the Bronze Age* (London, 1928). HAWES, C. H. and H. B., *Crete, the Forerunner of Greece* (4th ed., N.Y., 1922). NILSSON, M. P., *Homer and Mycenæ* (London, 1933) ; *The Minoan-Mycenæan Religion and its Survival in Greek Religion* (Lund, 1927) ; *Mycenæan Origin of Greek Mythology* (University of California Press, 1932). SHUCHHARDT, K., *Schliemann's Excavations* (N.Y., 1891). TOLMAN, H. C., and SCOGGIN, G. C., *Mycenæan Troy* (N.Y., 1903).

B. General and political histories. ABBOTT, E. A., *Pericles and the Golden Age of Athens* (N.Y., 1903). ABBOTT, G. F., *Thucydides, a Study in Historical Reality* (London, 1925). ALLCROFT, A. H., *Sparta and Thebes: a History of Greece, 404–362 B.C.* (London, 1895). ALLCROFT, A. H., and MASOM, W. F., *History of Sicily from 491–289 B.C.* (London, 1912). BOTSFORD, G. W., *Hellenic History* (N.Y.. 1924) ; *History of the Ancient World* (N. Y., 1921). BURY, J. B., *History of Greece*

(2d ed., London, 1924). BURY, J. B., and KIMBALL, E., *Students' History of Greece* (N.Y., 1916). *Cambridge Ancient History* (Vol. V, 1927), Vols. 1–VI, *passim.* CARPENTER, R., *The Greeks in Spain* (N.Y., 1925). CARY, M., *Documentary Sources of Greek History* (Oxford, 1927). CURTIUS, E., *History of Greece* (5 vols.; N.Y., 1902). FLEMING, W. B., *History of Tyre* (Columbia University Press, 1915). FREEMAN, E. A., *History of Sicily* (4 vols.; Oxford, 1891–1894). GOODSPEED, G. S., *History of the Ancient World* (N.Y., 1912). GRANT, A. J., *Greece in the Age of Pericles* (N.Y., 1897). GROTE, G., *History of Greece* (10 vols.; London, 1904–1907). GRUNDY, G. B., *The Great Persian War* (London, 1901); *History of the Greek and Roman World* (London, 1926); *Thucydides and the History of his Age* (London, 1911). HALL, H. R. H., *Ancient History of the Near East.* HENDERSON, B. W., *The Great War between Athens and Sparta* (London, 1927). HOLM, A., *History of Greece* (4 vols.; N.Y., 1899–1900). JAMES, H. R., *Our Hellenic Heritage* (N.Y., 1927). KELLER, A. G., *Colonization* (Boston, 1908). MACALISTER, R. A. S., *The Philistines* (London, 1913). McCARTNEY, E. S., *Warfare by Land and Sea* (Boston, 1923). MILLS, D., *Book of the Ancient Greeks* (N.Y., 1925). MYRES, J. L., *Dawn of History* (London, 1915). RAWLINSON, H. G., *Bactria* (London, 1912). ROSTOVTZEFF, M. I., *History of the Ancient World*, Vol. I. SANKEY, C., *Spartan and Theban Supremacies* (N.Y., 1899). SEIGNOBOS, M. J. C., *History of Ancient Civilization* (N.Y., 1910). SELTMAN, C. T., *Athens, its History and Coinage before the Persian Invasion* (Cambridge University Press, 1924). SHUCKBURGH, E. S., *Greece from the Coming of the Hellenes to A. D. 14* (London, 1905). WELLS, J., *Studies in Herodotus* (Oxford, 1923). WESTERMANN, W. L., *Story of Ancient Nations* (N.Y., 1912). WHIBLEY, L., *Political Parties in Athens during the Peloponnesian War* (2d ed., Cambridge University Press, 1889).

C. **Constitutional and institutional histories.** BONNER, R. J., *Aspects of Athenian Democracy* (University of California Press, 1933). CALHOUN, G. M., *Athenian Clubs in Politics and Litigation* (University of Texas, 1913); *Growth of Criminal Law in Ancient Greece* (University of California Press, 1927). FERGUSON, W. S., *Greek Imperialism* (Boston, 1913). FOWLER, W. W., *The City-State of the Greeks and Romans* (London, 1926). FREEMAN, E. A., *History of Federal Government in Greece and Italy* (2d ed., N.Y., 1893). GILBERT, G., *The Constitutional Antiquities of Sparta and Athens* (N.Y., 1895). GLOVER, T. R., *Democracy in the Ancient World* (N Y., 1927). GREENIDGE, A. H. J., *Handbook of Greek Constitutional History* (London, 1920). HALLIDAY, W. R., *The Growth of the City State* (London, 1923). HAMMOND, B. E., *Political Institutions of the Ancient Greeks* (London, 1895). PHILLIPSON, C., *International Law and Custom of Ancient Greece and Rome* (2 vols.; London, 1911). TOD, M. N., *International Arbitration amongst the Greeks* (Oxford, 1913). URE, P. N., *The Origin of Tyranny* (Cambridge University Press, 1922). WHIBLEY, L., *Greek Oligarchies* (N. Y., 1896). ZIMMERN, A. E., *Greek Commonwealth* (5th ed., Oxford, 1931).

D. **Economic and social life.** ABRAHAMS, E. B., *Greek Dress* (London, 1908). BECKER, W. A., *Charicles: or Illustrations of the Private Life of the Ancient Greeks* (8th ed., London, 1911). BLÜMNER, H., *Home Life of the Ancient Greeks* (3d ed., N.Y., 1910). BRITISH MUSEUM, *A Guide to the Exhibition illustrating Greek and Roman Life* (London, 1929). CALHOUN, G. M., *The Ancient Greeks and the Evolution of Standards in Business* (Boston, 1926); *Business Life of Ancient Athens* (University of Chicago Press, 1926). DAVIS, S. A., *A Day in Old Athens* (N.Y., 1914). DOBSON, J. F., *Ancient Education and its Meaning to Us* (N.Y., 1932). DONALDSON, SIR J., *Woman: her Position and Influence in Ancient Greece and Rome* (N.Y., 1907). FREEMAN, K. J., *Schools of Hellas* (3d ed., London, 1932). GARDINER, E. N., *Athletics of the Ancient World* (Oxford, 1930); *Greek Athletic Sports and Festivals* (London, 1910). GLOTZ, G., *Ancient Greece at Work* (N.Y., 1926). GUHL, E. K., and KONER, W., *Life of the Greeks and Romans* (tr. from 3d German ed., N.Y., 1898). GULICK, C. B., *Life of the Ancient Greeks* (N.Y., 1929);

Modern Traits in Old Greek Life (N.Y., 1927). JONES, W. H. S., *Greek Morality in Relation to Institutions* (London, 1906). KELLER, A. G., *Homeric Society* (N.Y., 1902). LIVINGSTONE, R. W. (Ed.), *Legacy of Greece* (Oxford, 1921). McCLEES, H., *Daily Life of the Greeks and Romans as illustrated by the Classical Collections* (Metropolitan Museum of Art, N.Y., 1925). MAHAFFY, SIR J. P., *Social Life in Greece* (7th ed., N.Y., 1898). QUENNELL, M. and C. H. B., *Everyday Things in Homeric Greece* (London, 1929). SEYMOUR, T. D., *Life in the Homeric Age* (N.Y., 1908). TOYNBEE, A. J., *Greek Civilisation and Character* (N.Y., 1924). TREVER, A. A., *A History of Greek Economic Thought* (University of Chicago Press, 1916). TUCKER, T. G., *Life in Ancient Athens* (N.Y., 1929). WHIBLEY, L., *Companion to Greek Studies* (4th ed., Cambridge University Press, 1931). WRIGHT, F. A., *Greek Social Life* (N.Y., 1925).

E. Religion and mythology. ADAM, J., *The Religious Teachers of Greece* (Edinburgh, 1923). BULFINCH, T., *Age of Fable* (Everyman's Library, N.Y., 1916). FAIRBANKS, A., *Handbook of Greek Religion* (N.Y., 1910); *Mythology of Greece and Rome* (N.Y., 1907). FARNELL, L. R., *The Cults of the Greek States* (5 vols.; Oxford, 1896–1909); *Higher Aspects of Greek Religion* (London, 1912); *Outline-History of Greek Religion* (London, 1921). GAYLEY, C. M., *The Classic Myths in English Literature and in Art* (Boston, 1911). HARRISON, J. E., *Mythology* (Boston, 1924); *Myths of Greece and Rome* (Benn's Sixpenny Library, London, 1928); *Religion of Ancient Greece* (London, 1921). HOWE, G., and HARRER, G. A., *Handbook of Classical Mythology* (N.Y., 1929). MOORE, C. H., *The Religious Thought of the Greeks from Homer to the Triumph of Christianity* (Harvard University Press, 1925). MURRAY, SIR G., *Five Stages of Greek Religion* (Oxford University Press, 1925). NILSSON, M. P., *History of Greek Religion* (Oxford, 1925). SABIN, F. E., *Classical Myths that Live Today* (N.Y., 1927). ZIELINSKI, T., *Religion of Greece* (London, 1926).

F. Art and archæology. *American Journal of Archæology*, 1885– . *Art and Archæology*, 1914– . BEAZLEY, J. D., and ASHMOLE, B., *Greek Sculpture and Painting* (N.Y., 1932). BELL, E., *Hellenic Architecture* (London, 1920). *Classical Weekly*, 1907– . FOWLER, H. N., WHEELER, J. R., and STEVENS, G. P., *Handbook of Greek Archæology* (N.Y., 1909). GARDNER, E. A., *Greece and the Ægean* (London, 1933); *Handbook of Greek Sculpture* (2d ed., London, 1920); *Six Greek Sculptors* (London, 1925). GARDNER, H., *Art through the Ages*. GARDNER, P., *New Chapters in Greek Art* (Oxford, 1926). GARDNER, P., and BLOMFIELD, SIR R., *Greek Art and Architecture* (London, 1922). HOPPIN, J. G., *A Handbook of Attic Red-Figured Vases* (2 vols.; Harvard University Press, 1919); *A Handbook of Greek Black-Figured Vases* (Paris, 1924). HUDDILSTON, J. H., *Lessons from Greek Pottery* (N.Y., 1902). JOHNSON, F. P., *Lysippos* (Duke University Press, 1927). JONES, H. S., *Select Passages from Ancient Writers Illustrative of History of Greek Sculpture* (London, 1895). *Journal of Hellenic Studies* (London), 1880– . LAMB, W., *Greek and Roman Bronzes* (London, 1929). LAWRENCE, A. W., *Classical Sculpture* (N.Y., 1929). LEAF, W., *Troy* (London, 1912). MAGOFFIN, R. V. D., *The Lure and Lore of Archæology* (Baltimore, 1930). MARSHALL, F. H., *Discovery in Greek Lands: a Sketch of the Principal Excavations and Discoveries of the Last Fifty Years* (Cambridge University Press, 1920). MICHAELIS, A. T. F., *A Century of Archæological Discoveries* (London, 1908). PFUHL, E., *Masterpieces of Greek Drawing and Painting* (N.Y., 1926). POLAND, F., REISINGER, E., and WAGNER, R., *The Culture of Ancient Greece and Rome* (Boston, 1926). POULSEN, F., *Delphi* (London, 1920). POWERS, H. H., *The Hill of Athena* (N.Y., 1924). RICHTER, G. M., *The Craft of Athenian Pottery* (Yale University Press, 1923); *Handbook of the Classical Collection* (new and enlarged ed., Metropolitan Museum of Art, N.Y., 1927). ROBERTSON, D. S., *Handbook of Greek and Roman Architecture* (Cambridge University Press, 1929). ROSE, H. J., *Primitive Culture in Greece* (N.Y., 1925). TARBELL, F. B., *History of Greek Art* (N.Y., 1927). WALTERS, H. B., *History of*

Greek Pottery (London, 1905). WHIBLEY, L., *A Companion to Greek Studies* (4th ed., Cambridge University Press, 1931).

G. **Literature, philosophy, and science.** ALLEN, J. T., *Stage Antiquities of the Greeks and Romans* (N.Y., 1927). BENN, A. W., *Early Greek Philosophy* (London, 1909); *Philosophy of Greece* (London, 1898). BOWRA, C. M., *Tradition and Design in the Iliad* (Oxford, 1930). BRETT, G. S., *Psychology, Ancient and Modern* (N.Y., 1928). BURNET, J., *Greek Philosophy* (London, 1914), Part I. BURT, B. C., *Brief History of Greek Philosophy* (Boston, 1896). BURTON, H. E., *The Discovery of the Ancient World* (Harvard University Press, 1932). CARY, M., and WARMINGTON, E. H., *The Ancient Explorers* (London, 1929). CROISET, M., *Hellenic Civilization* (N.Y., 1925). DRESSER, H. W., *A History of Ancient and Medieval Philosophy* (N.Y., 1926). FOWLER, H. N., *History of Ancient Greek Literature* (new and revised ed., N.Y., 1928). HAIGH, A. E., *Attic Theatre* (3d ed., rev. by A. W. Pickard-Cambridge, Oxford, 1907). HAMILTON, E., *The Greek Way* (London, 1930). JEBB, SIR R. C., *Attic Orators* (London, 1893); *Greek Literature* (N.Y., 189-); *Growth and Influence of Classical Greek Poetry* (N.Y., 1894). JEVONS, F. B., *History of Greek Literature* (N.Y., 1900). LANG, A., *Homer and the Epic* (N.Y., 1893); *Homer and his Age* (N.Y., 1906). LEAF, W., *Homer and History* (N.Y., 1915). MACKAIL, J. W., *Lectures on Greek Poetry* (new ed., N.Y., 1926). MURRAY, SIR G., *Aristophanes and the War Party* (London, 1919); *History of Ancient Greek Literature* (Appleton's Dollar Library, N.Y., 1927); *Rise of the Greek Epic* (3d ed., Oxford, 1924). NORWOOD, C., and DUFF, J. W., *Writers of Greece and Rome* (Oxford University Press, 1925). POWELL, J. U. (Ed.), *New Chapters in the History of Greek Literature* (3d series, Oxford, 1933). SANDYS, SIR J. E., *History of Classical Scholarship* (3d ed., Cambridge University Press, 1921), Vol. I. SHOREY, P., *What Plato Said* (University of Chicago Press, 1933). SINGER, C., *Greek Biology and Greek Medicine* (Oxford, 1922). SYMONDS, J. A., *Studies of the Greek Poets* (3d ed., London, 1920). TAYLOR, A. E., *Plato, the Man and his Work* (N.Y., 1929). TAYLOR, H. O., *Greek Biology and Medicine* (Boston, 1922). TAYLOR, M. E. J., *Greek Philosophy* (Oxford University Press, 1924). TOZER, H. F., *History of Ancient Geography* (Cambridge University Press, 1897). ULLMAN, B. L., *Ancient Writing and its Influence* (N.Y., 1932). WARBEKE, J. M., *The Searching Mind of Greece* (N.Y., 1930).

H. **Source selections.** BOTSFORD, G. W. and L. S., *Source Book of Ancient History.* BOTSFORD, G. W., and SIHLER, E. G., *Hellenic Civilization* (N.Y., 1924). CORNFORD, F. M., *Greek Religious Thought from Homer to the Age of Alexander* (N.Y., 1923). FLING, F. M., *Source Book of Greek History* (Boston, 1909). HILL, MRS. IDA C. (THALLON), *Readings in Greek History* (Boston, 1914). HOWE, G., and HARRER, G. A., *Greek Literature in Translation* (N.Y., 1924). LIVINGSTONE, R. W. (Ed.), *Pageant of Greece* (Oxford, 1923).

I. **Authors in translation.** ÆSCHYLUS, The Persians (L. Campbell (Tr.), World's Classics, London, 1925); complete works (H. W. Smyth (Tr.), Loeb Classical Library, N.Y., 1922–1926). ALCÆUS, songs (J. S. Easby-Smith (Tr.), Washington, 1901). ARISTOPHANES, plays (J. H. Frere (Tr.), Everyman's Library, N.Y., 1929; B. B. Rogers (Tr.), Loeb Classical Library, N.Y., 1924–1927). ARISTOTLE, On the Athenian Constitution (E. Poste (Tr.), 2d ed., N.Y., 1892); works (Loeb Classical Library, N.Y.). EURIPIDES, plays (Everyman's Library, N.Y., 1916; A. S. Way (Tr.), Loeb Classical Library, N. Y., 1925–1929). HERODOTUS (A. D. Godley (Tr.), Loeb Classical Library, N.Y., 1924–1928; G. Rawlinson (Tr.), Everyman's Library, N.Y., 1930). HESIOD (A. W. Mair (Tr.), Oxford, 1908; J. Davies (Tr.), Philadelphia, 1873). HOMER, Iliad (Edward, Earl of Derby (Tr.), Everyman's Library, N.Y., 1912; A. Lang, W. Leaf, and E. Myers (Trs.), London, 1929); Odyssey (W. Cowper (Tr.), Everyman's Library, N.Y., 1913; S. H. Butcher and A. Lang (Trs.), London, 1925). NEPOS, CORNELIUS, Epaminondas (J. C. Rolfe (Tr.), Loeb Classical Library, N.Y., 1929; J. S. Watson

(Tr.), London, 1910). PAUSANIAS, *Tour of Greece* (W. H. S. Jones and H. A. Ormerod (Trs.), Loeb Classical Library, N.Y., 1918–). PINDAR, odes (E. Myers (Tr.), N.Y., 1899; Sir J. Sandys (Tr.), Loeb Classical Library, N.Y., 1915). PLATO, Apology (H. N. Fowler (Tr.), Loeb Classical Library, N.Y., 1933; B. Jowett (Tr.), Vol. II, N.Y., 1892). PLUTARCH, Lives (the "Dryden Plutarch," rev. by A. H. Clough, Everyman's Library, N.Y., n.d.). THEOGNIS (J. Davies (Tr.), Philadelphia, 1873; E. Harrison, *Studies in Theognis*, Cambridge University Press, 1902). THUCYDIDES, History of the Peloponnesian War (C. Forster-Smith (Tr.), Loeb Classical Library, N.Y., 1919–1923; R. Crawley (Tr.), Everyman's Library, N.Y., 1929). XENOPHON, works (Loeb Classical Library, N.Y., 1918– ; H. G. Dakyns (Tr.), N.Y., 1890–1897).

Supplementary pamphlets and booklets may be obtained from the Service Bureau for Classical Teachers, 51 W. 4th St., Washington Sq. E., New York.

CHAPTERS XIX–XXI

A. **General works.** ADAMS, C. D., *Demosthenes and his Influence* (N.Y., 1927). ALLCROFT, A. H., *The Decline of Hellas: a History of Greece, 362–323 B.C.* (London, 1894). BEVAN, E. R., *History of Egypt under the Ptolemaic Dynasty* (London, 1927); *House of Seleucus* (2 vols. ; London, 1902). BURY, J. B., BARBER, E. A., BEVAN, E., and TARN, W. W., *The Hellenistic Age* (2d ed., Cambridge University Press, 1925). *Cambridge Ancient History*, Vols. VI, VII (1928), *passim. Cambridge History of India* (N.Y., 1922), Vol. I, chap. xv. CARY, M., *The Legacy of Alexander* (N.Y., 1932). CURTEIS, A. M., *Rise of the Macedonian Empire* (N.Y., 1916). DICKINS, G., *Hellenistic Sculpture* (Oxford, 1920). DODGE, T. A., *Alexander* (2 vols. ; Boston, 1918). EHRENBERG, V., *Alexander und Ägypten* (Leipzig, 1926). FERGUSON, W. S., *Hellenistic Athens* (London, 1911). HEIBERG, J. L., *Mathematics and Physical Science in Classical Antiquity* (Oxford University Press, 1922). HOGARTH, D. G., *Philip and Alexander of Macedon* (N.Y., 1897). JOUGUET, P., *Macedonian Imperialism and the Hellenization of the East* (N.Y., 1928). MACURDY, G. H.; *Hellenistic Queens* (Johns Hopkins Press, 1932). MAHAFFY, SIR J. P., *Alexander's Empire* (N.Y., 1902); *Greek Life and Thought from the Death of Alexander to the Roman Conquest* (2d ed., N.Y., 1896); *Progress of Hellenism in Alexander's Empire* (University of Chicago Press, 1905); *The Silver Age of the Greek World* (University of Chicago Press, 1906). MORE, P. E., *Hellenistic Philosophies* (Princeton University Press, 1923). POWELL, J. U., and BARBER, E. A. (Eds.), *New Chapters in the History of Greek Literature* (1st and 2d series, Oxford, 1921, 1929). RADET, G. A., *Alexandre le Grand* (Paris, 1931). ROBINSON, C. A., *The Ephemerides of Alexander's Expedition* (Brown University, 1932). ROGERS, R. W., *History of Ancient Persia*, pp. 261–376. ROSTOVTZEFF, M. I., *Out of the Past of Greece and Rome* (Yale University Press, 1932), pp. 93 ff. STIER, H. E., *Aus der Welt des Pergamonaltars* (Berlin, 1932). SUHR, E. G., *Sculptured Portraits of Greek Statesmen* (Johns Hopkins Press, 1931). SYKES, SIR P. M., *History of Persia*, Vol. I, chaps. xx–xxvi. TARN, W. W., *Antigonos Gonatas* (Oxford, 1913); *Hellenistic Civilization* (2d ed., London, 1930). TILLYARD, H. J. W., *Agathocles* (Cambridge University Press, 1908). WHEELER, B. I., *Alexander the Great* (N.Y., 1909). WILCKEN, U., *Alexander der Grosse* (Leipzig, 1931).

B. **Ancient authors in translation.** ARRIAN, Anabasis of Alexander (E. I. Robson (Tr.), Loeb Classical Library, N.Y., 1929–). CALLIMACHUS (A. W. Mair (Tr.), Loeb Classical Library, N.Y., 1921). DEMOSTHENES, *Oration on the Crown* and *Third Philippic* (A. W. Pickard-Cambridge (Tr.), *The Public Orations of Demosthenes*, Vol. II, Oxford, 1912). ISOCRATES (G. Norlin (Tr.), Loeb Classical Library, N.Y., 1928). JUSTIN, Abr., History of the World (J. S. Watson (Tr.),

London, 1910), Bks. IX, XI–XIII. PLUTARCH, lives of *Demosthenes, Phocion, Alexander, Aratus, Demetrius, Pyrrhus, Agis, Cleomenes,* and *Eumenes.* POLYBIUS, histories (W. R. Paton (Tr.), Loeb Classical Library, 6 vols., N.Y., 1922–1927). See also the general bibliography for Greek history, chaps. ix–xviii.

CHAPTERS XXII–XXVIII

A. General and political histories. BEVAN, E. R., *The World of Greece and Rome* (London, 1928). BOAK, A. E. R., *History of Rome to A.D. 565* (rev. ed., N.Y., 1929). BONUS, A. R., *Where Hannibal Passed* (London, 1925). BRYANT, E. E., *The Reign of Antoninus Pius* (Cambridge University Press, 1895). BURY, J. B., *Student's Roman Empire* (N.Y., 190-). *Cambridge Ancient History,* Vols. IV, VII, and VIII (1930), *passim.* DURUY, V., *History of Rome* (8 vols. in 16; Boston, 1890). FELL, R. A. L., *Etruria and Rome* (Cambridge University Press, 1924). FERRERO, G., *Greatness and Decline of Rome* (5 vols.; N.Y., 1909). FERRERO, G., and BARBAGALLO, C., *Short History of Rome* (2 vols.; N.Y., 1918–1919). FOWLER, W. W., *Rome* (N.Y., 1912). FRANK, T., *History of Rome* (N.Y., 1923). FREEMAN, E. A., *Story of Sicily: Phœnician, Greek, and Roman* (2d ed., N.Y., 1894). GREEN-IDGE, A. H. J., *History of Rome* (N.Y., 1905). GRUNDY, G. B., *History of the Greek and Roman World.* HAVELL, H. L., *Republican Rome* (London, 1923). HEITLAND, W. E., *Short History of the Roman Republic* (Cambridge University Press, 1916). HOLMES, T. R. E., *Cæsar's Conquest of Gaul* (2d ed., Oxford, 1911); *The Roman Republic* (3 vols.; Oxford, 1923). HOW, W. W., and LEIGH, H. D., *History of Rome to the Death of Cæsar* (N.Y., 1917). IHNE, W., *History of Rome* (5 vols.; London, 1871–1882). JOLLIFFE, R. O., *Phases of Corruption in Roman Administration in the Last Half-century of the Roman Republic* (Menasha, Wis., 1919). LONG, G., *Decline of the Roman Republic* (5 vols.; London, 1864–1874). McCARTNEY, E. S., *Warfare by Land and Sea.* MAGOFFIN, R. V. D., and DUNCALF, F., *Ancient and Medieval History* (N.Y., 1934). MASON, W. F., *Decline of the Oligarchy: a History of Rome, 133–78 B.C.* (London, 1895). MERIVALE, C., *History of the Romans under the Empire* (8 vols.; London, 1904). MOMMSEN, T., *History of Rome* (4 vols.; N.Y., 1911). MYRES, J. L., *Dawn of History.* NILSSON, M. P., *Imperial Rome* (N.Y., 1926). PELHAM, H. F., *Outlines of Roman History* (4th ed., N.Y., 1907). RANDALL-MACIVER, D., *The Etruscans* (Oxford, 1927); *Italy before the Romans* (Oxford, 1928). ROSTOVTZEFF, M. I., *History of the Ancient World* (Oxford, 1928), Vol. II. SMITH, R. B., *Carthage and the Carthaginians* (N.Y., 1902). TORR, C., *Hannibal Crosses the Alps* (2d ed., Cambridge University Press, 1925). WESTER-MANN, W. L., *Story of Ancient Nations.*

B. Constitutional and institutional histories. ABBOTT, F. F., *History and Description of Roman Political Institutions* (3d ed., Boston, 1911); *Roman Politics* (Boston, 1923). ABBOTT, F. F., and JOHNSON, A. C., *Municipal Administration in the Roman Empire* (Princeton University Press, 1926). ARNOLD, W. T., *Roman System of Provincial Administration* (3d ed., rev. by E. S. Bouchier, Oxford, 1914). BOTSFORD, G. W., *Roman Assemblies* (N.Y., 1909). BUCKLAND, W. W., *Manual of Roman Private Law* (Cambridge University Press, 1928). FRANK, T., *Roman Imperialism* (N.Y., 1921). GREENIDGE, A. H. J., *The Legal Procedure of Cicero's Time* (Oxford University Press, 1901); *Roman Public Life* (London, 1922). HADLEY, H. S., *Rome and the World Today* (2d ed., rev., N.Y., 1923). HADLEY, J., *Introduction to Roman Law* (Yale University Press, 1931). HUNTER, W. A., *Introduction to Roman Law* (new ed., revised and enlarged by A. F. Murison, London, 1921). MATTINGLY, H., *Imperial Civil Service of Rome* (Cambridge University Press, 1910). REYNOLDS, P. K. B., *The Vigiles of Imperial Rome* (Oxford University Press, 1926). TAYLOR, T. M., *Constitutional and Political History of Rome* (4th ed., London, 1915).

C. **Economic and social life.** ABBOTT, F. F., *Common People of Ancient Rome* (N.Y., 1917) ; *Society and Politics in Ancient Rome* (N.Y., 1916). BAILEY, C. (Ed.), *The Legacy of Rome* (Oxford University Press, 1924). BECKER, W. A., *Gallus; or, Roman Scenes of the Time of Augustus* (new ed., London, 1898). BRITISH MUSEUM, *A Guide to the Exhibition illustrating Greek and Roman Life.* BUCKLAND, W. W., *Roman Law of Slavery* (Cambridge University Press, 1908). CHARLESWORTH, M. P., *Trade-routes and Commerce of the Roman Empire* (2d ed., rev., Cambridge University Press, 1926). DAVIS, W. S., *A Day in Old Rome* (Boston, 1925) ; *Influence of Wealth in Imperial Rome* (N.Y., 1933). DILL, SIR S., *Roman Society from Nero to Marcus Aurelius* (London, 1925). FOWLER, W. W., *Social Life at Rome in the Age of Cicero* (N.Y., 1926). FRANK, T., *Economic History of Rome* (2d ed., Johns Hopkins Press, 1927) ; *Economic Survey of Ancient Rome* (Johns Hopkins Press, 1933), Vol. I. FRIEDLANDER, L , *Roman Life and Manners under the Early Empire* (tr. of 7th ed., rev. ; 4 vols. ; Vol. I, 2d ed., N.Y., 1909-1928). GWYNN, A. O., *Roman Education from Cicero to Quintilian* (Oxford, 1926). HARRISON, F. (Ed.), *Roman Farm Management; the Treatises of Cato and Varro* (tr., with notes of modern instances, by a Virginia farmer, N.Y., 1913). HEITLAND, W. E., *Agricola, a Study in Agriculture and Rustic Life in the Greco-Roman World* (Cambridge University Press, 1921). JOHNSTON, H. W., *Private Life of the Romans* (Chicago, 1932). LOUIS, P., *Ancient Rome at Work* (London, 1927). McDANIEL, W. B., *Roman Private Life and its Survivals* (N.Y., 1929). PELLISSON, M., *Roman Life in Pliny's Time* (Philadelphia, 1901). PRESTON, H. W., and DODGE, L., *Private Life of the Romans* (Chicago, 1900). ROSTOVTZEFF, M. I., *Out of the Past of Greece and Rome*; *The Social and Economic History of the Roman Empire* (Oxford, 1926). SANDYS, SIR J. E., *A Companion to Latin Studies* (3d ed., Cambridge University Press, 1921). SHOWERMAN, G., *Rome and the Romans* (N.Y., 1931). SOTTAS, J., "The Ship of St. Paul's Last Voyage," in the *Mariner's Mirror*, Vol. VII (1921), pp. 258–266. TOUTAIN, J., *The Economic Life of the Ancient World* (N.Y., 1930). TREBLE, H. A., and KING, K. M., *Everyday Life in Rome* (Oxford, 1930). TUCKER, T. G., *Life in the Roman World of Nero and St. Paul* (N.Y., 1929).

D. **Mythology and religion.** *Cambridge Ancient History*, Vol. VIII, chap. xiv. CARTER, J. B., *Religion of Numa* (N.Y., 1906) ; *Religious Life of Ancient Rome* (Boston, 1922). CUMONT, F., *Mysteries of Mithra* (2d ed., Chicago, 1910) ; *Oriental Religions in Roman Paganism* (Chicago, 1911). FOWLER, W. W., *Religious Experience of the Roman People* (London, 1922). GLOVER, T. R., *Conflict of Religions in the Early Roman Empire* (11th ed., London, 1927). HALLIDAY, W. R., *Lectures on the History of Roman Religion from Numa to Augustus* (Boston, 1923). PAIS, E., *Ancient Legends of Roman History* (N.Y., 1905).

See also section *E* in the general bibliography for Greek history, chaps. ix–xviii.

E. **Art and archæology.** BARKER, E. R., *Buried Herculaneum* (London, 1908). EHRENBERG, V., "Karthago," in *Morgenland*, Heft 14 (1927). ENGELMANN, W., *New Guide to Pompeii* (2d ed., rev., Leipzig, 1929). FERRERO, F. L., "That Amphora and the Death of Pliny the Elder," in *Art and Archæology*, Vol. XXIX (1930), pp. 51–55 and 75. HUELSEN, C. C. F., *The Forum and the Palatine* (N.Y., 1928). HUSSEY, M. I., "The Pompeii of Palestine," in *Art and Archæology*, Vol. XXXV (1934), pp. 3–17. JOHNSTONE, M. A., *Etruria Past and Present* (London, 1930). *Journal of Roman Studies* (London), 1911– . LANCIANI, R. A., *Ancient and Modern Rome* (Boston, 1925) ; *Ruins and Excavations of Ancient Rome* (Boston, 1897). LUGLI, G., *The Classical Monuments of Rome and its Vicinity* (Rome, 1929), Vol. I; *Horace's Sabine Farm* (Rome, 1930). MAGOFFIN, R. V. D., *The Lure and Lore of Archæology* (Baltimore, 1930). MAU, A., *Pompeii, its Life and Art* (N.Y., 1902). ORECCHIA, J., "*May I Show you Rome?*" (Rome, 1930). PLATNER, S. B., *Topographical Dictionary of Ancient Rome* (completed and revised by T. Ashby ; Oxford, 1929) ; *Topography and Monuments of*

Ancient Rome (2d ed., Boston, 1911). POULSEN, F., *Etruscan Tomb Paintings* (Oxford, 1922). RAMSAY, W., *Manual of Roman Antiquities* (18th ed., rev. by R. A. Lanciani; London, 1909). RIVOIRA, G. T., *Roman Architecture* (Oxford, 1925). ROSE, H. J., *Primitive Culture in Italy* (N.Y., 1926). SHOWERMAN, G., *Eternal Rome* (Yale University Press, 1924). STRONG, E., *Art in Ancient Rome* (Ars Una : Species Mille ; 2 vols. ; N.Y., 1928). WALTERS, H. B., *The Art of the Romans* (2d ed., London, 1928). WARSHER, T., *Pompeii in Three Hours* (Rome, 1930).

F. Literature, philosophy, and science. ARNOLD, E. V., *Roman Stoicism* (Cambridge University Press, 1911). BOISSIER, G., *Cicero and his Friends* (N.Y., 1925). *Cambridge Ancient History*, Vol. VIII, chap. xiii. CONWAY, R. S., *New Studies of a Great Inheritance* (London, 1921). DUFF, J. W., *Literary History of Rome, from the Origins to the Close of the Golden Age* (7th ed., London, 1927) ; *Literary History of Rome in the Silver Age* (N.Y., 1927). FOWLER, H. N., *History of Roman Literature* (N.Y., 1928). FRANK, T., *Life and Literature in the Roman Republic* (University of California Press, 1930). GUMMERE, R. M., *Seneca the Philosopher and his Modern Message* (Boston, 1922). HAMILTON, E., *The Roman Way* (N.Y., 1932). MACKAIL, J. W., *Latin Literature* (N.Y., 1925). NORWOOD, C., and DUFF, J. W., *Writers of Greece and Rome*. ROLFE, J. C., *Cicero and his Influence* (Boston, 1923). SELLAR, W. Y., *Roman Poets of the Augustan Age: Horace, and the Elegiac Poets* (2d ed., Oxford, 1899) ; *Roman Poets of the Augustan Age: Virgil* (3d ed., Oxford, 1897) ; *Roman Poets of the Republic* (3d ed., Oxford, 1905). SIKES, E. E., *Roman Poetry* (London, 1923). SUMMERS, W. C., *Silver Age of Latin Literature from Tiberius to Trajan* (London, 1920). TEUFFEL, W. S., *History of Roman Literature* (2 vols. ; rev. by L. Schwabe, London, 1900).

G. Source selections. BAILEY, C. (Ed.), *The Mind of Rome* (Oxford, 1926). BLAKENEY, E. H., *Pages from Latin Authors* (N.Y., 1924). BOTSFORD, G. W. and L. S., *Source Book of Ancient History*. DAVIS, W. S., *Readings in Ancient History* (N.Y., 1913), Vol. II. GREENOUGH, J. B., KITTREDGE, G. L., and JENKINS, J., *Virgil and Other Latin Poets* (Boston, 1930). HOWE, G., and HARRER, G. A., *Roman Literature in Translation* (N.Y., 1924). LAING, G. J., *Masterpieces of Latin Literature* (Boston, 1903). MUNRO, D. C., *Source Book of Roman History* (Boston, 1911).

H. Authors in translation. AMMIANUS MARCELLINUS, Roman history (C. D. Yonge (Tr.), London, 1887). APPIAN, Roman history (H. White (Tr.), 2 vols., N.Y., 1899). AUGUSTUS, *Monumentum Ancyranum* (W. Fairley (Tr.), *Pennsylvania Translations and Reprints*, Vol. V, No. 1 ; E. G. Hardy (Tr.), *Monumentum Ancyranum*, 1924 ; D. Robinson (Tr.), *The Deeds of Augustus as Recorded on the Monumentum Antiochenum*, 1926). AURELIUS ANTONINUS, MARCUS, Meditations (C. R. Haines (Tr.), Loeb Classical Library, London, 1924 ; M. Casaubon (Tr.), Everyman's Library, N.Y., 1919). CÆSAR, JULIUS, *Gallic War* (H. J. Edwards (Tr.), Loeb Classical Library, N.Y., 1917). CASSIODORUS, letters (T. Hodgkin (Tr.), London, 1886). CICERO, letters (E. S. Shuckburgh (Tr.), 4 vols., London, 1915–1920) ; W. G. Williams (Tr.), Loeb Classical Library, 3 vols., N.Y., 1927–1929) ; speeches (N. H. Watts (Tr.), Loeb Classical Library, N.Y., 1931). DIO CASSIUS, Roman history (E. Cary (Tr.), Loeb Classical Library, 9 vols., N.Y., 1914–1927). DIODORUS SICULUS, Historical Library (London, 1814). FLORUS, LUCIUS ANNÆUS, Epitome of Roman History (E. S. Forster (Tr.), Loeb Classical Library, N.Y., 1929 ; J. S. Watson (Tr.), London, 1889). HORACE (E. C. Wickham (Tr.), *Horace for English Readers*, in prose, Oxford University Press, 1930 ; H. Macnaghten (Tr.), in verse, Cambridge University Press, 1926). JOSEPHUS, works (W. Whiston (Tr.), 5 vols., London, 1890 ; H. St. J. Thackeray (Tr.), Loeb Classical Library, N.Y., 1926–   ). JUVENAL, Satires (G. G. Ramsay (Tr.), Loeb Classical Library, N.Y., 1928 ; J. H. Bolton (Tr.), London, 1930). LIVY, history of Rome (B. O. Foster (Tr.), Loeb Classical Library, N.Y., 1919-   ; D. Spillan and C. R. Edmonds (Trs.), 2 vols., N.Y., 1895) LUCRETIUS, *On the*

Nature of Things (W. H. D. Rouse (Tr.), Loeb Classical Library, N.Y., 1924; C. Bailey (Tr.), Oxford, 1929). OVID, works (H. T. Riley (Tr.), 3 vols., London, 1869; Loeb Classical Library: translations of various works). PLINY THE ELDER, *Natural History* (J. Bostock and H. T. Riley (Trs.), Bohn, 6 vols., London, 1855-1857). PLINY THE YOUNGER, letters (W. M. L. Hutchinson (Tr.), Loeb Classical Library, 2 vols., N.Y., 1915). PLUTARCH, Lives. POLYBIUS, histories (W. R. Paton (Tr.), Loeb Classical Library, 6 vols., N.Y., 1922-1927). PROPERTIUS, elegies (C. R. Moore (Tr.), in verse, London, 1870; H. E. Butler (Tr.), Loeb Classical Library, N.Y., 1916). SALLUST, *Jugurthine War* (J. S. Watson (Tr.), Bohn, London, 1889). STRABO, Geography (H. L. Jones (Tr.), Loeb Classical Library, 8 vols., N.Y., 1917-1932). SUETONIUS, *Lives of the Cæsars* (J. C. Rolfe (Tr.), Loeb Classical Library, 2 vols., N.Y., 1914). TACITUS, *Annals* (A. J. Church and W. J. Brodribb (Trs.), London, 1921). VIRGIL (H. R. Fairclough (Tr.), Loeb Classical Library, 2 vols., N.Y., 1916-1918; J. Rhoades (Tr.), World's Classics, N.Y., 1926).

I. **Biographies.** BAKER, G. P., *Hannibal* (London, 1930); *Sulla the Fortunate* (London, 1927). BUCHAN, J., *Julius Cæsar* (Edinburgh, 1932). CUTTS, E. L., *Constantine the Great* (N.Y., 1881). DODGE, T. A., *Hannibal* (2 vols.; 3d ed., Boston, 1896). DOVE, C. C., *Marcus Aurelius Antoninus* (London, 1930). FIRTH, J. B., *Augustus Cæsar and the Organization of the Empire of Rome* (N.Y., 1923). FOWLER, W. W., *Julius Cæsar and the Foundations of the Roman Imperial System* (N.Y., 1925). FRANK, T., *Vergil, a Biography* (N.Y., 1922). GREGOROVIUS, F., *The Emperor Hadrian* (N.Y., 1898). HENDERSON, B. W., *Five Roman Emperors* (Cambridge University Press, 1927); *The Life and Principate of the Emperor Hadrian* (N.Y., 1923); *The Life and Principate of the Emperor Nero* (London, 1903). HOLMES, T. R. E., *The Architect of the Roman Empire* (Oxford, 1928); *The Architect of the Roman Empire, 27 B.C.–A.D. 14* (Oxford, 1931) HOPKINS, R. V. N., *Life of Alexander Severus* (Cambridge University Press, 1907). LIDDELL HART, B. H., *A Greater than Napoleon: Scipio Africanus* (Edinburgh, 1927). LONGFORD, C., *Vespasian* (Dublin, 1928). MORRIS, W. O., *Hannibal* (new ed., N.Y., 1927). OMAN, C. W. C., *Seven Roman Statesmen of the Later Republic* (N.Y., 1902). PETERSSON, T., *Cicero, a Biography* (University of California Press, 1920). PLATNAUER, M., *The Life and Reign of the Emperor Lucius Septimius Severus* (Oxford University Press, 1918). ROSTOVTZEFF, M. I., "Augustus" (in *University of Wisconsin Studies in Language and Literature*, No. 15; Madison, Wis., 1922). SHUCKBURGH, E. S., *Augustus* (London, 1908). SIHLER, E. G., *Annals of Cæsar, a Critical Biography* (N.Y., 1911). SIMPSON, W. D., *Julian the Apostate* (Aberdeen, 1930). STRACHAN-DAVIDSON, J. L., *Cicero* (N.Y., 1903). TARVER, J. C., *Tiberius the Tyrant* (N.Y., 1902).

J. **History and culture of the provinces.** BOISSIER, G., *Roman Africa* (N.Y., 1899). BOUCHIER, E. S., *Life and Letters in Roman Africa* (Oxford, 1913); *Spain under the Roman Empire* (Oxford, 1914); *Syria as a Roman Province* (Oxford, 1916). HARRER, G. A., *Studies in the History of the Roman Province of Syria* (Princeton University Press, 1915). HAVERFIELD, F. J., *The Roman Occupation of Britain* (Oxford University Press, 1924). MOMMSEN, T., *The Provinces of the Roman Empire* (London, 1909). QUENNELL, M. and C. H. B., *Everyday Life in Roman Britain* (London, 1924). RAMSAY, W. M., *Studies in the History and Art of the Eastern Provinces of the Roman Empire* (Aberdeen, 1906).

CHAPTERS XXIX–XXX

A. **General works.** BAKER, G. P., *Constantine the Great and the Christian Revolution* (N.Y., 1930). BAYNES, N. H., *The Byzantine Empire* (London, 1925). BURY, J. B., *History of the Later Roman Empire from the Death of Theodosius I to the*

Death of Justinian (2 vols.; London, 1923); *Invasion of Europe by the Barbarians* (London, 1928). COTTERILL, H. B., *Medieval Italy* (N.Y., 1915). CUTTS, E. L., *Saint Jerome* (N.Y., 1878). DAVIS, H. W. C., *Medieval Europe* (N.Y., 1911). DILL, S., *Roman Society in the Last Century of the Western Empire* (London, 1921). EAKIN, F., *Revaluing Scripture*, chap. xvii. EMERTON, E., *An Introduction to the Study of the Middle Ages* (Boston, 1916). FERRERO, G., *Ruin of the Ancient Civilization and the Triumph of Christianity* (N.Y., 1921). FIRTH, J. B., *Constantine the Great* (N.Y., 1923). FISHER, G. P., *The Beginnings of Christianity* (N.Y., 1906). GIBBON, E., *History of the Decline and Fall of the Roman Empire* (7 vols., ed. by J. B. Bury; London, 1930). GROUSSET, R., *The Civilizations of the East*, pp. 133–162. HAARHOF, T. J., *Schools of Gaul* (Oxford, 1920). HATCH, E., *Organization of the Early Christian Churches* (N.Y., 1901). HAY, J. S., *The Amazing Emperor Heliogabalus* (London, 1911). HEITLAND, W. E., *The Roman Fate* (Cambridge University Press, 1922); *Iterum* (Cambridge University Press, 1925). HODGKIN, T., *Dynasty of Theodosius* (Oxford, 1889). HUTTON, W. H., *The Church and the Barbarians* (N.Y., 1906). IORGA, N., *The Byzantine Empire* (London, 1907). KIDD, B. J., *A History of the Church to A.D. 461* (3 vols.; Oxford, 1922). MUNRO, D. C., *The Middle Ages, 395–1500* (rev. ed., N.Y., 1928). OMAN, SIR C. W. C., *The Byzantine Empire* (London, 1922). STEVENS, C. E., *Sidonius Apollinaris and his Age* (Oxford, 1933). WRIGHT, W., *An Account of Palmyra and Zenobia* (N.Y., 1895).

    B. **Sources and source selections.** BONIFACE, SAINT, *English Correspondence* (E. J. Kylie (Tr.), King's Classics, London, 1911). BROOKE, D. (Ed.), *Private Letters, Pagan and Christian* (London, 1929). EUGIPPIUS, *Life of St. Severinus* (G. W. Robinson (Tr.), Harvard University Press, 1914). JORDANES, *The Origin and Deeds of the Goths* (C. C. Mierow (Tr.), Princeton University Press, 1908). *Notitia Dignitatum* (Department of History of the University of Pennsylvania, 1899). ROBINSON, J. H., *Readings in European History* (Boston, 1904), Vol. I, pp. 14–27, and chaps. iii–vi. TACITUS, *Agricola; Germania* (M. Hutton (Tr.), Loeb Classical Library, N.Y., 1914).

    See also the general bibliography for Roman history, chaps. xxii–xxviii.

    Atlases and miscellaneous reference books. AMERICAN COUNCIL OF EDUCATION, COMMITTEE ON MATERIALS OF INSTRUCTION, Achievements of Civilization Series (5835 Kimbark Avenue, Chicago, Illinois). BREASTED, J. H., HUTH, C. F., and HARDING, S. B., *Ancient and European History Atlas* (Denoyer-Geppert Co., Chicago, 1920); *Ancient-Medieval-Modern History Maps* (2d ed., Denoyer-Geppert Co., Chicago, 1918). GRUNDY, G. B. (Ed.), *Murray's Small Classical Atlas* (2d ed., London, 1917). KIEPERT, H., *Manual of Ancient Geography* (London, 1881). LOGASA, HANNAH (compiler), *Historical Fiction and Other Reading References for History Classes in Junior and Senior High Schools* (Philadelphia, 1930). NEUBERGER, A., *The Technical Arts and Sciences of the Ancients* (London, 1930). PUTZGER, F. W., *Historischer Schulatlas zur alten, mittleren und neueren Geschichte* (44. verm. und verb. Aufl., Leipzig, 1923). SHEPHERD, W. R., *Historical Atlas* (7th ed., N.Y., 1929). SIEGLIN, W., *Schulatlas zur Geschichte des Altertums* (5 Aufl., Gotha, 192-). SMITH, G. A., and BARTHOLOMEW, J. G., *Atlas of the Historical Geography of the Holy Land* (London, 1915). SMITH, W., *A Classical Dictionary of Greek and Roman Biography, Mythology, and Geography* (London, 1925); *A Smaller Classical Dictionary* (rev. by E. H. Blakeney; Everyman's Library, N.Y., 1927). SWINDLER, M. H., *Ancient Painting from the Earliest Times to the Period of Christian Art* (Yale University Press, 1929).

INDEX

KEY. ă *as in* at; ā *as in* ate; â *as in* senate; ä *as in* arm; à *as in* ask; â *as in* care; ą *as in* sofa; ĕ *as in* met; ē *as in* be; ê *as in* enough; ē *as in* her; ę *as in* novel; ĭ *as in* it; ī *as in* ice; ŏ *as in* not; ō *as in* note; ŏ *as in* obey; ô *as in* horse; ǫ *as in* anchor; ŭ *as in* us; ū *as in* use; û *as in* unite; û *as in* fur; ų *as in* stirrup; ü *as in German* grün; oo *as in* foot; ōo *as in* food; ṇ *like* ng *in* song; th *as in* then; zh *like* z *in* azure; ĸ *like* ch *in German* ich *or* ach; N *like* n *in French* bon

CDEFGHIJ 069

PRINTED IN THE UNITED STATES OF AMERICA

101   B   F
101   C   E